THE TEXAS QUARTERLY

A Special Issue:

IMAGE OF AUSTRALIA

Summer 1962

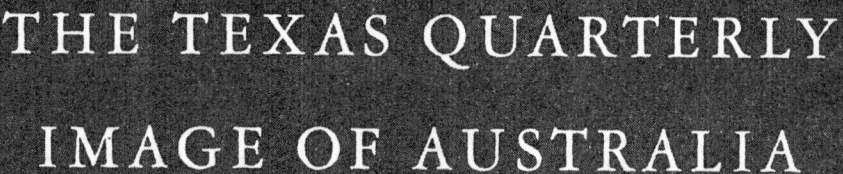

THE TEXAS QUARTERLY
IMAGE OF AUSTRALIA

A Special Issue edited by JOSEPH JONES
General Editor : HARRY H. RANSOM

THE UNIVERSITY  OF TEXAS, AUSTIN

This volume was originally published as a special supplement to *The Texas Quarterly*, Summer 1962, Vol. V, Number 2.

Requests for permission to reproduce material from this work should be sent to:
Journals Department
University of Texas Press
P.O. Box 7819
Austin, TX 78713-7819
www.utexas.edu/utpress/journals/jperm.html

Library of Congress Catalog Number 58-8635

ISBN 978-0-292-74424-0,

The cover shows bark paintings by Australian aboriginal art-ists. The front shows the Moon-Man, *Yumaria*, and the Tides. Water flows into and fattens *Yumaria* when the tides are high; escapes and slims him when they are low. The horizontal strip is the sea; below is the moon.

Throughout the book are other aboriginal art motifs taken from bark and cave paintings and other sources. Their essen-tial forms have been retained by photocopying but they have been adapted to line reproduction with background shapes that are arbitrary and imposed.

The cartoons by the Australian artist George Molnar are from *Australian Accent* by John Douglas Pringle, and are printed here by kind permission of the publishers, Chatto & Windus, London.

CONTENTS : THE TEXAS QUARTERLY / Summer 1962 Vol. V No. 2

About the Contributors

MOLNAR

JOSEPH JONES : *Encounter with Australia*

AUSTRALIA, TO MANY BRITISH OBSERVERS IN THE NINETEENTH CENTURY AND some in the twentieth, has faced the perennial peril of sliding into an abyss labeled "Americanisation." Australians themselves, although by no means hostile towards America or Americans, would rather be thought to resemble nobody else in particular. At this they succeed very well.

It has been our aim, in this number of *Texas Quarterly*, to explore what it is that has made Australia *sui generis* and keeps it so. We offer here a number of critical interpretations of Australian life and a sampling of current creative writing by Australians. Since any single issue must be selective, not nearly all the best-known figures in Australian literature are included, but neither have younger writers been overlooked; and it is hoped that the fiction and verse will be found representative of the quality and variety observable in Australian publications. Urban and rural Australia alike may be approached through the articles, the stories, and the poems.

To the special editor, these preliminary pages offer the welcome opportunity of setting down a few recollections and reflections out of a multitude attaching to a residence of some months at Melbourne, Canberra, and Sydney, with brief calls at other places.

Perth is two days from Johannesburg by plane, in the same hemisphere but in a different century. Or so it seemed to me, when late in 1960 after nine months in South Africa I landed there. Had there been two weeks at sea, the contrast might not have been so dramatic; as it was, I felt I was home already. During the months to follow, differences became apparent. But upon final departure—by ship this time, from Cairns, at the northeast corner, directly opposite where I came in—it was still difficult to believe I was leaving foreign soil.

As an academic visitor, gravitating towards libraries and literary associations, I was hardly the best qualified to receive and report a wide spectrum of impressions. What I did *not* see of the country would constitute a formidable list of omissions, among which the most important would be the lonely far interior, the edge of settlement, where one might expect to encounter a cattle drive, a kangaroo hunt, a "Flying Doctor" plane, a "bush" school, a party of aborigines, or a mine.

Many, possibly most, Australians have not seen these things, either, for well over half of them live in cities. Their awareness, however, of the "bush" and "outback" tradition remains keen, and not a few of them try to work out some kind of personal accommodation between town and country. For example, not so long ago there was a train in and out of Sydney, running as far west as towns in the Blue Mountains, which arrived in the city early in the morning and left in the late afternoon, carrying clerks and other workers back and forth from their sub-suburban homes to their jobs. For some reason or other this train became known familiarly, for years, as "The Fish." When subsequently another train was added to the same line, departing later in the morning so as to accommodate the more leisurely executives, this one immediately was called "The Chips."

It is an Australian habit to look to the future. One feels the urge of futurity on many sides, though he may come to realize at the same time that it is not an Australian habit to be oversanguine. Understatement excels overstatement, except possibly for the merits of a cricket team or a racehorse. But if expectation were not part of the national character there would be far fewer immigrants—"New Australians" —being invited and responding to the invitation by annual scores of thousands. There would be no such projects as the Snowy Mountains scheme (being built by immigrants, in large part) which proposes and is already beginning to realize the reversal of a whole watershed into a gigantic power and irrigation system. Other signs of confidence are abundant. Sydney dares to commence an opera house of the most advanced design, and before the foundations are barely out of the ground—or, more appropriately, out of the water, since the building is flanked by the harbor on three sides—fortune provides Australia with one of the great soprano voices of our time. The artist Dobell paints an "experimental" portrait of Dame Mary Gilmore, about which a hue-and-cry goes up until Dame Mary herself (well past ninety at the time) says she entirely approves of the picture and, moreover, the rest of the family like it too!

The crowded streets of Melbourne, the suburban proliferations of Perth and Adelaide and Brisbane, the astonishing growth rate of Canberra (rapidly living down its reputation as "the best-lighted piece of bush in all of Australia"), the appearance at newsstands of foreign-language newspapers published locally, the thrust of skyscraper skeletons through a lower crust of Victorian and Georgian scroll-and-pillar masonry, the presence of Colombo Plan students at the universities, the foundation of whole new universities as older ones become overcrowded, the open, easy talk of trade relations with the Orient and the inevitability of junking the "White Australia" policy—all this, and much more, sets the tempo of present-day Australia.

The arts there, especially in the urban centers, have pretty thoroughly domesticated themselves, one feels, and are ready for inspection by visitors or for export as the case may be. Galleries contain canvases in quantities more than sufficient to show the successive presence of a variety of styles and modes, in addition to housing treasures from overseas acquired during various periods of mineral and pastoral prosperity. Such painters as Dobell and Drysdale are already to be counted among the "older" masters in the face of a contemporary upsurge. A new school of art, combined with an extensive exhibition and concert center, is shortly to open in Melbourne; and with these and other facilities available to artist and patron, there should be no flagging of interest. Aboriginal painting, handcraft, and dancing are all subjects of both public attention and scholarly investigation. New histories of art, on widely regional bases, are appearing. Likewise in the theater there is much that the

Northern Hemisphere will in time become better aware of. Several generations of poets and novelists have already contributed thousands of volumes to render the collection of Australiana a very special and sometimes expensive pursuit. Library collections are increasing not only in bulk but in intrinsic importance, with authors' manuscripts beginning to find their way into archives outside the traditional centers of Sydney and Melbourne. Bookstores thrive, and publishers now explore the market with paperback reprints of Australian classics in addition to expanding their facilities for handling more adequately the work of present-day authors. Broadcasting and telecasting under state sponsorship have done much to encourage individual writers and artists, avoiding the worst pitfalls, at least, of the sort of commercial debauchery only too well known and too meekly tolerated in some places, including Texas. Authors, artists, publishers, critics, collectors, scholars are easy to meet and easy to talk to, on Australian and international subjects as well.

Everywhere, I found, Australians were kindness itself. However much the land may withhold from them—and they expect they can induce it to withhold less and less—they do not withhold fellowship from each other, or from strangers. (On occasions—political and otherwise—they of course can hate each other, too, but it is still a fact that in all the earth, Australia is the only populated land mass of any size which has never been the theater of a major, or even a minor, war.) The concept of "mateship" which tied men together for mutual protection and survival in the bush may no longer be much talked about except at ceremonial functions, but its legacies are to be seen and felt, and "mate" is by no means an archaism.

If occasionally, amidst neo-puritanical concerns with our neighbors' orthodoxy and dark suspicions of global depravity, one wonders whatever happened to American optimism, he may take a little comfort in realizing there are still people who can look ahead without being frantically exhorted to do so. But if he supposes that Australians forget their past, let him work for a spell in the great Mitchell Library at Sydney, visit the Eureka Stockade at Ballaarat or the Joseph Furphy cottage—"Tom Collins House"—at Perth, or better yet, be taken for a cook-out to the Blue Mountains and shown traces of the early coach road where the rock cuts still bear the marks of convict picks. Let him attend an annual meeting of the Henry Lawson Society at Footscray Park, Melbourne, or a performance of Douglas Stewart's *Fisher's Ghost,* or talk with the Melbourne bibliographers Anderson and MacLaren, the Sydney bibliographers Ferguson, Mackaness, and Stone, or read FitzGerald's *The Wind at Your Door.* For that matter, let him even read *The Texas Quarterly:* "Down Under" begins at the top of the next page.

MARY DURACK : *In Search of an Australian Frontier*

"If Kit Carson, Daniel Boone, Davey Crockett and any other frontiersmen were around today, the chances are they would quit America and hotfoot it to the new Wild West—Australia. That is the view of millionaire rancher ———— who is doing just that. He is selling up his own ten square miles of rich cattle country in Florida to 'find a new frontier' in Australia . . . .

" 'You see, we are frontier kind of folks, and we like frontier living,' he said. 'But that's dead here now. Life is gotten to be too soft cushioned. We are going to Australia just as my own people trekked to Carolina before the revolution and my great-grand-daddy came to Florida with old Hickory Andrew Jackson in the early 1800s.'

"The rancher's sons recently returned from scouting Australia with the news that it is at the same stage as America was 100 years ago."

THIS RECENT NEW YORK ITEM FROM THE LONDON *Daily Express* HAS prompted me to consider the question of the Australian frontier and the rancher's chances of finding it.

If just any sort of outback life will answer his definition of a frontier he should have little difficulty in finding a suitable pastoral property in any state in the Commonwealth—a going concern where he and his family will have plenty of room to move. Conditions that seem fairly luxurious to the Australian may appear rugged enough to our millionaire Floridan, and he might feel a genuine frontiersman even with electricity, refrigeration, radio, telephone, good roads, and a convenient township. But supposing in simple earnest he wants not to take over an already developed property in a district that hasn't been an outpost in a hundred years, but to pioneer a new one—to forge a true frontier outside the existing bounds of settlement? What then?

This is where we take out the map and consider the problem conscientiously. *Frontiers.* Yes, there is all this spare land around the centre where the last sheep properties run out. There is the immense emptiness of the Nullarbor Plain where a few hardy optimists believe they have only to tap the artesian in order to throw the area open to settlement. The rancher might be prepared to back this proposition in spite of carping scientific pessimists who doubt that an adequate water supply alone would bring productivity to this arid wilderness.

What then, the enthusiast may ask, of this tract of unoccupied country in northwest Kimberley, showing an annual rainfall of thirty inches? If our frontiersman is really dedicated to discomfort, isolation, and difficulties that others have found insuperable it might be worth considering. Should he go in undeterred by an aerial impression of rugged inaccessibility he will find it wild, romantic looking country with palm-fringed rivers and lily-clad billabongs, abounding in bird life and crocodiles (which should not disturb a Floridan), its huge boabs, spreading white gums and paperbarks shading pockets of good grazing country interspersed with limestone

MARY DURACK

outcrops and picturesque ranges. Any experienced bushman will tell him that it is ideally suited to the development of a fine independent breed of scrub cattle and brumby horses and that cattle tick and wild dogs thrive splendidly there as well. He should be warned, however, that until such time as the area is opened up with roads and a port it is a poor risk for the man with capital and a hopeless one for the man without.

This fairly seems to cover Australia's frontier prospects in the old-fashioned sense, and we face the rather depressing fact that the boundaries of agricultural and pastoral settlement as defined in the nineties remain virtually unaltered. Some ascribe this to the refusal of a softer-skinned generation to leave the overcrowded cities for the all-too-empty land, but the trend is inevitable, for everywhere in the world while modern mechanisation diminishes the need for rural labour the development of urban industries holds out ever-increasing opportunities. It would be difficult for a hard-headed businessman to escape the conclusion that although roughly the size of the United States, Australia's resources have never been comparable and that our "great empty spaces" remain so because their occupation has not yet been practicable. A survey of the bald facts will reveal that over one million square miles, or approximately one third of the continent, must be classified as unexploitable desert, while three quarters of the map, lacking the discovery of hitherto unknown scientific aids, is incapable of carrying more than a very sparse population. History reveals how the land's limitations were learned the hard way and at great cost, how overconfident development in the booming eighties precipitated national disaster in the drought-stricken nineties, while overstocking turned vast, light-carrying areas into desert wastes.

Though seeming of all countries in the world to offer the least tangible resistance to European settlement, Australia was to prove in many respects the most baffling. Understanding could be reached only through hard experience, her land laws and methods of development established by a tough process of trial and error without some clue to which the newcomer may find the Australian frontier situation today as puzzling as it ever was.

After the penetration of the Great Dividing Range in the early 1820s the Australian inland drive from the east coast was as rapid and vigorous as the American, her first footers as impatient of restraint and as quickly outdistancing official surveys to take up land not yet legally open to settlement. In both countries early land laws were desperately contrived to fit patterns established by individuals who had become a law unto themselves but the different methods of development and conceptions of democracy were largely inclined by the contrasting nature of their lands.

While America's frontier moved into a fertile west before consolidating ranks of small farming families, in Australia thin spearheads of settlement strung on into the mirage of an increasingly arid interior. Britain's demand for wool and the land's natural suitability for sheep raising strongly influenced early Australian enterprise, especially since agriculture, possible only in the higher rainfall areas, was difficult and not highly profitable.

Up to the 1850s the big leaseholders, or "squatters," representing one tenth of the community, had been a power in the land. In a series of heated battles they had won the purchase rights to the plums of their districts and by buying up for a few pounds all permanent waterholes and river frontages could tie up hundreds, even thousands of acres of grazing land. With the discovery of gold in 1851, however, the picture swiftly changed and the squatter found his rights challenged on all sides by a new influx of population. Land-hungry little men gained confidence through exponents of new democratic ideologies and from colonists returning from the California gold rushes with stories of how the prairies of America had been opened by free selectors unhampered by the widespread preëmptions of the squatters and the locked areas of crown reserve.

The resulting Free Selection Act of the early sixties, designed to uphold the rights of the small settler, somewhat paralleled the United States Homestead Act of the same period, but though both were subject to the same abuses the American Act was vastly more successful. In Australia it soon proved much harder for the majority to develop their small farms than they had imagined. Land that could be used by the pastoralist in its natural state required clearing at great cost for agriculture and small farming. The revolutionary age of the "stump jump plough" had not arrived and the land did not yield readily to primitive farming equipment. Added to these difficulties a succession of bad seasons ruined and discouraged many who had started with high hopes on their new selections. Little wonder that the more unscrupulous big men could so readily find "dummy" selectors to occupy parts of their estates that had been resumed!

But the Act had the over-all effect of breaking up the higher rainfall areas. The struggling "cockies," or small farmers, introduced a new era of encroaching fences and of widespread horse and cattle stealing to harass the once all-powerful big holders. Many of these, nostalgic for the good old days of "open range" grazing and unchallenged boundaries, moved west and north to new frontiers in country capable of carrying sheep and cattle only over increasingly large areas.

The law, in recognition of their useful enterprise, gave them as much as it deemed prudent. Homestead areas were granted in freehold, leases extended in time and size, and rentals reduced, but the Crown, mindful of its duty to posterity in dealing with land of untried potential, retained the title deeds, the mineral rights, and the right to resume land, with due compensation, for "other purposes." The quandary of the law makers should be appreciated. The small men must be placated on the one hand, but it was obvious, on the other, that the threat to the squatters of being driven off either by drought or resumptions did not foster land husbandry: that it led in fact to a tendency, so often cited politically against the big estates, to exploit or "mine" the land while the going was good.

No one in this country was ever satisfied with the land laws. Every attempt to mollify the big holders in their demands for the greater security of tenure that would

MARY DURACK

encourage them to improve their properties and develop the pastoral industry brought from the landless or small holders louder protests against "favouritism" for the grasping sheep or cattle "kings."

My Irish grandfather, who had carved out properties on the boundaries of Western Queensland settlement, voiced the sentiments of all such "outside" pastoralists: " 'Cattle Kings' you call us, then we are kings in grass castles that may be blown away upon a puff of wind."

That Australia's land laws, rightly described as "a jungle penetrable only to the initiate," did tend to favour the big holder was actually a reluctant concession to harsh reality. As many a determined trier or "battler" learned to his sorrow, it was only men with enough capital to improve and maintain large pastoral leases who could make out in those drought-menaced, light-carrying areas and they were depriving nobody of land that could have been used for "other purposes."

In time, when the discovery of the artesian flow made smaller holdings practicable, many of the bigger properties were broken up but the Australian frontier remained the province of the relatively big pastoral holder.

The country, however, was never really at ease with the situation or happily resigned to the fact that so few should control so much. The voice of Australian democracy was always the voice of the struggling majority against the more fortunate few.

Sometimes, to be sure, individuals starting from scratch could, with a rare combination of luck, good timing, drive, and sagacity, win through to be prosperous landholders, but the average man had no such prospect and the farther out he got the less were his chances of being anything other than a wage earner. For this reason labour was always one of the greatest problems in the far outback, for few men were attracted by the isolation, hard living, and poor chances of advancement offering in remote areas.

The frontier, however, did attract a certain, perhaps uniquely Australian type: the itinerant stockman or drover, who, ambitious within the limitations of the bush, took pride in his horsemanship, his knowledge of handling stock, and his "bushmanship" which covered a variety of skills such as setting a course in trackless country, living off the land, coping with the aborigines, and generally surviving under the toughest circumstances. Almost all these men, knowing their only chance of a breakthrough to lie in a stroke of phenomenal luck, combined their stockwork with a constant search for gold. With this added incentive there was no corner of the continent they were not prepared to probe, mapping with extraordinary perception the areas of possible settlement, blazing new trails in the big stock drives of the seventies and eighties. In their nomadic calling few of them ever gathered moss or settled into ordinary home life. Some of them found gold, or indications of gold, and even started rushes to various remote parts of the country, but others usually got the credit and the reward for their discoveries. Others occupied the country they opened up while they rode on to ever-receding horizons and lonely graves.

But none of these men, or even the pioneer pastoralists who employed them, ever thought of themselves as "frontiersmen" or saw any of the excitement and romance in their lives that they readily acknowledged as belonging to America's "Wild West." My father expressed precisely the Australian attitude in letters written to his bush associates while on a visit to the United States and Canada in 1906. Everything thrilled and excited him, but the highlight of his experiences was a short sojourn "out on the open prairies among the cowboys of Western Canada." "They ask me about Australia," he wrote, "but time is precious and I keep them going nonstop about life in this fabulous west . . . ."

He relates how, sitting around a roaring fire under the cold Canadian stars, wrapped in a huge beaver coat, he thrilled to the tales of expanding American settlement and the tough frontier towns, the verve with which he writes in striking contrast to the terseness of his comments on his own frontier-forging days. Tales of covered waggon treks across the Rockies and the penetration of the white man with his flocks and herds into Indian country he would ever afterwards relate with zest but he made only the most casual reference to his own first memories of a covered waggon jolting a thousand miles north from Goulburn, New South Wales, into the still unexplored aboriginal hunting grounds of Western Queensland. Nor did he then see as the epics they were the overlanding feats of his own and other families, three thousand miles from Queensland to the new promised land in the Kimberley district of the northwest where at twenty years old he established a million-acre property on the virgin pastures of the Ord.

"Now I must tell you," his Canadian letter continued, "of some of the colourful characters of this 'outfit' as they call it here. The stories we read of this great country are not exaggerated . . . . One of my companions, when turning in, quietly slipped me a six-chambered Colt revolver, saying that I probably wouldn't need it but that its possession at all times in this country established a certain amount of reverence or respect . . . . I slept well and undisturbed, however, dreaming that I was back in Kimberley telling you chaps there all about Western Canada and these wild, young, reckless chaps of the prairies . . . ."

One wonders why the incident of the Colt revolver would have appeared remarkable when neither my father nor those to whom he wrote would, in their right minds, have travelled or slept without a firearm in the bush.

"Slippery Bill" from Mexico, "Deadly Dick" from Wyoming, "Slim" from 'way down Montana, and the rest of them would have seemed colourful indeed to the hard-living, hard-riding men of the Kimberley cattle camps, in their strictly utilitarian stockmen's garb. It is doubtful, however, whether any outpost in the world could have claimed such an odd and interesting assortment of characters as the Kimberley district at that time. For many it was the last retreat from the law, from society, from political intrigue. Many were survivors of the overland trails, some of the best and toughest stock riders in the world, whose adventures would have outclassed the wildest fiction, and yet we are told they would ride for miles to get news bulletins from the traveller. They were simply "stockmen," or "bushmen," and the country they pioneered the "back blocks," or "back o' beyond" if you like, but nothing as "high falutin'" as a "frontier." While their American counterparts galloped the prairies with swinging lariats, creating legends to delight the world, these men rode on in obscurity, performing real feats of bushmanship and triumphs of endurance that left little country to be officially "opened up" by the end of the last century.

A newcomer looking for frontiers and wanting to be a frontiersman will amuse Australians, but he may well insist that our use of the term is sadly limited, that there are new kinds of frontier jobs to be done today. And this is true. Every year fresh vistas are being opened up in Australia in hitherto bypassed or little developed areas. The use of trace elements has brought fertility to large, naturally poorly productive areas; new equipment has made possible the large-scale and economic clearing of brigalow and acacia scrub, opening up a future of more intensive development beyond Queensland's Darling Downs, while large-scale irrigation schemes are bringing an era of long-dreamed-of closer settlement in many areas. It is encouraging too that far from being reluctant to take up the challenge of the land Australians are flocking eagerly to each new field.

In this age of rapid technical development where much of today's science fiction may be tomorrow's scientific fact it has become the fashion to conjure up fantasies of blossoming deserts irrigated with sea water condensed by atomic power, while scientists and technicians, like initiates in the immense problems of space who speak cautiously of its "conquest," are often dismissed as defeatist and unimaginative. But in truth these are now the frontiersmen without whose work the highest visionary flights, the boldest enterprise and hardiest optimism, can achieve little. Australia *is* a land of opportunity. She *is* a land of expanding development, but for the outriders of modern development, as dedicated and matter-of-fact as the old, there are no short cuts to the goal of man's imagination. With all the old-time prospector's longing for the "lucky break" they must cover the distance step by step within the discipline of today's reality, knowing as the pathfinders before them that others will inherit their discoveries. They will never concede a destination—only a horizon.

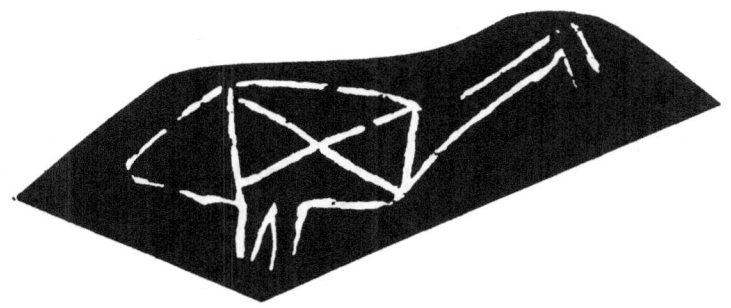

GOLD HAD BEEN KNOWN TO EXIST IN AUSTRALIA LONG BEFORE IT WAS discovered.

This kind of Irishism was quite in keeping with the upside down values of Antipodean life during the early part of the nineteenth century. After all, the Irish themselves were there in large numbers, mostly as unwilling exiles from recurrent political troubles at home. A good proportion of the population was, or had been, convicts. As Governor Lachlan Macquarie (1810–1821) expressed it, the colony of New South Wales was inhabited by "those who had been transported and those who ought to have been." There were, in fact, two classes: the mass of assigned labourers, with or without broad arrows on their working dress, and their masters (among them a fair number of emancipated convicts) who had achieved social status in the New World as military officers, men of property, merchants, traders, and pastoralists. From the second decade of the century King Wool began to emerge as the monarch of Australia's destinies.

The discovery of payable gold would have upset the balance of established society, for anyone might dig it out of the ground and become wealthy, or at least independent. Hence the fact that gold-encrusted stones were to be picked up on New South Wales sheepwalks, west of the Blue Mountains, was met with a conspiracy of silence. When Governor Sir George Gipps was told in 1839 of nuggets found near Bathurst, he advised his informant "to keep the matter secret for fear of the serious consequences." During the 1840s a Sydney jeweler used to buy native gold from a shepherd named M'Gregor, who cunningly refused to reveal the locality. In 1841 the Rev. W. B. Clarke, a keen geologist, found gold in the Cox Valley, behind the Blue Mountains. "Put it away, Mr. Clarke," said Gipps when shown a specimen, "or we shall all have our throats cut." But it was gold strikes in distant California that finally overcame the reluctance of Australian authorities to face the facts.

Among the thousands who crossed the Pacific to join the great rush of 1849 in the Sacramento Valley was Edward Hammon Hargraves, an English migrant who had been raising sheep in New South Wales for many years. The Californian landscapes reminded him of the country he had known beyond the Blue Mountains, so two years later he returned and struck gold almost as soon as he dismounted from his horse. Officialdom then received him with a very different air. "If this is gold country, Mr. Hargraves," said the Colonial Secretary, "it will stop the Home Government from sending us any more convicts, and prevent emigration to California." As Brian Fitzpatrick has pointed out, the situation had by then become crucial. The loss of manpower represented "a drain as great as that of the Australian Sixth, Seventh and Ninth Divisions . . . when they sailed for the wars ninety years later."

By May 1851 more than a thousand men were washing creeks for gold in country too poor for grazing cattle. Three months later three thousand were working along the Turon River alone. Pastoral centres like nearby Bathurst were immediately drained of their population. Large numbers left capitals like Sydney, Melbourne, Adelaide in the hope of quick-won riches. In the newly separated colony of Victoria this mass exodus was looked upon with misgivings, and leading citizens offered a reward for anyone finding gold within two hundred miles of Melbourne. Almost at once a big strike was made at Ballaarat. Hundreds of excited diggers began to demolish the beauty of landscapes that had hitherto known only the quiet browsing of sheep, while the sheepruns themselves were swept clean of labour.

This sudden lust for gold, with its promise of freedom and rich living, hit Australia with the force of a revolution. The cities and towns were left with empty streets; stores, offices, workshops, and wharves had virtually no employees to carry on; seamen deserted from ships, police threw away their uniforms, government clerks left the dust to gather upon files. Those who did remain shocked employers with their demands for higher pay. Wages jumped as much as two hundred per cent, while prices for commodities rose accordingly. It was Australia's first taste of inflation. Coupled with this was the impossibility of carrying on stable overseas trade. Shipping lay idle; wool remained on the wharves. And in the bush itself squatters—as the Australian stockbreeders were called—found their flocks abandoned and land values deteriorating so fast many decided to sell out.

No wonder the *Sydney Morning Herald* wrote in 1851, "Let us cling to the hope that the treasure does not exist in large quantities. Should our gold prove to be abundant in quantity, rich in quality, and easy of access, let the inhabitants of New South Wales and the neighbouring colonies stand prepared for calamities far more terrible than earthquakes and pestilence."

The Sydney newspaper was apparently fearful from tales filtering back from California, where life on the diggings was alleged to be wild and ruffianly. It was a charge rebutted by American gold seekers in Australia who pointed out that such lawlessness as did exist could be attributed largely to ex-convicts escaping Sydney life for the wider freedom of American diggings. History has its own genius for irony.

At all events, the opponents of these "winds of change" took a narrow view. In the long term the country was to achieve enormous benefits. Gold was the making of Australia. It transformed the social and economic scene almost as fundamentally as any change from feudal to industrial regimes. This, however, did not become apparent for some years.

The first result was a wave of immigration. In 1851 Australia had only 405,000 persons. Within ten years the figure had reached 1,145,000. The gold rushes not only brought them in at an initial rate of nearly 100,000 a year, but attracted men of a completely different type. No longer were they the victims of England's industrial revolution, those "who left their country for their country's good," as the convict-playwright Barrington once put it: criminal elements and those driven by necessity to petty crime. They were in the main adventurous, free-living spirits who had no intention of adapting themselves to the social climate of "old lags," poverty-haunted shepherds, and simpleton hut keepers. No wonder the self-made aristocracy of squatters saw them as dangerous elements.

Pastoral leaders called for a total ban on gold digging. Others urged governments to declare martial law. New South Wales did the next best thing: it declared gold to be Crown property and issued licenses for which diggers had to pay thirty shillings a month. When the Victorian government followed suit it opened the way to later political upheavals—and to a radical change of government in Australia as a whole. Meantime, officialdom could only deplore the mass movement into the once neglected countryside.

The infant colony of Tasmania alone lost one seventh of its population of 70,000. In Melbourne only two police constables were left to keep order. The wharves there, and in Sydney, seemed to be constantly crowded as newcomers disembarked from European sailing ships. They came from everywhere; Scots, Irish, and English predominating, but also Germans, Frenchmen, Italians, Swiss, Dutch, and Danes. Forty-Niners from California joined the interminable procession crossing the Blue Mountains or toiling up the Victorian roads to Ballaarat and Bendigo. They went by bullock dray, buggy, on horseback, and by foot. They camped in lean-tos roughly built of saplings, in bark humpies and bough sheds. They toiled all day down insecure shafts and winzes and drives, or beside windlasses and mullock heaps under the hot summer sun, or in bitter winds sweeping over plains and up stony gullies, and at nighttime they caroused and tossed nuggets or pouches of gold dust over the bars for their grog. Almost every district had its legends of men shoeing their horses with gold, using ten-pound notes to light their pipes, or drinking champagne by the gallon. And, if there were more luckless ones than lucky, for the average weekly earning was less than £4 a week, at least these adventurous souls brought a new breath of life to landscapes where it was once said no one could live.

If gold gave colonial society a great lift, it was a great leveller, too. Describing everyday life in the canvas town of Solfala, along the Turon River, Colonel G. C. Munday (*Our Antipodes,* London, 1852) wrote of "merchants, cabmen, magistrates and convicts, amateur gentlemen rocking the cradle merely to say they have done so, fashionable hairdressers and tailors, cooks, coachmen, lawyers, clerks and their masters, colliers, cobblers, quarrymen, doctors of physic and of music, aldermen, an ADC on leave, scavengers, sailors, shorthand writers, a real-life lord on his travels —all levelled by community of pursuit and of costume . . . ." It was, in fact, the beginnings of a democratic community.

And that, no doubt, was what prompted the *Sydney Morning Herald* to warn of worse calamities than earthquakes and pestilence. For the autocrats of the period democracy was a fearsome word, as emotive as communism today. They recalled what they had heard of recent unrest in Europe; the Paris Commune revolution in

GEORGE FARWELL

Germany, the English Chartists defying law and order in the "hungry forties." The secret tide of democracy was unquestionably starting to seep into Australian soil.

What fostered it, unwittingly, was the harsh outlook of officialdom. At first it seemed not unreasonable to charge miners a fee to search for gold. The New South Wales and Victoria governments had to find revenue for services somewhere. They had to police the goldfields, provide armed escorts for the wagonloads of bullion despatched to the cities, build roads and other amenities—though the tracks to the fields long remained mere strings of potholes under a choking cloud of dust. But the diggers felt their 30/-license fee too high, especially since it had to be paid every month, and most individual yields began to drop after the first few lucky strikes. It was not every day a man found sudden wealth like Holtermann at Hill End with his famous five-foot nugget weighing 630 lbs. The resentment against license fees, whether a man won gold or not, began first in a passive way. Had it not been for the peremptory manner of the goldfields' police, who insisted on frequent inspections, the issue might never have come to a head.

Trained police were then in short supply, so that fresh men had to be recruited wherever they could be found. In many cases the new acquisition of power went to their heads. In others, the recruits were brought from convict Tasmania, and many relished this rare taste of authority.

From inspections of licenses these daily forays by police turned into "digger hunts." They became only too reminiscent of searches for bushrangers, then beginning to harry the countryside, or for runaway convicts. Sometimes the police foraged in parties with fixed bayonets; sometimes they marched diggers away under arms when they failed to produce licenses, or chained them to logs outside the Gold Commissioner's tent for interrogation. No wonder the Ballaarat diggings eventually burst into flame.

The political flashpoint was not reached until December 1854, when Australia's much romanticised "Bunker Hill" took place at the Eureka Stockade. But it is necessary first to examine the rather complex series of events that led up to this short-lived rebellion. Its beginnings were not political at all. An unsuccessful move in the New South Wales Legislative Council dominated by squatters, to abolish license fees (which were not great revenue producers there) encouraged Victorian miners at Bendigo to ask their government for a reduction. A deputation was sent to discuss the question with Governor Latrobe in Melbourne. His answer was that the monthly "head tax," recently doubled, was even then insufficient to pay for governing the fields, whereupon the delegates told a huge city audience they would bring down 100,000 men to ring Melbourne with fire. Their sentiments met with wild applause. Back on the Bendigo field big meetings resolved to boycott licenses. The government panicked and reduced the fee to £2 for three months. It was too late for such bargaining.

Had the fairly tolerant Latrobe not returned to England at the end of his three-year term, no crisis might have matured. But his successor, Sir Charles Hotham, was a naval man with stern ideas on discipline. Moreover, he found an economic crisis developing because normal trade had come to a standstill. His government was faced with a deficit of a million pounds, and the only possible revenue appeared to be from licenses. This time popular opposition arose from a different region, in the newly discovered Eureka Valley. It was an extension of the usually well-behaved Ballaarat field, but there were some pretty wild elements among the newcomers to this rush.

In October 1854, a brawl developed outside the notorious Eureka Hotel, and a digger was stabbed. The owner, an ex-convict from Tasmania, was charged with murder but acquitted by a venal magistrate. A hostile mob, numbering several thousand men, burnt down the hotel in protest. At once Hotham intervened, dismissed the magistrate, ordered a new trial, and had the publican convicted of manslaughter. Three of the men who burnt down the hotel were gaoled as well. This led to further protest meetings, and a detachment of four hundred and fifty soldiers and police were sent up from Melbourne.

At this stage a group styling itself the Ballaarat Reform League began to assume leadership of the diggers. It was severely tainted with democratic ideas. Hotham preferred to talk of "foreign agitators." Formed in November, it was pledged to campaign for the abolition of licenses—but also adopted the aims of the People's Charter of 1838 in England. These Chartist leaders encouraged the Ballaarat diggers to demonstrate against Hotham's armed detachment. When shots were fired by the soldiery, a fiery mass meeting resolved to burn the detested licenses. At once the Riot Act was read and the Gold Commissioner ordered his troops to hunt for licenses, using arrogant and aggressive methods. There was a clash with a large crowd, eight diggers were arrested for disorderly conduct, and the League's supporters marched en masse to a small rise known as Bakery Hill.

It was here that a new symbol of resistance appeared. A blue flag with the silver stars of the Southern Cross was hoisted on the hill; a flag that was to become an almost legendary affair in later years. A stockade was built around this hill; men armed themselves and began to make pikes out of any iron they could find. A new set of leaders emerged, more resolute and political minded than their predecessors. It was true, as Hotham suggested, that there were some "foreigners" amongst them; but not many. The main two were a picturesque Italian named Carboni Raffaelo, who claimed to have fought for Mazzini and Garibaldi and who later wrote a colourful if somewhat romantic account of the Eureka rebellion; and a German radical called Vern, who tried to introduce the rudiments of military drilling among the miners. But the main figures were English and Irish; notably Peter Lalor, an Irishman and Roman Catholic who was elected "commander in chief."

Raffaelo has left us a richly coloured narrative of how, beneath the Southern Cross flag, Lalor made his followers kneel and swear "to defend our sacred rights and liberties." In that excited atmosphere, the melodramatic gesture did not seem out of place. When dawn broke on December 3, the scene was almost the classic one of the ill-prepared but heroic band of martyrs facing superior arms. It was David against

GEORGE FARWELL

Goliath, the ancient Greeks at Thermopylae, the rebels of the Paris Commune. On one side, crouching behind the stockade of logs and mining timber, were some one hundred and fifty miners with muskets, pikes, and pistols. On the other, facing the grassy knoll, were the redcoats in orderly ranks, led by an officer with revolver and sword.

Someone opened fire; the soldiery charged; a wild struggle took place by the stockade; and in a few minutes it was all over. Thirty of the defenders were killed, and four soldiers, including their captain. Peter Lalor was wounded but escaped. Those of the rebels who failed to get away were put in chains and marched off to gaol. So ended what the Labor Movement has since tended to call "Australia's only rebellion." As the conservative historians insist, it achieved nothing in itself. However, like the classic British defeat, it led on to future victories—of a kind.

Four days later thirteen men were committed for trial on charges of high treason. Including Lalor, who gave himself up, there were five Irishmen among them, as well as one Italian, one German, and an American Negro. The subsequent trial in Melbourne, though there was no further trouble at Ballaarat, aroused mass demonstrations. (A significant fact is that the mass of the miners were never involved, preferring to look upon the stockade incident as a kind of spectator sport, once again suggesting that social changes are created by minorities.) The political impetus, in fact, had shifted to the city. There, a strong democratic movement drafted a constitution (which Hotham considered revolutionary), circulated it in secret, and aroused mass support for the captive thirteen. A demand for an amnesty was made. When that failed, funds were raised to engage Melbourne's leading barristers for the defense.

All thirteen were acquitted, given a welcome fit for heroes outside the court, and returned home to live subsequently respectable lives. Lalor, in fact, was soon to be returned to the newly constituted Victorian Parliament and eventually became Speaker of the House. The operative factor was, of course, the creation of this parliament. Even if the conservatives claim that the Ballaarat rebellion achieved nothing, that representative government was on the way anyhow, it must be conceded that the mass indignation of the mining community forced the British Colonial Office to speedier action. The Victorian Legislative Council, appointed on a property basis, remained as an upper house, but a democratically elected parliament came into being as well in 1856. The move was swiftly followed in other Australian states.

By resisting change to the last, the Victorian Council simply speeded up the inevitable, because of population pressures and a shifting economy. The conventional historian tends to overlook these implications. He points to the fact that Hotham —and Latrobe before him—initially favoured a more liberal policy but were held back by an intransigent Council. Then, when the Ballaarat Reform League grew truculent, they adopted a tough attitude instead—and finally declared martial law. The real question is just why did the Legislative Council act in this way? And whether, had it been more flexible, the miners would have resorted to violence. This is fundamental to the understanding of subsequent Australian history, especially in relations between capital and labour.

The Legislative Council largely represented pastoral interests, which have always played a reactionary role. Yet in 1854 half the total population was engaged in mining. It had no say whatever in making the laws; no representation. The Council was elected by, and spoke for, some six hundred squatters and perhaps twice as many farmers, merchants, and manufacturers. The latter feared they would be swamped in any move towards democracy. Yet, as it happened, representative government merely helped to broaden the economy and consolidate their interests.

The pastoralists, whose revenue was declining because they could sell no wool overseas for lack of shipping and labour, soon began to find a new market at home —for meat to feed the rapidly growing population. The infant banks, faced with a slump in land values, found they had some £3,000,000 of deposits from the gold-fields in their vaults, but no way of investing it. They decided to set up as indent merchants and fostered large imports from Britain. Then, as the easily won surface gold began to peter out, new methods of production began to create a class of wealthy private owners.

Towards the end of the 1850s mining in Victoria ceased to be a small man's occupation. It became a matter of developing deep leads, big companies, capital. The sprawling, rough-living shanty towns of Ballaarat and Bendigo became prosperous, conservative; they were converted into solid bourgeois centres with broad and tree-lined avenues, dignified mansions, stock exchanges, and gilt-edged investments. Certainly the gradually awakening labour movement kept alive the tradition of Eureka, but it ceased to be militant. If Ballaarat Town Hall continued to fly the South Cross flag each anniversary—as it still does today—it was little more than a token gesture.

Though the beginnings of Australia's strong trade union movement can be dated from that period, the agitation for wages and standards came from the cities and not the goldfields. Likewise the struggle between capital and labour—an ever present feature for the next century—shifted to another scene; to the campaign to unlock the pastoral lands. Again it was the squatters versus the rest.

Parliamentary government did not lead, as most expected, to an easing of the land monopoly. As gold digging declined, thousands began to seek the chance of taking up a few acres as farmers or fruit growers. Liberals like (Sir) John Robertson, later premier of New South Wales, felt that the future lay in creating a yeoman class, a buffer between big landholders and a rootless proletariat. Those who had prospered from gold also looked to the land as an investment. They found their ambitions once more challenged by what the late Professor G. V. Portus described as "the landowning politician of the Whig type who wanted government of the squatters, by the squatters, for the squatters." Their political struggle became the major factor of the 1860s, and large areas were thrown open for free selection only after much bitter agitation. Later the conflict shifted again to become a war of attrition between squatters and bush unionists, mainly shearers, eventually flaring into the great strikes of the 1890s, which gave birth to the Australian Labour Party. As an American observer, G. H. Allen, has recently expressed it, "Mistrust of the squatter provided fertile soil for the swift development of a proletarian party."

Allen, who sees Australia as having been dominated since the gold rushes by "collectivist ideas," admits that unionism and class consciousness have been mainly "a city, not a frontier phenomenon." All the same, he describes the bush as a potent force in the same direction. "In the United States the frontier preserved individualist opposition to collectivist ideas and slowed down the economic use of the State's political power. In Australia the pressure of city and country alike created a strong labour movement that in the 1890s was to lead the world."

In general principles, maybe. But Allen overlooks the fact that the gold era also fostered a number of vital individual traits in the Australian character. The legendary swagman stems from this period; the man who rejected city orthodoxy and the rule of the squatter alike, preferring to tramp the bush alone—or with a mate—carrying all his possessions in a swag slung over his shoulder, dependent upon nobody, except for an occasional "handout," and sleeping freely under a wide sky. Mateship—the creed of the Australian outback, as developed to its most eloquent expression in the stories of Henry Lawson—was also the creation of this free-roving period, when men had to hang together in order to survive in the hostile, or at best indifferent, outback. The peculiar genius of the prospector—usually a lone hand—also arose out of the necessity to search for new diggings as the old ones were abandoned.

Often enough these were small shows, worked by small syndicates or single men. But the prospector—in his thousands—has remained a potent factor in the back country to this day. Moreover, he had to be a bushman. In common with the cattleman and the drover, he had to be able to find his way across the huge, featureless landscapes, the deserts and rugged mountain regions where less resourceful characters would soon have perished of hunger or thirst.

It was men of this calibre who opened up large areas of the back country to settlement throughout the nineteenth century. They were the foragers who located the first, short-lived Queensland goldfield at Canoona, near Rockhampton, then unearthed the great riches of Charters Towers, Mount Morgan, the Palmer field in tropical junglelands behind Cooktown, Gympie and Croydon, where a few crumbling tenements and huge mullock piles alone recall the wealth mined near the lonely Gulf of Carpentaria sixty years ago.

In the 1870s the phrase "Rich as Mount Morgan" carried its echoes around the world and helped to place once remote Queensland on the map. One after another thriving towns grew out of the silent and empty plains, all upon much the same pattern as E. B. Kennedy described it (*Four Years in Queensland,* London, 1870): "The night par excellence was Saturday night; the whole length of the street was so full of diggers we could hardly move at all, and what with singing, swearing, fighting, drinking, bargaining for loaves, beef and sausages for Sunday's dinner, the noise was tremendous, while every public house was crammed with men discussing their various finds . . . while they frequently paid for their drinks with small samples of gold . . . ."

The prevalence of drink in such accounts was by no means accidental. There are times when the history of Australia seems littered with rum casks and bottles. Natural perhaps in a tough climate, with primitive conditions of life, no amenities, few womenfolk but those you paid for, and half a continent to cross to return to civilization. It was a gambler's world; and you lived for the day. That outlook too has etched its way into the Australian temperament.

Nowhere was that more in evidence than in Western Australia, the most arid, most unpeopled sector of the continent. Covering 900,000 square miles, this state consisted of little more than the embryo city of Perth and sparse cattle-raising lands until Southern Cross broke out in 1892. Two years later a really big strike was made at Coolgardie, a hundred miles farther into the desert. Today the "Golden Mile" between Coolgardie and Kalgoorlie is still yielding more than 800,000 fine ounces of gold a year. It is West Australia's greatest revenue producer. Unlike Queensland, which followed its gold discoveries with the exploitation of fertile lands for sugar, sheep, and cattle, the sun-dried western state has had to eke out a more precarious livelihood.

All the same, the Australia-wide pattern has been remarkably uniform. It was gold that made the break-through from the narrow, static hegemony of the early squatter, forced him to revise his economic outlook, and flooded the country with a tide of unexpected wealth later to be invested elsewhere. Gold became the basis of the youthful nation's capital. From early Victoria and New South Wales it flowed not only into local industries and real estate, but passed over the state borders to enrich the continent at large—in Queensland, sheep and cattle stations, big mining enterprises, sugar; in Tasmania tin, copper, and more gold; in the great outback it led to further mineral discoveries such as the rich silver-lead field at Broken Hill, Coolgardie, and Kalgoorlie. It transformed the profile of a continent and the character of a nation.

Nowhere has this been more effectively summed up than in the Proem to Henry Handel Richardson's *The Fortunes of Richard Mahony,* one of the great Australian novels. Evoking the atmosphere of the early Ballaarat diggings with its toiling, tippling, temperamental thousands subjected to an alien environment, digger hunts, unexpected wealth, and nostalgia for a far-off homeland, Mrs. Richardson writes:

"This dream it was, of vast wealth got without exertion, which had decoyed the strange, motley crowd, in which peers and churchmen rubbed shoulders with the scum of Norfolk Island, to exile in this outlandish region. And the intention alike had been: to snatch a golden fortune from the earth and then, hey presto! for the old world again. But they were reckoning without their host; only too many of those

GEORGE FARWELL

who entered the country went out no more. They became prisoners to the soil. The fabulous riches of which they had heard tell amounted, at best, to a few thousands of pounds; what folly to depart with so little, when mother earth still teemed! Those who drew blanks nursed an unquenchable hope, and laboured all their days like navvies, for a navvy's wage. . . . There were also men who, as soon as fortune smiled on them, dropped their tools and ran to squander the work of months in a wild debauch; and they invariably returned, tail down, to prove their luck anew. . . . A passion for gold itself awoke in them, an almost sensual craving to touch and possess; and the glitter of a few specks at the bottom of pan or cradle came, in time, to mean more to them than "home," or wife or child.

"Such were the fates of those who succumbed to the 'unholy hunger.' It was like a form of revenge taken on them, for their loveless schemes of robbing and fleeing; a revenge contrived by the ancient, barbaric country they had so lightly invaded. Now, she held them captive—without chains, ensorcelled—without witchcraft; and, lying stretched like some primeval monster in the sun, her breasts freely bared, she watched, with a malignant eye, the efforts made by these puny mortals to tear their lips away. . . ."

Here, in fact, is the end product of the wealth these variegated pioneers gave to a nation then only on the verge of being—its later cultural achievements. From the folk ballads sung around campfires in the gold-digging and pastoral era to the tales of Henry Lawson, mostly drawn from life in the abandoned goldfields of New South Wales; from the lithographs of men like S. T. Gill, who followed the coaches and bullock wagons of the Victorian diggings to the Impressionist landscape painters of the 1890s; from Henry Handel Richardson and a host of bush writers who etched the Australian character, first moulded in the quest for gold, to the more sophisticated artistic tradition of today—the rich and variegated leads can mostly be traced back to the mother lode of the gold discoveries that made this continent a misbegotten utopia for half the nations of the globe.

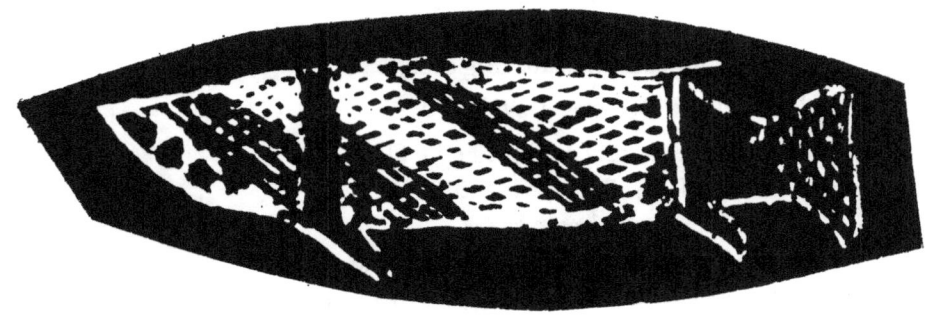

JAMES MCAULEY : *Festival at Santa Cruz*

(From a narrative poem, *Captain Quiros*)

The mountain is awake, with utterance
Of flame and burning rock and thunderous sound—
Abode of the ancestral spirits who dance
In blissful fire!   Tremors run through the ground
And through men's hearts.   The people stand dismayed
By prophecies as mantic ghosts invade
With alien voice the soothsayers in their trance.

Therefore Malope has begun to hold
A feast at his own ground.   The pigs are killed;
The scarlet feather-money is unrolled;
The conch is blown; and while the drums are stilled
Cooked strips of flesh from the boar's chine are placed
Before the ancestral stock, the vision-faced,
So that all ancient ritual is fulfilled.

Malope is the Chief, the central pole
Supporting the whole house by wealth and merit,
Acquired as he identifies his soul,
In sacrifice, with his ancestral spirit,
Till to his folk he seems to represent
The *duka,* as its live embodiment:
A man instinct with power, authentic, whole.

High-pitched men's voices chant unwearying
Above the slotted drums' sonorities,
With women's shrill harmonics flickering
Higher, like lightning over choppy seas.
Then silence, in the stop of voice and drum,
Opens a void wherein inrushing come
The spirits from the listening cycas trees.

And now the dancers move in single file
Tracing the Path of Fire, which all must tread
To Tinakula, the volcanic isle,
When after death they go to join the dead.
Along that path the She-Ghost gives them pause,
The guardian monster with black waving claws
And huge malignant eyes of burning red:

For in a cave-mouth, spider-like, she sits,
A maze-design half-finished at her feet,
Which the wayfaring soul with trembling wits
Must labour from his memory to complete,
Or be devoured.   So now the dance rehearses
Those labyrinthine windings and reverses
In token of the test that all must meet.

And then ecstatically they imitate
The dance of blissful spirits deified,
And rapt in deep communion celebrate
The tutelary beings who provide
Health, harvests, wisdom, prowess, progeny,
Protection in the night and on the sea,
And pleasure to the bridegroom and the bride.

This is that island world, Malope's place,
Much like our childhood world of presences
That look out from a mythic time and space
Into the real: a land of similes
Where man conforming to the cosmos proves
His oneness with all beings, and life moves
To the rhythm of profound analogies.

Nightlong the ancestral voice from the log-drum
Has urged the dancers till they seem to find
The nodal point in their delirium
At which all living things are intertwined:
Cycles of man and pig and yam and tide
In endless intervolvement unified,
Repeating all that's past in all to come.

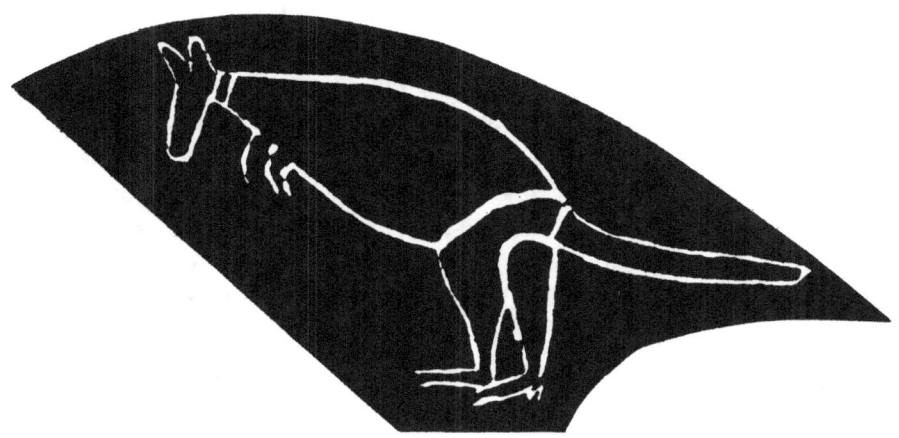

HEARTY CURTIS LEANED INTO THE OFFICE UNDER THE STAIRS. "Hullo, Ma. Thought you might like to know Whiner's on the pots." That was at three o'clock on the Monday afternoon. At three-ten Ma handed a telegram across the Post Office counter. "City Registry Office. Send relieving barman tonight's express. Cosmopolitan Hotel, Southern Cross." At four o'clock she put Whiner on the train for Kalgoorlie with a cheque for £50 in his pocket. Then she went back to the Cosmopolitan and took over in the front bar from Hearty.

Hearty leaned on the other side of the counter, then pushed over the three bob that Ma had paid him and, dripping his straggly ginger moustaches in his beer, he was able to save Ma the trouble of telling Whiner's story, a story that had to be told, because the customers asked questions.

"Hullo, Ma. Mine's a dash. Whiner not on the job today?"

"Whiner 's on the pots and Ma's sent him off to Kalgoorlie. Has to. Once he gets on it . . ."

Seemed Whiner had been at the Cossie since he hit the town after Gallipoli back in 1915. Old Grubstake Reedy had his name over the door in those days, though Ma, who was then Miss Carter, as cunning a barmaid as ever signed on for six months on the 'Fields, was doing most of the managing. Old Grubstake's wife was a lady that didn't have to soil her hands with a counter swab or even just handing a whisky bottle; she sat upstairs in her sewing room and made pretty clothes for herself and had a baby every year. Always belle of the ball she was, at Southern Cross, with her soft black curls and her lovely curves; and well old Grubstake knew it. He'd work from sun-up to midnight in that pub to keep her in silks and satins and moire antique; and she had a turn-out, the smartest on the 'Fields or down at the Coast either, for that matter; and on Sundays she'd drive up to church with old Grubstake and no man could have been prouder. And when they'd get back to the pub again, she'd sit upstairs and play the piano while Grubstake and the barmaid worked over the stocktaking in the closed-up bar.

Then one day he drove this wife of his down to the railway station with the three youngest and off she went to spend the summer by the seaside. She stayed there with the four others that had been in the convent, learning to be ladies like her and gentlemen, not like their father, until the Christmas holidays were over; but then she didn't come back to old Grubstake in the Cosmopolitan like he expected.

"No, Mr. Reedy," she said, when he went down to find out what was the matter, "I won't be returning. I think it would be wiser if I stayed at Cottesloe. The children should have a better home life . . . after all, those rough miners . . . the language . . . and the climate . . . and the children's schooling. I want Leo to be a doctor and Mary should be a nurse and the twins must be lawyers. . . ."

"And where's all the money to come from, Mrs Reedy dear, now tell me that?"

Mrs. Reedy knew the Cosmopolitan was a bonanzer and she said as much. So old Grubstake came back to Southern Cross and closed up her sewing room and moved Miss Carter, the barmaid, up into the room next door. She worked like a slavey in those days did old Ma. She was only a girl then, thin and gingerly but she was quick on her feet and sharp with her tongue and witty. Blokes 'ld come out of their way from Salt Hill and Marvel Vale and 'round about for miles, just to spend their cheques over her bar and hear her stories and tell their own. Even at that, the Cossie wasn't doing well enough to make ladies and gentlemen out of the seven Grubstake kids down at the Coast; so presently Ma, that was Miss Carter then, puts it to him that just grubstaking other people into bits of claims here and there isn't good enough; why doesn't he get into the mining game himself? So he did. And spent his time out at the "Spinning Jinny" while Ma looked after the pub.

It went on like that for years, with people calling her "Ma Reedy" and forgetting she's only the barmaid. Until a bit of earth hit old Grubstake behind the ear and the real Mrs Grubstake and Leo and the twins came up to Southern Cross and gave him a fine funeral while Ma kept the till ringing with the help of Whiner, making the most of the burying and the gossip about the will. Everyone heard that old Grubstake had left the mine to his wife and a half share in the pub to her too; the other half went to Ma. And the town was wondering what Ma was going to do.

All Ma did was act as though she was just the barmaid. "Yes Mrs Grubstake, no Mrs Grubstake," until after a decent interval of two days the family all went back to their fine house at the Coast and left Ma to carry on at the Cossie. Ma and Whiner. Whiner, he'd come back from Gallipoli and settled in in that front bar as though he was born there.

Bar minding, it's a ticklish business in its own way. You either got the knack or you haven't. Whiner, he had it. For the front bar. Takes something different for the saloon. In the front bar you got to be quick and you got to know the tricks of the trade to make the percentage without letting the customer know you're putting them over. You got to know your customer's likes; you got to be able to talk about things the bloke on the other side 's interested in; but most of all you got to know when to talk and when not. If a bloke comes in in the middle of the afternoon when there's only you and the blowfly on the window in the bar and if he asks you to have one, well, he's out for a wongi, that's plain as an outcrop of pommy gold. But if he comes in 'round about knock-off time with a couple of mates, well you just say "Evening gents. Dash and two straights? Thanks." Then you swab up the counter and straighten the shelf and don't pratt your frame into their conversation. But if they drag you into it . . . well you got to look as though their conversation's the most interesting thing in the whole of Southern Cross and when you have to leave their end of the counter to serve someone else you just have to look as though it hurts you to drag yourself away.

That's the way it goes in the front bar. But that's not Whiner's way. Not by a long chalk. He's not built that way. Ever since he first came to the Cossie he's run the front bar his *own* way. Slow and sure and "take it or leave it." And whining all the time. If it isn't the weather, it's his stomach; if it isn't the flies, it's the dust; whining all the time. But he's been here so long he's a fixture; like that lemonade machine on the counter, there. People say "Look in on old Whiner when you're passing through the Cross." He's an institution, if you see what I mean.

And then, once every two or three years, old Whiner he goes on the pots. Just out of the blue. For months on end he don't have a drink; anyone doesn't know him shouts, he says "I'll take smokes." Anyone knows him, they don't ask him. Then one day he goes on them. Take my word for it, the whole of Southern Cross don't hold old Whiner when he's properly on the pots. Remember one time he finishes up in a new-dug grave out in the cemetery; another time he falls down a bit of an old working out on the flat. Old Whiner, he can get into more trouble than a left-handed bogger working with a right-handed mate, when he starts.

So now old Ma, she knows what to do. Puts him on the train and when he wakes up he'll be in Kalgoorlie with his thirst and his cheque. When he's ready to come home, when he's worn out his welcome in Paddy Hannan's town, old Whiner, he'll wire Ma for his fare and he'll come home. And believe me, he won't look sideways at it for years.

So Hearty told his tale while Ma handled the front bar and the floosy barmaid flirted with the new bank clerk in the saloon. In the middle of the night, the express passed through and left the new barman that the Registry had sent from the city. At six next morning he got the keys from Ma, very surprised and still in her curlicues; there was a great scrubbing and swilling and washing and polishing and when he opened up at nine oclock the front bar was so full of spit-and-polish that Mullocky Jones who slept on the doorstep, they used to say, was too scared to set foot over the sill. At ten, when the barmaid came on to open up the saloon, she put on an act about the Brasso and the lino cream that were missing from her cleaning box; not to mention the clean embroidered shelf covers and the glass towels. Ma said, "Don't make a song about it." She wanted to see how he went with the customers, which, as she pointed out to the girl, is the main thing about a barman, isn't it? That and the percentages.

Yes, Harold went well with the men. They didn't seem to mind his curly hair with the slight sideboards or his pink hands with the manicured nails; they opened their eyes at his clean starched white coats and they laughed at his stories. Young Buller Smeed was even heard to suggest it mightn't be a bad idea if he wrote out a few of them for old Whiner to use. And Blue Allen from the Shell Depot thought it wouldn't hurt if Whiner learned to sling a pot like Harold, that didn't have a tie on it as well as a collar. All in, Harold was a great success and Ma said to the bar-maid that she didn't mind if Whiner stayed away a week or two longer. Do him good to have a real break while he was about it.

Then young Gavin arrived. One of the Grubstake twins; the one that Mrs Grub-

LYNDALL HADOW

stake had made into a lawyer. He wasn't really young but Ma remembered him from when he was a little chap always trying to get a look into the bar and his lady-mother keeping him back. Now he'd grown a trifle officious, more than a trifle pompous, and he couldn't hide how annoyed he felt when he heard people calling the old barmaid "Mrs Reedy" or even "Ma." He was careful to call her "Miss Carter," which after all was her real name, notwithstanding and in spite of the irregular relationship that had existed between her and his father for so long. He found it difficult to congratulate her on the way she'd run the Cosmopolitan, making profits for the Grubstake family all these years; he never so much as said "thank you." The local auditor gave him the report instead of posting it to Perth and Gavin poked around the place and next day he said to Ma,

"Well, Miss Carter, I'm returning to the city tomorrow. Before I leave I'd like to discuss a few changes with you."

Ma said, "We'll be sorry to see you go" . . . (always the diplomat, though the cook had said only that morning, "It's that long-nosed lawyer or me! How many serves out of a roast? and him pretending he don't know how many-a them poor jokers on the track look for a hand-out here. Him or me!") Still, Ma said to the lawyer,

"We'll be sorry to see you go. And what might the changes be?"

"First, I've had in mind for some time now that we should modernise the Cosmopolitan."

Ma smiled. She'd heard it so often. Every visit that any of the family paid, they always left crying "We must modernise the old Cosmopolitan"; every time, nothing was done. So Ma said, "Yes. Not a bad idea," and Gavin, squirming, knew that *she* knew that nothing would ever be changed.

"Then there's the staff."

That startled Ma. "The staff?"

Gavin said, "I know the staff's always been your show, Miss Carter, and I've never interfered; but I feel now that it's time we made a change. That fellow . . . the old barman . . ."

"Whiner? Used to make your kites . . . ."

"Yes, Whiner. A very apt name."

Seemed Gavin didn't like Whiner's ways. Harold now, *there* was a barman, a real barman, an excellent type of employee. Harold was the boy for Gavin's family's pub.

"There's a smart, well-conducted fellow, Miss Carter. Knows his job. How was his percentage last week?"

"Near enough for a new man. Next week 'll tell a better tale."

"It 'll be all right. Anyway, when that old fellow gets back, give him his notice and get rid of him. That's a start."

She could look at him, the city lawyer, with those knowing old eyes with the twinkle of unexploded mirth in them; she could keep her secrets about his father, disreputable Grubstake Reedy; she could have her half share in the Cosmopolitan;

she could be called "Ma Reedy"; she could grin about the alterations; but he'd be adamant over Whiner. "He's been here too long. They get to think they own the place."

Ma smiled. Perhaps she'd been here too long?

Then, that night, after they'd closed up at eleven they took the tills and locked the bars and the office and left the night light on outside, and the glimmer in the side hall, and the slate with the vacant-bedroom numbers on it, and they all went off to their beds. Around three o'clock there was a clatter and a crash and they trooped downstairs, Ma in her curlicues and Gavin not so pompous with his bottom teeth still in the tumbler on his washstand. There was Harold, the smart barman, down in the bar. He'd got himself a key and he'd been lashing into the grog. Bit of a quiet drinker, it seemed. When they picked him out of the mess of broken bottles and sent him off on next day's train and did a snap check of the front bar stock, they found out plenty.

His stock was all right; his percentage as good as Whiner's ever was. What Ma found in the saloon bar on the top shelf was just nobody's business.

Harold knew the barmaid went driving on Sundays with the new bank clerk. He knew she didn't check her top shelf properly . . . just counted along, head craned from the floor. Didn't bother to climb up and shake the bottles and make sure they were full of what they were supposed to be full of. And Ma hadn't worried much, so long as the customers were happy in the saloon and clustering around like flies and the honeypot. Harold had decided water was good enough if you do your stock-check that way. He emptied her gin and whisky and brandy bottles off that top shelf and drank it up in his bedroom at night with his friends; sold what he couldn't drink and put the cash in his pocket. And he filled up the top shelf bottles with ginger ale and water and put the caps back carefully. When the bank clerk gets tired of taking the barmaid out driving on Sundays, the barmaid 'll have a clean-up in her bar and might get around to climbing up to the top shelf. But by that time Whiner will be back and Harold down in Perth again, with a good reference as a relieving barman in his pocket.

That's how he'd planned it but it didn't work out that way due to his tripping on the coconut matting in the dark at three o'clock in the morning; and not even his fare paid back to the city.

Next Monday, Hearty Curtis leaned into the office under the stairs.

"Hullo, Ma," he said wiping his hands on his bar apron that he'd just taken off, "thought you might like to know that Whiner's back." From the bar came Whiner's whine,

"Who the 'ells been muckin' around in this bar? Nothin' where I left it. Take weeks to get right. Eh? Whadda y' want? Beer? The beer's off, see?"

Ma and Hearty grinned happily and the Cossie settled back into its rut.

LYNDALL HADOW

GEOFFREY DRAKE-BROCKMAN : *Engineering in Australia*

THE FIRST AUSTRALIAN SETTLERS WERE FACED BY A HOSTILE COUNTRY—IN this instance not so much by the hostility of the aboriginal inhabitants as by the harsh nature of the land itself. The discovery of Australia offered no new vegetable food of marketable value to the world; all species since developed have grown from imported stock. On the other hand, a plentiful supply of fresh meat, in the form of marsupials, wildfowl, and emus, was readily available if hunted with persistence.

The majority of rivers soon proved to be merely dry, sandy watercourses for a large part of every year. Except for a relatively short distance from the sea, very few Australian rivers are permanent waterways; thus in the dry season even these are affected by tidal flow and become salt to brackish. One notable exception—the Murray River, which drains a large part of the States of New South Wales and Victoria, and flows through South Australia to empty in the Southern Ocean—remains navigable and fresh for hundreds of miles. Although so many of the other rivers cease to flow in the dry season, fresh-water pools and billabongs* are constant. These were originally well stocked with fish and waterfowl, and remain so today when remote from closely settled areas.

The first ships sailing from England with their complements of men, women, and children destined to begin settlements at various points on the Australian coast brought not only building materials, furniture, plant, stock, and seeds so that production might proceed, but also sufficient provisions to sustain the new arrivals for some time. As there was never any certainty as to when the next ship might arrive, the growing of crops was a matter of immediate urgency. The firstcomers and their goods were landed by means of ships' boats, and the stock swam ashore. But soon temporary improvisations for better landings were replaced by properly constructed jetties and berthing facilities. Thus engineering practice began, and from the beginning of settlement, engineering services have been of paramount importance to all of Australia.

The earliest active agricultural settlements were built up successively around Sydney, Hobart, Brisbane, Perth, Melbourne, and Adelaide, in that order—towns that in time became the capital cities of six states. Whilst the settlers were struggling to create homes and learning how to cope with the growing of food under the strange and difficult conditions prevailing in the new continent, engineers set to work to develop water supplies, from the very beginning an urgent necessity. At the same time, they opened up dirt tracks leading from landings to settlements so that horses might be used to haul goods and housing materials throughout those areas, and farther on to nearby farming allotments.

* Branch of river that comes to a dead end (aboriginal name).

Since much of the land near the coast is infertile, the difficulty experienced in making crops grow was not surprising. Large areas of coastal country remained unused until recent times, when fertilizer in the form of superphosphates, with the addition of trace elements, induced poor sandy soil to produce in abundance. Thus scientific aids to agriculture have made naturally poor, almost worthless, soils grow grain and nurture stock profitably. Land that could not feed one sheep to several acres now frequently feeds several sheep to one acre.

The isolated nature of the early colonizing efforts scattered round the vast coast-line of Australia resulted in the establishment of six separate colonies. Funds and settlers continued to come from Great Britain. Throughout the nineteenth century, these six Crown colonies gradually increased in population and production to a point when self-government was requested and granted by the British government.

Self-government, however, did not bring political unity. The six developing and governing authorities of the expanding colonies created, at length, six separate public works organisations. Each department, in fact, such as health, land settlement, or mines, had its corresponding number in each colony. But in time all the other departments, as a matter of course, became the clients of the works organisations. No other department could function until accommodation was supplied and access provided to its spheres of operation.

For a time dirt and macadam roads satisfied the communication needs of the early settlers; when population was increased by the arrival of more and more immigrants, however, it became necessary to seek suitable farming and grazing lands farther inland. Surveyors explored and mapped new areas; engineers considered problems of communication and water supply. But the ever-increasing demand for agricultural land necessitated striking farther and farther inland, and such pressures inevitably led to the construction of railways on a large scale. Thousands of miles of permanent way were pushed out into virgin land, often enough well ahead of settlement. These railways first opened, then serviced, lands soon given to wheat farming, grazing, dairying, and fruit growing. Railways were also built to develop timber milling in natural forests and the mining of gold and base metals. Gold was frequently discovered in areas of very low rainfall. This had not encouraged settlement in the surrounding country; thus in many instances, when the rush came, there was no fresh water available on the goldfields. Engineers did what they could to meet immediate minimum needs by the installation of plants for condensing water from salt lakes or wells. Since condensed water was too costly for anything but drinking, as much rain as possible was collected from rock or hard catchments and run into storage reservoirs, scooped out of the earth itself wherever good holding ground could be located.

The most notable engineering work undertaken by any Australian colony during the self-governing period before Federation was the Coolgardie Water Scheme, designed to cater for goldfields in Western Australia. A reservoir capable of supplying 5,000,000 gallons a day was constructed at Mundaring in the Darling Ranges, 26 miles from Perth. Water is pumped from this storage reservoir first to Coolgardie (the site of the first rush in 1892) and then on to Kalgoorlie, where thousands of pounds worth of gold are still annually won from the world-famous Golden Mile —in all, a distance of 348 miles. (The American Ex-President Herbert Hoover lived for some years in Kalgoorlie, where he was a mining man of importance.) On this long journey, the water is raised about 1,400 feet by means of eight pumping stations with small intermediate regulating reservoirs. Sixty years ago this pumping of water more than 300 miles inland was a major undertaking. It is quoted in *Engineering Wonders of the World* (London, 1910) as being one of the outstanding engineering feats of the modern world. That, of course, was fifty years ago, but the glamour still clings: some of the original steam-pumping plants are still sending 5,000,000 gallons of water on a journey of 348 miles every day. The pipeline has a diameter of 30 inches, and it takes two weeks for a gallon of water to travel from Mundaring Weir to Kalgoorlie.

A more recent example of pioneering work in Australian transport is the inauguration in 1922 of what was, I understand, the first long-distance commercial air service in the world. A weekly service was established between Perth, the capital of Western Australia, and Derby, a far north cattleport, a distance of 1,500 miles. Commonwealth engineers pioneered those first landing grounds. They were little better than cleared areas of level ground. Since then the Commonwealth government has provided hundreds of aerodromes throughout the continent. City terminals, of course, are now major works costing millions of pounds—very different from those first landing grounds on the Perth-Derby route. A modern development also pioneered on this same first long-distance commercial route is the slaughtering of bullocks on inland, isolated, and inaccessible cattle runs (Glenroy being the pioneer station). Dressed on the spot, the carcasses are flown from the local meatworks to refrigerated stores on the coast, there to await shipment overseas. Air freight may come to play a still more important part in the development of outback areas.

Indeed, for the first hundred years of settlement in Australia, transport was a major concern for engineers; first by opening up dirt tracks, then metalling them as traffic increased. When the distances became too great for horse-drawn traffic, government railway construction was put in hand. Generally speaking, all railways have been developed as systems to increase the trade of the state capitals. The railways running inland from the coastal towns of Queensland were the chief exceptions: there they were individual lines, at first unconnected, although a coastal line now joins all but the most northerly port to the capital. Building these thousands of miles of pioneer railways kept many of the engineers in the outback. They lived under canvas and for many months were far away from cities or towns of any size.

The first and main railways from the capital cities were followed by branch lines and spurs, with feeder roads. The construction of these branch railways greatly increased the area of land served. The main railway systems of the six states were built in the horse-and-buggy era and the routes had of necessity to lie twenty-five miles apart to permit a horse-drawn vehicle to transport produce from farm to siding and return on the same day.

The internal combustion engine has now completely taken over road transportation. Farms can therefore be serviced at a much greater distance from a railway. This means that in Australia there are now thousands of miles of government railway track that have become surplus to requirements, or very soon will. Increasing motor road transport has required the construction of thousands of miles of new roadways, whilst railway spurs are being abandoned. It is generally accepted that the transfer of farm produce, other than bulk grains and fertilizer, from motor truck to rail wagon is not economical unless the distance is greater than one hundred miles. The actual distance is debatable and of course varies according to local conditions. And although we are now in the road-and-internal-combustion-engine age, engineers often wonder how many of the new roads will become nearly useless, as many of the railways already are, when heavy air transport becomes practicable and economical.

Diversification and specialization of engineering effort was in time, of course, inevitable. As earlier noted, the Australian capital cities all lie on the coast—Sydney, Hobart, Brisbane, Perth, Melbourne, and Adelaide. They have grown from their small beginnings—the first founded in 1788, the last in 1836—until now the six capitals together have a population of over five million. The number of persons in Australia has not yet reached eleven million, so it can be seen that approximately half the inhabitants live in the cities. The development of industry has taxed the imagination and skill of the engineers. Water supplies alone have presented a continuing problem in a country of few permanent running waterways.

Electric power supply plants have kept pace with the continuing growth of the cities, as have extensions and improvements to harbours. Some provision has been made for docking, and harbours have been dredged to cater for the ever-increasing draft of modern ships. Shipbuilding started at Whyalla in South Australia more or less as a war necessity and has since continued. There are large steel manufacturing plants at Newcastle, Port Kembla, and Whyalla, and thousands of industrial plants of all sorts are scattered throughout the continent, nearly all of them adjacent to the cities, and run by private companies.

Essential public works, roads, railways, bridges, harbours, water and sewerage schemes, irrigation undertakings, power plants and steel structures of all kinds are extending and expanding rapidly as population and trade increase. The opening up of mining enterprises keeps pace with new discoveries. Important mines have been developed and produce regularly, such as those for lead and zinc at Broken Hill in New South Wales, gold at Kalgoorlie in Western Australia, iron at Iron Knob in South Australia and Yampi Sound in Western Australia, coal at Newcastle in New South Wales and at Yallourn in Victoria, copper at Mt Isa in Queensland, and uranium at Rum Jungle in the Northern Territory.

Some engineering undertakings stand out from amongst the many works in Australia. A few of these may be worth mentioning. The Sydney Harbour Bridge is an important structure by world standards. Built for the State of New South Wales, it carries a tremendous volume of traffic—rail, motor-vehicle, and even pedestrian. It has a single arch span of 1,650 feet, a measurement within two feet of the span of the Kill-van-Kull Bridge in New York.

The Eildon Dam in Victoria, recently completed, is an earth-filled structure. A huge quantity of earth-moving plant, most of which came from America, was employed on its construction. The Utah Construction Company of the U. S. were the contractors.

The Graving Dock in Sydney Harbour, named after Captain Cook, who first took possession of Eastern Australia in 1770 in the name of Great Britain, was built during World War II. Though labour and material were scarce at the time, the construction of the Dock was hurried on to completion to cater for war-damaged vessels of the Navies of the U. S. and Australia.

Years ago, a Murray River Commission was set up to coördinate the utilization of the Murray River waters for irrigation in New South Wales, Victoria, and South Australia. One of the major works of the Commission was the earth-filled dam at Hume with an overflow section of concrete. It is situated on the western slope of the continental divide near Albury on the border between New South Wales and Victoria. The last sixty miles of the Murray River in South Australia being tidal, a barrage has been constructed near the mouth at Goolwa to prevent the ingress of sea water.

Today, the Snowy River hydraulic undertaking (in the Snowy Mountains, New South Wales) is probably the greatest engineering project yet put in hand in Australia. It provides for the diversion of the Snowy River by tunnel through the continental divide to augment the supply of water to the Murray Valley irrigation schemes. Advantage has been taken of the high elevation of the Australian Alps to generate electric power, distributed to the States of Victoria and New South Wales. The final cost is likely to be about £450,000,000 Australian.

Hydroelectric works in Tasmania have been of major importance to that state. The Great Lake is practically in the centre of the island and at a high elevation. Engineers planned the harnessing of the effluent streams to provide electric power for many industries—the manufacture of paper and the recovery of aluminium from the large bauxite deposits of Tasmania being probably the most important. The most recent dam constructed at the Tasmanian hydroelectric works is a prestressed one: the amount of concrete in the retaining wall will, by prestressing, be reduced by approximately 40%, thereby reducing the over-all cost of the wall by about 20%.

All these works and enterprises have resulted in a shortage of engineers—civil, electrical, and mechanical—especially in State and Commonwealth Government Departments throughout Australia.

Historically, the administration of Australian engineering has followed the pattern originally set, with gradual modifications in more recent times. The six self-governing colonies, known as New South Wales, Victoria, Queensland, South Australia, Western Australia, and Tasmania, federated in 1901. The people of each state elected a quota of members to a federal parliament, known as the Commonwealth Parliament of Australia. This body consisted of two Houses: the Senate, an upper chamber with a fixed number of senators representing each state, and a House of Representatives with members elected from the many constituencies into which each state was divided for the purpose of federal government. As there were already six Parliaments in existence, this has meant that from 1901 onwards Australia has maintained seven Parliaments and seven separate governments. The Commonwealth government determines policies and controls certain services common to Australia, such as defence, post, customs, broadcasting, and civil aviation. In addition, the federal government has formed its own works organisation to provide facilities for its client departments.

During the period required to select a federal capital and to construct Parliament House and administrative buildings, the administrative centres of the Commonwealth were housed in Melbourne. Nowadays the headquarters of the federal government is at Canberra, a city specially built for the purpose, on territory resumed from New South Wales. The federal capital has grown to a city of 50,000 persons, of whom a large proportion are civil servants employed in the Commonwealth Public Service. Today, practically all administrative responsibilities of the Commonwealth are centred in Canberra; but this transference has taken nearly sixty years to complete.

Each of the six states remains responsible for the internal government and development of its own territory. The state engineers undertake the construction of harbours, roads, water supplies for towns and country, power houses, sewerage schemes, hospitals, schools, and all other public works and buildings required to meet the public needs of individual states as their population increases.

What, at present, is the professional status of the Australian engineer? Again, the historical background is the key to an answer. During World War I (1914–1918) hundreds of young and not so young engineers went overseas to war fronts in Egypt, Gallipoli, or France, and were finally based on England. They learnt what was happening abroad in their special spheres of engineering activity. In those days Australia was extremely isolated—a month's journey by sea to anywhere of importance. Australian engineers, until then, had little or no opportunity of seeing any works of magnitude at first hand. They had to rely on textbooks, periodicals, and papers read at their various professional societies. The mass opportunity afforded by the war of benefiting by seeing, provided an impetus for more, bigger, and better-designed works in Australia.

During World War I the principal professional societies of engineers existing in Australia themselves federated to form The Institution of Engineers, Australia. This body includes qualified and experienced men from the civil, mechanical, and electrical branches of the profession. Members are known as chartered engineers. The

GEOFFREY DRAKE-BROCKMAN

Australian Institution has grown into a great and powerful body of more than 14,000 members. Its journals and its state and general meetings keep the whole profession throughout Australia in touch with everything new and of importance to engineers that occurs within the Commonwealth and abroad. The Institution largely determines the standard of training and ethical behaviour of the professional engineer in Australia.

Australian engineers have up to the present been lower in the salary scale than men of other professions. This lack of financial recognition of professional training and service has annoyed the younger generation of chartered engineers, prepared as they are to give service to their country under trying conditions. They have willingly lived in camps and in outback small towns far removed from the amenities of the cities, but they are now demanding improved status. The general body of engineers think it their due to be able to earn incomes commensurate with their training and responsibilities. They consider that their earnings should be more in line with their contemporaries who graduated to other professions or to industry and commerce at the same time. As engineers are now in short supply, it is considered that improved status would quickly assist in overcoming the shortage.

With improved status as their objective, a large proportion of engineers have combined in an association outside The Institution of Engineers, Australia, known as the APEA (Association of Professional Engineers, Australia). This Association is now seeking higher salaries through the Commonwealth Arbitration Court—a judicial court, free of government interference, which controls the earnings of the mass of Australians.*

What I have been trying to indicate is that Australia was, and still is, a difficult country to develop. Its early settlement followed closely on the work of engineers, often enough struggling against odds to provide urgent communications and amenities, with little or no plant except manpower and horses, and such items as shovels, barrows, and drays.

Without the pioneer work of the various public works authorities, development beyond the coastal fringe would have been slow indeed. From the landing of the first settlers to the exploration and occupation of inland areas, first by track and road and later by the construction of railways and aerodromes, engineers have directed and expedited the progress of Australia.

The ideal of service, fostered by the engineering profession and their institutions, has led engineers to accept their lot, to live lonely lives, separated from their families for a great part of their working days. For instance, over fifty years ago, in 1908, as a young man I was one of four engineers engaged on the location of the Trans-Australian Railway, Western Australian section. The route stretched approximately 450 miles from Kalgoorlie to the boundary between Western Australia and South Australia. There was no motor transport at that time. On this location job our drink-

* Since this article was written, the APEA has attained a first award that materially increases the salaries of chartered engineers.

ing water was carted up to 150 miles in small tanks on the backs of camels. We struck and pitched our tents on a new site every day for seven days a week month after month. We saw no one, not even a native, outside our own party, throughout the whole distance.

When we reached the South Australian border, we ran a line south for sixty-five miles to Eucla, a tiny telegraph-repeating station on the Great Australian Bight, in order to check our longitude. Here we camped for a few days before turning back with our camels along our pegged route to Kalgoorlie. On the way we made rock catchment surveys for railway water supplies. Riding a camel is rather like being on a small boat on a rough sea, but you either got your "camel legs" or you walked thirty miles a day.

The job just described, where we lived for six months on tinned meat, etc., and a gallon of water a day, amidst the smell of camels, would have seemed like the worst job on earth to persons working in cities in the Old World.

As World War I was responsible for improving engineering design and construction methods in Australia, so did World War II (1939–1945) improve techniques—notably by the arrival in Australia of American Service Engineers with their many labour-saving devices. When war broke out, we in Australia were only just beginning to use modern earth-moving plant. The Australian Army immediately ordered earth-moving plant to the value of some millions of pounds; thus we were enabled quickly to follow the American example. What the Army more or less started, the civilian authorities followed up as soon as it was practicable. At the present time Australia employs labour-saving plant, new and old, wherever it can be used economically. We are also prepared to try out anything new as it comes on the market.

During World War II long land supply lines became necessary to reach Darwin in the north of Australia where American and Australian troops were based. It so happened that the Japanese suddenly and unexpectedly gave Darwin a miniature Pearl Harbor raid, destroying the jetty berthing facilities and sinking about a dozen naval and supply ships at the Darwin anchorage. The extensive damage, and the likelihood of further raids on shipping, made it necessary to abandon regular sea communication to Darwin. Road supply lines had of necessity to be provided. The rapid improvement of the main road routes into Darwin became urgent.

A railhead existed at the town of Alice Springs, about 980 miles north of Adelaide. (Alice Springs is considered the geographical centre of Australia, and is often just called "The Centre.") The railway from Alice Springs to Adelaide is 3'6" gauge. It makes connection with the railway systems of Australia, but several breaks of gauge occur. The road distance from Darwin to Alice Springs is 950 miles. A dirt track and a short length of 3'6" gauge railway extending south from Darwin to end at a railhead called Birdum was all that existed when the emergency arose.

This drovers' track for horse and cart from Alice Springs to Darwin was graded, gravelled, and surfaced with bitumen in quick time. It became known as the North-

　　　　　　　　　　　　　　　　　　　　　　　GEOFFREY DRAKE-BROCKMAN

South Road, and was often referred to as "the bitumen." It has since been renamed The Stuart Highway. A second line of communication to Darwin was also established by the construction of a bitumen-surfaced road from Tennant Creek (about 360 miles north of Alice Springs on the North-South Road) to Mt Isa, a distance of 420 miles.

This 1,370 miles of bitumen roadway was a war emergency work. The rapid construction was possible only through the cooperation of state governments. For various stages of its construction the States of New South Wales, Victoria, Queensland, and South Australia were called on to transfer their state-engineer road organizations to this work. Several army field and construction units also assisted. Army service units supplied rations and canteen services. An American Negro transport unit distributed most of the bitumen required along the route from the railhead at Mt Isa.

(Mt Isa is the centre of one of the greatest mining ventures in Queensland, or for that matter in Australia. Silver, lead, zinc and copper are won in large quantities there. Tennant Creek at the Northern Territory end of "the bitumen" is a gold mining town. Mines there were profitably producing gold before the war, and still are. Rum Jungle, a mining area sixty miles south of Darwin, situated between the railway from Darwin to Birdum and the route of the North-South Road, is a large producer of uranium.)

Whilst the 1,370 miles of roadway to service the Darwin army base was being constructed, an additional war emergency road, of about 1,000 miles in length, was being graded and gravelled from Norseman (ninety miles south of Kalgoorlie in Western Australia) to Port Augusta in South Australia by the State Road Authorities of Western Australia and South Australia. The Army also supplied rations, canteen, and medical services for this work.

The war thus taught Australia the value of cooperative endeavour between Commonwealth and State Governments and Service Departments. At the time, in no other way could the roads described have been built rapidly enough to meet the necessities of war.

What of the future? In little more than 170 years from the date of first settlement, Australia has developed to a point that enables her to exert at least the influence of a small nation in world affairs. It is now possible to envisage the time when Australia's population will have increased to fifty or a hundred million. It already seems likely that the twenty million mark will be reached before the end of the present century. Increasing our population, first to twenty million, and then possibly to a hundred million, will call for great engineering effort.

I foresee the damming of all streams in the north of Australia, as well as those in the south. Northern rivers, that for most of the year are now only long sandy beds, become raging torrents for some months every year. During the greater floods, which frequently occur, larger areas of land are inundated; thousands of millions of cubic feet of water race to the sea. Australia is a water-hungry country; we badly need the tremendous volume of water thus wasted every year.

Someday large areas of the north will be irrigated by this water. Conceivably, Australia will then supply much of the world with high grade beef. Beef production, and possibly the growing of cotton, rice, and sugar, could help to populate the climatically difficult northern country. In recent times the sheep-carrying capacity of millions of acres in the southern portion of the continent has been greatly increased by scientific methods already mentioned.

Irrigation from conserved water provided by many small streams, as well as that from the Murray River system, has also been the means of improving pastures and expanding the fruit-growing and dairying industries. This conservation of water for irrigation is likely to continue to be one of the main developmental activities of engineers until all possible water has been conserved.

Australia's population growth in the foreseeable future will be limited only by its water supply. After advantage has been taken of all streams and catchments available, engineers will be forced to provide artificial catchments and so conserve as much as possible of the rain that falls in low-rainfall areas. Small bitumen-surfaced catchments will supply the needs of individual farms.

Underground salt water is prevalent throughout the continent. Thus conversion of salt water into fresh, when such becomes economically practicable, will be a tremendously important aid to closer settlement in now waterless regions. Nuclear power may eventually help to solve this problem.

What I really envisage is that engineers in Australia, in addition to providing the amenities necessary to cope with an ever-increasing population by the construction of bigger and better harbours, more and more power houses, steel structures, industrial plants, more and more water for cities and the countryside generally, more and more sewerage undertakings, more and larger aerodromes, and more highways, will find their most important work still to be the provision of water to bring arid and sparsely populated areas into economic production.

The successful occupation and development of Australia has been made possible primarily by the patience, skill, and leadership of engineers and scientists. In many instances professional engineers have remained strictly behind the scenes, usually getting little or no acknowledgement from politicians. It is difficult to understand why, in their own country, they have not been advanced either economically or socially to the same extent as other professional men or executives in commerce and industry. It is perhaps even more difficult to understand why they have hitherto accepted such status without protest. The only reason that I can suggest for this is that, in Australia, the greater percentage of engineers have been working directly for the government, and, as a body, they have chosen to maintain an ideal of service to the community.

The position of the profession, however, is changing; more chartered engineers are becoming private consultants, and more graduate engineers are joining industrial and commercial undertakings, often enough not strictly in the practice of their own

GEOFFREY DRAKE-BROCKMAN

profession but as executives. This widening of scope is assisting the younger generation in its demand for better status.

In my opinion, unless the position of government engineers is greatly improved, state and government services must ultimately be obliged to secure only the second best and even too few of them. If this miserable condition should arise, then state and Commonwealth planning must inevitably deteriorate. The blueprint of the future will compare unfavorably with the achievement of the past and the growth of population become less than the geographical position of Australia demands.

MARY GILMORE : *Two Poems*

Man

Life in the veins,
In spite of years,
An outlet asks
As force appears—
Appears as thought
That lifts a pen,
And man is born
Anew again.

Life

Man may create
A plough, a wheel,
But only life
Begets.

But what is life?
Life is demand;
The primal cell
Heard its command—
Heard and took shape,
For, wanting form,
Power lies inert,
Unknown its norm.

Only through form
Can life create:
Or man, or cell
Perpetuate.

AUSTRALIA IS A MODERN COUNTRY DEVELOPED ON A STONE-AGE BASE. The last continent to be discovered, its recorded history goes no farther back than 1606 when the little Dutch ship *Duyfken*, voyaging to discover "the Iland called Nova ginnea, which, as it is said, affordeth great store of Gold", sailed south into the Gulf of Carpentaria and lit on the west coast of the Cape York Peninsula. Even then, nothing material happened until Lieut. James Cook discovered the eastern seaboard and landed at Botany Bay, south of Sydney, in 1770; eighteen years later Governor Arthur Phillip arrived, with a band of soldiers and convicts, to occupy the new land Cook had claimed for England. Thirteen more years had to elapse before Matthew Flinders circumnavigated the coast to establish, finally, the existence of one solid land mass, and suggested that the sixth continent be called Australia. The name was not officially adopted until 1817. Quite modern; indeed but a short gap of sixty-two years, less than one man's lifetime, stretched between the date of Phillip's landing and the building of the first railway in 1850 when the speed of nineteenth-century mechanical techniques took charge.

That brief interval was all the time Australia had to span the gap between neolithic practice and modern methods. Little progress was made; European or Asiatic methods of soil culture proved precarious; the white population clung to the coastal fringe. Yet fifty years after that first railway began, telegraphs, telephones, electric light, tap water and bathrooms, tinned foods and ice works, hospitals and primary schools, were widely distributed and in far more common use than in many lands that had been civilised for centuries; by 1930, motorcars and aeroplanes had practically ousted horses (except for stock work) and superphosphates dealt with recalcitrant soils.

Symbolic of this colossal contrast between Australian past and present is the mining town of Mary Kathleen in arid northwest Queensland. Building it in 1956 to house a thousand persons employed in uranium mining—complete with pastel-tinted buildings, air conditioning, reticulated water, refrigeration, modern design, every conceivable domestic amenity, and green gardens—the construction party unearthed an enormous collection of aboriginal artifacts: stone adzes and grinding stones, flint knives, spearheads. Nor were these unearthed in layers, one civilisation piled upon another. They might have been left long ago; they might have been left comparatively recently, buried by wind-blown soil. Today white women and children live in luxurious comfort where even the blacks had no permanent waters.

No example could better underline the extent of the Australian debt to modern scientific methods, or the fact that Australian women probably owe more to the engineering profession than do women of any other country.

Not only was Australia the last-discovered continent, it was also the most undomesticated. For centuries before the arrival of the British settlers the aboriginal women wandered naked with their men, who were hunters and nomads (and artists, as their own decorated weapons and more recent paintings in Western style proclaim). The men were skilled in the manufacture of that unique weapon, the boomerang, and of spears and woomeras, or wooden shields. Forty years ago I was invited to watch spearheads being fashioned from flint and quartz by a tribal expert. No mechanical tool could have worked with greater precision and skill than the deft hands of Pompey, squatting half-naked in a dry Kimberley river bed; a process that I had imagined laborious was a matter of seconds. Having selected his flint with care from a collected stockpile, Pompey used a small stone as an anvil, another stone as a hammer, and in less than ten minutes a pile of beautifully even, serrated spearheads lay beside his thigh.

But these primeval engineers did not extend their skills (except as hunters of food) in service of their women, who were left with no domestic aids other than coolamons, or boat-shaped wooden dishes of all sizes, and digging sticks to aid their search for edible roots, lizards, and similar additions to the menu. Both sexes rolled fur and hair or vegetable fibres into string, using a winding stick; this was made into "dilly-bags" for carrying purposes or, in the north, into quite large fish nets; in the southern areas animal sinews also were used to sew kangaroo-skin cloaks with bone needles. In the north, in spring, many of the Western Australian plains appear like immense fields of grain. But the grass seeds are small. Nevertheless, the women used a long, shallow, oval wooden dish called a yandy to separate grain from husks by means of a complicated rocking and shaking movement of forearms and wrists. This unusual skill has now been successfully extended (generally with a similar dish made of sheet iron) to separate mineral from mullock in small native mining shows. Now known as "yandying" this skill was originally exclusively feminine. In the past no permanent homes were ever built, nothing but quickly constructed shelters made of branches or of bark—mia-mias, wurleys, gunyahs, humpies (probably *oompi* in dialect), according to district. These would shelter a family for at most a few days, serving as protection against the sun, but more usually the rain. In the far north, dug-out canoes, or other canoes fashioned from immense strips of certain barks first soaked in water and then shaped by moulding in hot sand, were propelled by one or more paddles.

And that was all. When the whites arrived there was neither garden nor cooking pot nor house nor domesticated bird or beast other than camp dogs (no horses or any bovine species inhabited the new continent), no garment or tool they might use, to assist in settlement. And they were too unsettled and uninterested to learn the native languages, the legends and bushcrafts (or intimate knowledge of the countryside) that are now being eagerly sought, much too late in the day, in order to establish some sort of link between the Australian past and present.

From the beginning Australia was a man's country, with tribes of nomadic hunters expressing themselves imaginatively in the masculine art of corroboree dancing.

Then came the whites: firstly, soldiers in barracks and convicts in jails, road camps, and chain gangs, to be followed by free settlers clearing, hoeing, scratching a living from the hostile bush with incredible hardship—acquiring stock, striking inland at last, enduring long days in the saddle—their minds preoccupied with bare subsistence or animal husbandry. The drovers came, and the teamsters; the gold rushes poured in thousands from China to California, prospectors tramped after explorers. Any interest in the arts was confined to horsemanship, bush ballads, or campfire songs and yarns. There was no time to spare for more than essentials. Any type of soft living was considered "sissy". By extension, so were the sophisticated arts. Moreover, a man's "mate" was not his wife, but, in American terms, his "buddy" or male companion. It was not the lonely, highly individual rider of the range, with his heroic cowboy honour, that captured Australian imagination to create both legend and ideal; it was the hard, unspoken, unsentimental devotion of man for man, united in the face of nature or other men, and derived from all the "mates" at sea and on shore, who attend a job together.

Travelling always on foot, the aboriginal men carried only their weapons; their women followed piled up with string bags, coolamons, babies, digging sticks. In much the same manner, cluttered with more complicated furnishings, carts or wagons conveying them, did the white women follow their men. But at first there were few to follow. A handful of soldiers' wives, from Governor's lady to an occasional private's missus; a larger number of "depraved women," as the wretched female convicts were frequently dubbed. The latter were in considerable demand as assigned servants, paramours, or, sentences served, as wives. There was neither time nor place (nor servants—assigned convicts were hardly either gracious or devoted, and later free immigrants responded with alacrity to the atmosphere of a land where Jack could soon overtake his master) for the cultivation of the social graces that had flourished in Europe and Asia for so long and were also, by then, burgeoning in the U.S.A.

Moreover, for centuries European minds had been exposed to the influence of the young Madonna, portrayed a million times with adoration as the incarnation of tender charm, and to a lay concept of feminine beauty in either princess or peasant as a quality to be much desired. Before that the Greek goddesses, chaste or passionate, amorous, wise, maternal, or jealous, but always the deified personifications of womankind, had also exerted considerable influence on social thinking. Goddesses, princesses, and peasants had no place in early Australia (nor since); the image of the gentle Madonna has doubtless been cherished in many individual hearts, but the immense impact of great masterpieces devoted to supreme womanly grace did not even brush the early Australian consciousness. Australian art itself, especially in the hands of contemporary painters now busy embalming legend and incorporating myth, reflects the masculine ethos with quite startling emphasis.

The male preponderance and masculine nature of the environment was soon seen and deplored (on moral grounds) by an officer's wife, Caroline Chisholm. Her eager

HENRIETTA DRAKE-BROCKMAN

wish to help became her life's work: a steady stream of respectable young women, and, later, family groups, were enabled by her efforts to migrate from Great Britain. Margaret Kiddle, in her biography *Caroline Chisholm,* gives an accurate but nonetheless fascinating picture of this stirring period. In *Portrait with Background,* Alexandra Hasluck has broadened a biography of Georgiana Molloy to cover the early history of Western Australia and in particular the difficulties that faced the wives of free settlers, many of them gentlefolk, who founded that colony. A third book, *Kings in Grass Castles,* by Mary Durack, begins no earlier than 1850, the date associated with the first railway, but moves from the rough goldfields of Victoria through the centre to the northwestern plains of Kimberley in the tracks of her grandfather and his sons, who were frequently accompanied or followed by their families. This book recounts one of the most famous Australian cattle drives across the continent to occupy unknown country; at the same time it dispassionately re-creates the hardships of the women situated at the spearhead of advance. Taken together, these three books by women give a valid account of the conditions faced, accepted, and endured by women in Australia before modern engineering skills came to their assistance.

Today, Australians are prone, in their thoughts, or perhaps it would be better to say subconsciously, to compare their country with the U.S.A. Early ties with England and the consciousness of a close British blood relationship remains as strong and as frequently acknowledged as ever; but never at any time has it been possible to relate the Australian way of living to that of the Old Country, no matter how hard a few early landowners tried. Size, geographical features, climate, social diversions, land tenure, offer no imaginative comparisons. When American troops first landed in Australia during World War II the local populace was genuinely astonished to discover them, not close cousins with a similar background of thought, but rather men who employed the same mother tongue to express alien (though comprehensible) attitudes to past, present, and future. Possibly the fact that during the period devoted to Australian federation the Constitution of the U.S.A., in default of any similar British document, was freely discussed and consulted, made earlier generations feel some affinity. But the close similarity of size, the open-air life of the western plains, the gold rushes, the stories of Bret Harte—so readily striking a familiar note—set the tendency. American films, preponderant in Australian programmes, confirmed it: here were a similar people inhabiting a large, expanding country, unfettered by ancient traditions, themselves rugged individualists. (Individualism is a characteristic which Australians like to regard as one of their own national traits, although in fact their ideal myth of "mateship" very soon extended to embrace organised workers' unions that frown on individualistic enterprise; marked social consciousness became part of the Australian scene from an early date.)

But this pairing with the U.S.A. reflects an inflated viewpoint. There was, in fact, little similarity in first settlements (although England exported her convicts to both countries originally). The fertile and friendly east coast of America was thriving and closely settled long before the wagon trains moved west—a large number of

European countries had well-established communities on both seaboards. The Middle West had rich, comparatively well-watered plains. The natural resources of the U.S.A. were (and still are) immensely superior to those of Australia. Mountains were watersheds, not barriers; great permanent rivers crossed the plains for thousands of miles; the rainfall was consistent; oilfields followed goldfields. The U.S.A. was closer to Europe, it received and was able to accommodate floods of migrants in an era before the advancements of science raised the general standards of education as well as of living, or before the later-known benefits of medical practice made women reluctant to take young children hundreds of miles into sparsely settled country.

Haunted, then, by an inward comparison based on size and hearsay, Australians today unquestionably and unreasonably strain towards the luxuries, amenities, and large-scale developmental works, both public and private, of American living. They forget that the 3,022,000 sq. miles of the U.S.A. supports a population of 177,130,-000 (1959), while Australia's 2,971,081 sq. miles can boast but 10,280,742 (1960) —more than a million *fewer* than Holland sustains on 34,000 sq. miles—and that our national income until recent years depended entirely on primary exports, whereas, to an enormous extent, home markets maintained the U.S.A. To Australians, Holland is a small country not much larger than many cattle stations; Australia is a large one. Ergo, comparison goes by physical size, and desired services and amenities are not reckoned on a just basis of population or production. The 1947 census figures show distribution as 50.72% metropolitan, 17.98% provincial, and only 31.06% rural. It is doubtful that the recent census will materially alter the proportions. It should be remembered that all our capital cities lie on the seacoast and that any other city is negligible in comparison and in any case, with the exception of Kalgoorlie, merely fringes the vast inland areas.

This disproportion has given, and still gives rise to much political discussion and considerable pious planning in the air. The people themselves are aware of it, but the standards of living widely prevalent in the past half century and within the grasp of the majority (at least since the last war), have been far too attractive to tempt many to face what are still rough pioneer conditions both inland and in the far north. While there was, and still is, much development possible within comparatively close distance of city lights, amusements, comforts and education, and since fortunes can no longer be made from rural pursuits without considerable capital investment as well as possible physical hardship, the problem of the empty north and the uninhabited inland does not exercise the masses; at best it hovers on the edge of consciousness: it would be a good idea, of course, if somebody did something about it ("but not me!").

Nor can Australian women be censured for subscribing to this attitude. At the beginning of the century general education in Australia was well in the vanguard. From 1902 on, universal franchise enabled all women over twenty-one to vote, although this was not obtained in Great Britain until 1928 (limited female suffrage

HENRIETTA DRAKE-BROCKMAN

for women over thirty had been won in 1918 after hard fighting). In 1921 Mrs. Edith Cowan was elected to the Western Australian parliament, the first woman member in Australia. Following the pattern set in New Zealand by Dr. Truby King, infant welfare centres were established in suburban areas during the twenties. Women worked on the land very little, even during the war years. Industrialisation was small by American and European standards and there was not a high proportion of female factory workers; in short, the majority of Australian women were housewives, and, as has been mentioned, enjoyed the privileges of tap water, electricity, and gas to an extent proportionally unknown in Europe. As far as social services were concerned—I can recall eagerly opening a newspaper in Collins Street, Melbourne, to read the recommendations of the much-publicised, reputedly very advanced Beveridge Scheme, released in 1942, and my staggered surprise which found vent in the remark, "Why we've had most of these things for years!" Exaggeration perhaps, but near enough to demonstrate the difference in the tone of social thinking in Australia and Britain at that time.

Strangely, Australian women have not greatly increased their interest in government or their use of political power since they received the vote sixty years ago. Female suffrage was never an issue; possibly that is one reason why the undoubted power of female vote could exercise has not so far been exerted; possibly also the fact that the Australian community pattern was really set in the mid-Victorian era, when housewifely virtues were preëminent and the wife-husband relationship sentimentally enshrined by Queen Victoria herself, has as much to do with feminine political apathy as the more apparent predominance of middle-class values and attitudes: "woman's place is the home." A point of view reflected, not in daily business, or in educational curbs, or in restraining women from professional careers, but in what appears to be a reluctance in women themselves to seek office in government.

Thus the Australian woman of today is a modern-minded housewife, living with reasonable comfort and security in a more or less urbanised environment, whilst behind her stretches an enormous expanse of country still but little altered from its ancient condition; the aboriginal inhabitants linger only in a few reserved areas, or else, when they cannot obtain stock work on stations or farms, for the most part cluster near the border towns of civilised districts in a somewhat lethargic condition of slow social advancement. The aboriginal Australians, although they are excellent with cattle and horses (some also become good mechanics and tradesmen) and although their women can be trained in all domestic tasks, including nursing, have not yet shown sustained interest in agricultural pursuits, nor were there ever sufficient numbers to employ as coolie labour, even had they shown any such inclination. Thus the full settlement of Australia has come to depend on what developments can be made in modern civil and mechanical engineering, more especially on the part played by electrical and aeronautic techniques in creating a quickly habitable environment for modern white women, and making it safe for them to embark on family raising in the outback.

This is most dramatically demonstrated by what has happened in the isolated northern areas. Railways, roads, water supplies (windmills and dams for farms), government hospitals, and schools had prevailed in the south for at least a quarter century when forty years ago I visited the Kimberley district of Western Australia for the first time. Kimberley had no air service, no motor roads (indeed, I went with my husband in the first car ever to travel from the port of Wyndham to Hall's Creek, three hundred miles inland, our petrol stores sent on ahead by camel pack); no more than three white women lived on the cattle stations between Wyndham and Derby, a more southerly port yet another three hundred miles west of Hall's Creek. A telegraph line ran between these three points, but to ride into town to telegraph was not a jaunt lightly undertaken. Ships called at Derby fortnightly during the cattle season, at Wyndham only once a month. A pack-mail carried letters and parcels inland. At Hall's Creek there were five women: the policeman's wife, the publican's wife, the storekeeper's wife, and two nurses resident at a tiny Presbyterian Inland Mission hospital. Rumour had run ahead that I was a medical woman. The nurses had a difficult case; their disappointment on discovering the mistake was the bitter measurement of their heavy responsibilities. Already legendary was the story of an operation performed ten years earlier when there was not even a nursing outpost. With a sterilized penknife, on a patient anaesthetized by a bottle of whisky, the then postmaster carried out a major operation at the direction of a surgeon more than a thousand miles away in Perth, step by step transmitted over the cleared telegraph wires.

Today there are made roads, with all-weather river crossings, cars and trucks race everywhere, and homesteads that were without any amenities other than a few native women to do the rough chores, are now comfortable, even luxurious. One we visited during our first trip was kept going by a male cook half dead with malaria; there was nothing to sit on but old wooden oil cases. Completely rebuilt today, this homestead now houses the owner's family and has more than once sheltered the Governor General (who is the Queen's representative) when he tours the continent; a journey unthinkable, in terms of time alone, before air services became widespread and regular.

Communication was the greatest stumbling block to closer settlement, even in the south. The vast distances were intimidating. Aeroplanes have made a major, possibly even a preëminent, contribution to Australian civilization. In 1922 Western Australia saw the inauguration of the first long commercial air route in the world, soon stretching from Perth to Wyndham, approximately 1,500 miles. Mails and quick transport, fresh fruit and procurable drugs almost overnight changed the feminine state of mind towards the outback. Other conditions did not greatly improve until after World War II, but with the coming of aeroplanes the pall of isolation no longer stultified thought: it was possible to envisage a life in the outback no longer dangerous or deprived, for young families.

The Presbyterian Australian Inland Mission (AIM) lost little time in beginning to provide what has now come to be called "a mantle of safety" for the inland popula-

HENRIETTA DRAKE-BROCKMAN

tion. The little mission hospitals had been introduced in 1912; as early as 1917, the Rev. John Flynn, Superintendant of the AIM, saw the possibility of employing aerial ambulances. But to make such a service feasible, it was first necessary to have means of communication with bases. Some type of transmitter that would be able to transmit key signals over a distance of three hundred miles and for which no technical knowledge was required—this was the question. In answer, an electrical engineer, Alfred Traeger of Adelaide, designed a pedal radio with a crystal-controlled transmitter able to maintain a steady wave length regardless of whether the generator was driven evenly or not. Cloncurry, a Queensland town with hospital and airstrip, became the first base; the service began in 1928. A transmitter was installed in the vestry of the Presbyterian church, and pedal sets were gradually distributed to station homesteads. One disadvantage was the need to know the Morse code; but Traegar continued to experiment, finally evolving a Morse typewriter that could transmit Morse letters at governed speed. This also solved the question of widespread telegraphic communication, since messages could be handed on to the postal authorities and despatched as ordinary telegrams. Today there are at least seven such bases, but radio transceivers have displaced the old pedal sets and verbal communication is spread far and wide across two thirds of the Australian continent.

Other aerial medical services were begun, some by group enterprise. One, based at the Northern Territory town of Katherine, was started by Dr Clive Fenton, who bought and flew his own Gypsy Moth. Eventually becoming the Northern Territory Aerial Medical Service, this operation was maintained until the Japanese bombing of Darwin in 1942, when the Royal Australian Air Force took over. After the war, the Federal Government reintroduced the service.

Meantime other doctors were being flown many hundreds of miles, attending patients or bringing them in to hospital if necessary. By then the project was known as The Flying Doctor Service, and the first report of activities to be published fired public imagination. Subscriptions poured in to augment a government subsidy. The subsidy was withdrawn during the Depression, but rather than see the service fail, John Flynn made a tour of the continent to raise funds. So great was his success that in 1934 a group in Melbourne formed themselves into a council to advise and raise funds. This group, and others formed later, eventually amalgamated to create a Federal Council. Today the Royal Flying Doctor Service is one of the most famous and dramatic features of life in Australia, a remarkable and highly efficient safeguard to health, and, by various extensions, the great ameliorator of outback conditions.

Most outback homesteads now have some sort of airstrip. There are special "doctors' rounds" run by the air companies. Medical chests have been installed at suitable outposts; a trained nurse often travels, infant welfare nurses do occasional tours to teach mothercraft; the Education Department conducts a "school of the air" from Alice Springs over the Flying Doctor base. The West Australian Health Department conducted an ophthalmic survey of the Kimberleys made by world-famous eye specialist Dr Ida Mann. The service is for everybody; no distinctions of colour, creed, or finance ever interfere with the treatment of patients. Many a sick outback native has found himself in a large metropolitan hospital within twenty-four hours, perhaps his first close contact with civilization: last year, one such was a youth said to have been "boned," or bewitched, by the wirinuns, or "clever-men," of his tribe. He recovered.

Aeroplanes and airstrips, pedal wireless, radio—these are the engineers' skills and inventions that have most of all lifted the terrifying fear of personal failure from the minds of outback women. Australians know the immense capacity of modern medical practice: they are not any longer prepared to subject their children to the risks of isolation in uninhabited country. A hundred years ago infant mortality was so high, infant welfare so little understood, that mothers could bow the head and say, "The Lord gave, the Lord has taken away." Today, the Scottish saying of, "The Lord helps them who help themselves" is more nearly applicable. In short, women feel immeasurably more responsible for the physical care of their families; and for this reason, more than any other, engineers must be credited with an immense contribution towards assisting Australian women to follow their men into the vast unsettled areas of the continent.

It is still necessary for children to leave the outback areas for secondary education. But as well as correspondence classes conducted by air mail and special radio sessions to enable children to hear their teachers' voices (exchange of photographs also establishes a vital link), the government supplies a teacher wherever there are enough children, white and native, to warrant primary instruction. The Australian Broadcasting Commission conducts a "Kindergarten of the Air" for preschool children in the more closely settled areas and also for Western Australia. This was in fact a wartime measure begun in 1942 to circumvent the difficulties caused by the evacuation of young children from coastal city areas to the country, under the threat of Japanese invasion. So successful did this imaginative use of radio prove to be, that far from being discontinued after the war, it spread to every state in Australia. It has since been taken up overseas, by Britain, Canada, Norway, and New Zealand.

In the older settled areas, electric power becomes more and more widely distributed throughout the countryside, carrying with it a thousand domestic benefits bestowed. Small plants, some run by wind power, are privately installed; solar heat is being used to produce hot water for baths and washing up; good roads and motor vehicles cut down distance and create and consolidate social intercourse. If a country woman needs must still bake her own bread, she has every modern convenience to help her. But it is the recent mining towns that really point the difference between past and present pioneering.

At Mary Kathleen, already mentioned as a symbol, the daily milk supply comes 825 miles from the Atherton Tableland, by truck first from the dairy farms to be pasteurized; then in refrigerated vans by rail to Cloncurry; then once more into trucks, also refrigerated, to its destination in the wild spinifex hills. Like Hall's

Creek which sprang up round a gold strike in 1885, this little uranium town lies amid arid, stony copper-coloured hills—an eroded region with land virutally undisturbed for three hundred million years; the metamorphosed limestone ranges date back to Cambrian times, the red granite in some of the valleys is pre-Cambrian. The area has attracted prospectors for gold and copper since 1870, but all that remains of an old copper town once boasting a population of 5,000 is a mass of abandoned shafts and a host of gravestones. Hall's Creek has at least lived to become a centre for post, police, and Flying Doctor and air services; but it remains three hundred miles by road from any other centre, and I expect goats still supply the milk for tea or puddings, just as they did forty years ago.

Mary Kathleen is no more than forty miles from a railhead at Cloncurry, but the new road put out in 1958 cost half a million pounds to bitumenize. Until then it was a country fit only for horses or camels. The first project for the new town was to build a dam, once mining leases were taken up in 1955. The wall was thrown across the Corella River, a dry watercourse in winter, but a copious stream in the wet summer season. Now Lake Corella, with a capacity of three billion gallons, stretches blue and shining for more than three miles; birds and fishes abound. Mary Kathleen, named after the wife of Norman McConachie, the man who discovered the uranium field, has been called "the most modern little town in Australia." Mrs McConachie died less than a fortnight before her husband made his discovery; a touching memorial, the up-to-date town thus pays tribute to a woman whose menfolk had been drovers, prospectors, and bushmen in the old tradition. The shopping centre is an ultramodern square with tubular steel supports, with white painted timber sun awnings over the concrete sidewalks, and with lawns, gardens, cafeteria, a beer garden surrounded by those ghost gums that the aboriginal painter Albert Namatjira has made so famous, a drive-in theatre, and an AIM hospital. The surrounding homes have either two or three bedrooms; they are built to a standard design suitable for the climate, with cross vents and louvres, but it is an elegant design, and far from boring with differing colours and gardens. To see this town, built where fifty years ago rough shanties between mullock dumps, scrounging goats, water carted from some precarious hole, or even more precarious rainwater in small rusty tanks that would be the most that Australian women could expect, is sufficient proof of what engineers can do to break the resistance of a country difficult to tame for the use of Western man. But it is the women who must finally take up the challenge and people the land.

Strangely, this so obvious fact is scarcely mentioned in the innumerable articles, dissertations, political speeches and conferences devoted to the settling of Australia's "vast empty spaces." At present the daily papers are filled with plans and projects: a dam is at last being constructed across the Ord River where it winds in splendour through the red and purple gorges of the Carr Boyd Ranges in Kimberley. A site which I was enabled to visit sixteen years ago (they told me I was the first white woman to do so) will soon be given over to experimental irrigation. A planned settlement, already begun, will replace the lonely camp of the two drillers then engaged in testing rock foundations; pegged-out crocodile skins bore witness to their sole week-end amusement, and their pedal wireless diverted a 'plane to pick up an accident case in our party. Better beef, rice, cotton, sugar, fodder grasses, tropical fruits—there is no end to the vision splendid of closer settlement on irrigated land. The one commodity never seriously mentioned is women.

The average Australian woman is highly efficient. She is a capable housewife even if she has outside employment. She is a good plain cook, until recently unused to processed food except as emergency rations. She likes to own her own home, and is frequently an enthusiastic gardener. She is, in fact, a hard-working domesticated person.

Yet until Australian women are willing not only to make homes in the northern areas, but also to live out their lives and die there, watching their children's children grow to maturity, it will remain impossible to create stable and expanding communities no matter how numerous parliamentary grants and departmental reports may be, or how grandiose masculine schemes and projects. If this happens, and the women do set out to settle the land, their success will be made possible by modern engineering methods capable of providing the necessities of decent living. Only in domestic security can be developed the physical and moral strengths necessary for national maturity. It would seem that the future of Australia lies at present very much in the hands of the engineers and the women.

JOHN BLIGHT : *MUD*

       Fat, flabby as a woman's belly, jellylike mud;
       Neither land nor water, but a black, rude
       Substitute, lying primitive and crude
       In squalor and poverty; a quadroon of the blood
       Which the sea and the land mixed, with a skeleton of wood;
       Belonging to neither; conceived in the flood,
       The blind surge, and low urge of flats that intrude
       Under the white sea; the worm-infested nude
       Land, deserted by the tide, gross and unclad;
       Black flesh, fat flesh, flesh that's never had
       The bones of ice to brace it; black, filthy mud
       Conceived in the mad swirl of torrent and flood;
       Yet, stone in embryo, firming into nationhood.

GAVIN CASEY : *The Minister for Thingamejig*

T HE ROAD BOARD CHAIRMAN, WHO WAS INTRODUCING THE MINISTER, SEEMED LIKELY TO BURST.

His face was purple, and his eye rolled wildly and pitifully. He kept on talking, because there was nothing else to do, but he was in trouble.

"This here young feller," he said. "This here young feller that lots of us knew as a boy."

He seemed astonished that anybody who had ever been a boy should have grown to be a man, and taken part in the affairs of the world. But he was in acute distress over something. The old fool can't have forgotten my name, the Minister thought.

"This young chap that grew up in this here town," the Chairman was saying. "This young kid that didn't seem any different from all the others, except that our late respected schoolmaster, our late respected schoolmaster, I refer to Mr. Bates, Mr. Bates, I mean, he once said to me, he said, 'Charlie, you keep your eye on young Masters, he'll get somewhere, that boy,' he said."

Well, he had the name, anyway. What the devil could the matter be? The Minister started to fidget, and feel most uncomfortable.

"And here he is with us, here he is with us again after all these years, a Minister, a Minister in the Government of the country, a Cabinet Minister, no less."

The Minister scowled, because he was not a Cabinet Minister, and without being exactly a sore point it was at least a touchy one. When the Big Boy had again enlarged the Ministry he had done away with the Assistant Ministers, and given them all portfolios, but only the ones of senior rank were in the Cabinet. The Minister was not in the Cabinet. After all his years as a most frustrated sort of back-bencher, he was glad for any sort of lift, and properly grateful to the Big Boy. But he was touchy about references to himself and the Cabinet.

"So here's Joe Masters, young Joe Masters who some of us remember with bare feet and no seat in his pants, young Joe Masters, who unknown to himself impressed our late respected school head, and I mean the late Mr. Bates, who once told me he would get somewhere, here's young Joe Masters with us again to open our Annual Show for us."

Well, what about letting me open the bloody thing? the Minister thought. But the Chairman was in the grip of his own difficulty, whatever it was, held and hypnotized by it, as orators and actors sometimes are when they lose a line and, the further it recedes from their minds, grow more and more determined to remember it and say it. The Minister knew all too well how it happened sometimes. He was sorry for the Chairman, but impatient.

With a painful gulp, and a glazing of his eyes through the effort, the Chairman blundered on.

"An' there's nobody it could give me greater pleasure to ask to open this great display of our district's wealth, of our district's wealth and skill, than this man some of us knew as a boy, this man who stands beside me on this here platform—I refer to the Hon. Joseph Masters, the Minister for—the Minister for—" (He gulped again, desperately) the Minister for Thingamejig."

He had meant to mumble the last word but, frantic as he had become, it erupted out of him in a loud, agonised croak, hoarse but clear, easily heard by everybody. The lips of the Minister's wife set into a thin, hostile line of furious disapproval, and the Minister himself froze with horror for a second. But the shout of mirth he expected did not come. There was a snigger or two, and somebody yelled, "Good old Charlie!" Then the crowd applauded vigorously and seemingly warmly, and the Minister moved forward and raised his hand.

But it had put him off his stroke. He spoke creditably and suitably, but a lot of what he had wanted to say had vanished out of his mind, apparently along with his Ministerial title which had fled from the Chairman's. He could feel that it was not going to be one of his good days.

He was careful to emphasise that he was Minister for Loans and Insurances and, of course, he gave no hint to these people of how subservient he had to be to the Treasurer, or how closely old Scrooge McDuck supervised all his activities. He got away well enough with creating an impression of his own importance in the inner councils of the nation, without being revealingly specific about anything. But he didn't grip or hold them, and he cut it short when too many of them started to drift away from around the rostrum to go and look at the exhibits and displays.

What he had intended to say would have been much warmer. This was his home town, though it was not in his electorate, and he cherished a sentimental regard for it and its people. He wanted them to think well of him, even if they could not vote for or against him. He was a sentimental man, not a cynic—or not more than he had to be.

The trouble was that the goat of a Chairman had upset him, right at the start. Now, when he looked at the people, they were not his people, not the ones from whom he had sprung. The older ones looked dull and dopey, with too much straw in their hair, and the younger ones had weird clothes and mad hair styles. There were even louts scattered among the crowd who lounged against rails and trestles and listened intently to transistor radios while he was speaking. It was enough to put anybody off, and he felt a distaste for the people, and felt that they probably deserved what they got.

"Did you hear what that old lunatic said?" his wife hissed at him, indignantly, when his speech was over.

He laughed indulgently, being the imperturbable man-of-the-world, who shrugged off trifles and enjoyed a joke against himself. He said, "Doesn't matter, dear. All over, now."

But it did matter, of course. It had upset his balance, and his whole day, and it

56

nagged at him, following him about as he inspected the stands and met people, and said the appropriate things. It irritated him, and created an urge in him to say inappropriate things. Minister for Thingamejig, eh? It was just about what he was, and damn old Charlie.

When his sweat was running freely, and Mary had been taken off by the women, and the dust and dry grass kicked into the air by the mob was beginning to tickle his hay-fevery nose, a time of relief came, as one always does.

"Well, Mr. Masters," said the Chairman, who knew some of the right things to say, anyway. "The sun's over the yardarm. What say we adjourn to the Committee Room?"

They adjourned, and everybody went on earbashing him. They wanted things. They wanted everything. He'd have had to be the Big Boy himself, the boss, to be able to give them a fraction of what they asked for. Minister of Thingamejig! he thought, for a moment tempted to tell one of the supplicants that he had better see the Minister for Whattayacallit about that.

Anyway, there was always the grog, and good grog and plentiful it always was, at these country shows. He lapped it up thirstily, and after a while he felt a bit better. Even the Chairman, for whom he had developed an immediate distaste that morning, began to seem not a bad old sod, and as for the earbashing, the liquor restored his long-cultivated ability to grunt impressively at suitable intervals and hear hardly a word of it. The hour before lunch, soothed by Scotch and spent inside in the shade, was good.

His lunchtime speech, to the Agricultural Society Committee and its guests, was better and livelier than the morning one. Almost too lively, his wife told him, disapprovingly, later, and what had he meant by referring in front of all those people to the Treasurer as Scrooge McDuck, instead of by his proper name as the Rt. Hon. Sir Pursepuller Threadneedle? But that was a long time later, and much happened before then.

For instance, by midafternoon the Minister was sweating again, even in the shade, and uncomfortably aware that he had, perhaps, taken a little too much Scotch. Wouldn't do! He was a convivial politician, not an austere one, and everybody expected a good fellow like him to put away his share of the grog. But enough was enough. People sniggered. Sort of thing that eventually reached the Big Boy's ears, and made him devastatingly sour and sarcastic. Sort of thing in the long run that got even a Minister for Thingamejig tossed out of the Ministry altogether.

The Minister went to the men's room, discovered there was a second door out of it, emerged near the back fence of the Showground, and went wandering off on his own, with the intention of pulling himself together. He looked over the showground fence and was rather charmed to see Golliger's place there, where it had always been.

What a man! Golliger must have been there on his few acres for fifty years now, forty of them defying the town to grow over the top of him and change his place into rows of streets and houses, as it should have done long ago. Golliger was no doubt as fiercely and arrogantly intolerant as ever, quarreling as energetically as he had for years with increasing numbers of neighbors, their dogs, their children, and their motorcars. The recollection of Golliger and his eccentricities brought a strong flood of memories of his youth and the Minister was filled with nostalgia.

He climbed two fences, and was on the old man's land, among overgrown grape-vines he had once helped to prune and pick in school holidays. There was the big, old, dead warren which had once been lively and thick with rabbits, which he and Vic. Simpson had spent a couple of days digging out. The marks of their spades were long gone, of course, but disturbed earth retains its shape in spite of weather and the years, and there were still signs of all the digging and trenching.

What a tiger old Golliger had been, what an absolute tiger, the Minister thought, walking slowly among the overgrown, thickened, too lush vines. The terror of all the kids in the district, and of half the grown-ups, too. There was the house, much the same as ever, though the stables and sheds looked in bad repair. Still, even old Golliger could hardly use horses still, and no doubt all they housed nowadays was a tractor and some sort of old car.

Then, suddenly, Golliger himself was storming down out of the house, and the Minister felt, for a moment, all the fear he had experienced years ago, as a ragged-trousered boy, when the old man had come after him for trespassing, orchard-robbing, and such villainy. He had an impulse to take to his heels, as he certainly would have then, but he giggled a trifle, and stood his ground.

"What the hell are you doing here?" old Golliger bawled, looking much the same as ever, tall and gaunt and cranky, like one of the rulers of the earth of a bygone age, which was just what he was.

"My name's Joe Masters, Mr. Golliger."

"Your name? I didn't ask your silly damned name. I asked what the blazes you were doing here."

"I was just looking. I thought you'd remember me, sir," said the Minister, disappointed that the old boy did not. "I was born and brought up here, in the town. Used to do odd jobs for you, weekends and holidays, sometimes. Joe Masters."

Golliger glared at him. "Masters? Don't remember anybody called Masters. Wait a minute, though. There was that drunken sot that worked at the chaff merchant's. You his son?"

The Minister didn't relish the description of his father any more than he relished Golliger's nonrecognition of him, either as a one-time resident or as a Minister of the Crown. He admitted his paternity, rather snappily.

"Looks like a case of like father, like son. You're drunk, my man," barked Golliger.

"I'm not," the Minister barked back, angrily, feeling his blood pressure soaring among clouds that were composed of the fumes of Scotch. "I've been—well, I was opening the annual show, over the fence there."

"The show? What would a drunken, disreputable sot like you be doing, opening their silly, blasted show?"

"I'm not," bawled the Minister again, in fury and despair. "I'm a guest of the Committee. I'm a Minister."

"Well, it must be a funny sort of church that puts a drunkard in the cloth," snorted Golliger, poking his long nose out suspiciously. "Where's your collar? No, that's right, most of you don't wear 'em any more, do you? First step downhill, I said when they started dropping them, an' now here you are, trespassing on my property, and drunk into the bargain. It's as well you don't wear the cloth, my good man. You'd be a damned disgrace to it."

"I'm not that sort of Minister," the Hon. Joseph Masters shrieked, retreating a cautious step or two as old Golliger advanced menacingly. "I'm a Minister—well, a Minister of the Crown."

"Oh, well that's a different kettle of fish, isn't it? Now you're a Minister of the Crown, boozing on the taxpayers' money. Well, I'm a taxpayer, and I don't like it."

"I haven't been boozing. I just had one or two with the Committee, after I'd opened the show."

"One or two! One or two over the eight, by the look of it. Now, if you're a Minister, tell me what you're Minister for, before I break your leg and call the dogs to chew it off."

"I'm the Minister for—the Minister for—" said the Minister, and then his jaw dropped, with horror and confusion.

He couldn't remember! He could remember Scrooge McDuck bossing him around, and the Big Boy giving him the good news that he was now in the Ministry, if not the Cabinet, and he could remember the lean, sour, domineering face of Stringy Leanrope, Secretary of the Treasury, the permanent civil servant who was really his boss. He could remember the House, and his colleagues, and even some of his so-called duties. In a very short time he would remember it all, but just for this stunned moment the thing that evaded him was which of the new, minor portfolios his insignificant Ministerial duties came under.

"Come on, what is it?" Golliger snarled. "Housing? Agriculture? Trade? Industrial Development? Likely story, you being a Minister—wandering around my paddocks drunk in broad daylight."

"I'm not," Masters bawled. "I am. I mean I'm not drunk and I am a Minister. I'm the Minister for—the Minister for—I'm the Minister for Thingamejig."

The fearful Golliger's maniac laugh exploded in his ears just as the old lunatic grabbed a pitchfork out from behind one of the vines, and came at him. He broke and ran, and fell through the fence into the dust in a most undignified manner. Golliger still roared with laughter, but he stayed on his own side of the fence.

The Minister went off along the dusty road, nearly weeping with mortification and anger. The Minister for Bloody Thingamejig! That's just about what he was, and no mistake.

Then, in his anger and sweat and confusion, he had a moment of perception. Were any of them much more? Was even the Big Boy really big enough to handle the things they had to tackle? Was old Scrooge, who always looked so wise, really wise, or just cunning? Were they all, in their Homburg hats and solemnity, blundering about with things that were too vast for them? Was he, or even the best of them, really much more than the Minister for Thingamejig?

The Minister was a decent and fairly honest man, who really wanted to do the best for his country and its people, so he had had occasional doubts before that were not unlike these.

But never before or after were they as strong as on that day when he opened the show, and the Road Board Chairman called him the Minister for Thingamejig, and Scotch and anger had made him briefly forget his own title, and mad old Golliger had chased him, as a grown man and one of importance too, out of the ancient vineyard with a pitchfork.

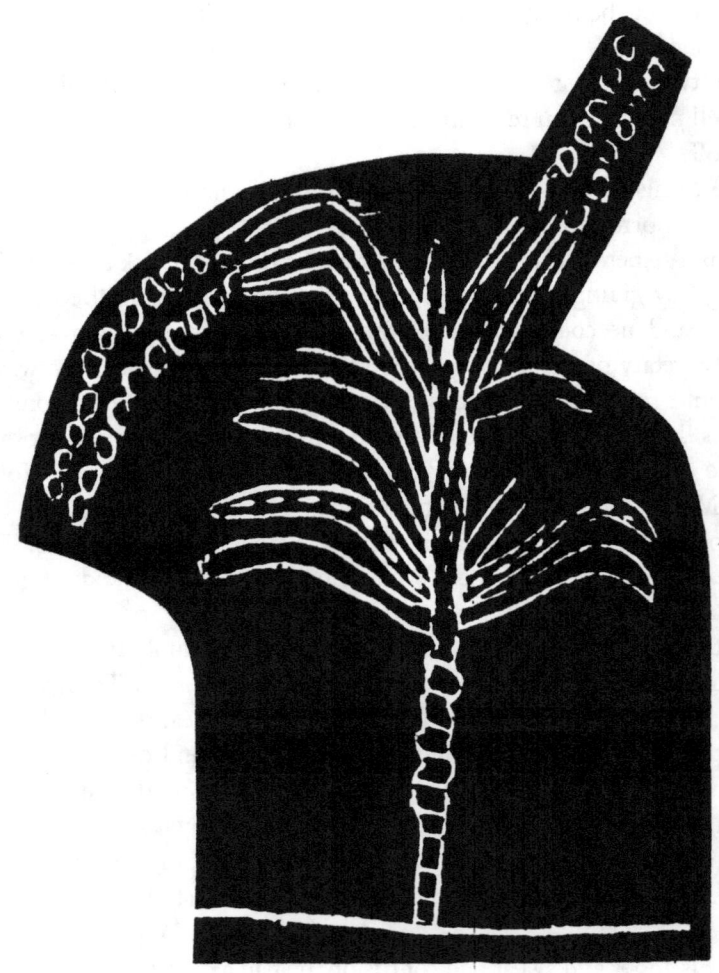

GAVIN CASEY

ROBIN BOYD : *Architecture in Australia*

T HREE NATIONAL INFLUENCES HAVE ACTED ON AUSTRALIAN ARCHITECTURE.
One is the English tradition, which was the fountainhead of nearly all building ideas through the nineteenth century. Another is the more recent influence of the U.S.A., which may be subdivided into two kinds: Hollywood and
serious. Thirdly, there is the complicated set of indigenous influences, ranging from
the native materials to the psychology of isolation. These influences were represented
by three men, all now dead, who struggled to bring modern architecture to life about
the time of the first world war.

First, the Englishman, Robert Haddon, a Romantic-functionalist inheriting a little
from Morris and Mackintosh: a scholastic man, fond of his new land but always
nostalgic for the Old Country.

Second, an original member of the Chicago School—and one of the last of them—
the American, Walter Burley Griffin, radiating gentle warmth, organic theory, and
democratic New World idealism.

Third, the Australian, Harold Desbrowe Annear, who was born in Bendigo in
1866 when it was still hardly more than a gold-rush canvas town. Annear never left
Australia. He was impatient with such tuition as he could get in Melbourne. He was
an experimenter, improviser, inventor of architectural gadgetry. He was self-confident
and rebellious. He ridiculed "good taste" and traditions, preferring what he
imagined were his own answers, whatever their faults. He was inconsistent, unstable,
and not altogether reliable, but among his best works are some which deserve passing
recognition alongside the earliest European and Chicagoan pioneers of the modern
movement. (Not that Annear, working in isolation from hearsay and first principles,
would have known the others' names or expected recognition outside the smarter
streets of Toorak or Portsea where he worked.)

The antipodean isolation has since been modified by radio and jets, but still the
three elements are to be found separately, each in a fairly pure state. The Old World
is now represented architecturally by a persistent, if slowly shrinking, streak of con-
servatism that diverts attention from form to detail. The results of this are never
exactly academic, but on the other hand not quite as dowdy as Europe at her stodgiest.
The New World is represented by a more than usually hysterical worship of the
American image: we might call it "Austericanism." This leads to violent primary-
hued delinquency—not clever enough to be fashionably smart but on the other hand
never quite as mad as Miami. The physical isolation of Australia from her spiritual
sisters of the West is not in fact felt strongly enough to be valuable; it is not sharp
enough to free architects to work out their own solutions. The oceans have worked
as a valve permitting only a one-way passage of ideas: inwards always from the
higher-pressure areas, continuously inflating feelings of inadequacy or frustration

among the local practitioners of all arts. The supremacy of the importation is a popular concept against which the Annear spirit of indiscipline has rebelled at intervals and has produced one vital strain of modern Australian building.

But the average unintrospective Australian architect and his client are not, of course, disturbed by the action of the valve. There is no serious suggestion of aggressive artistic nationalism. Any Australian flavour in everyday building appears to be involuntary, in some obvious ways related to the qualities which visitors usually discover in the Australian human character. He is (observers often say) easygoing to an extent which exasperates urgent North Americans and exact Central Europeans. "Near enough" is the national philosophy: a deliberate cult of antifinesse, of outbackmanship. But (they admit) he answers up to challenges. He is resourceful, an ingenious improviser, a born mechanic, the sort of fellow you like to have close by in an emergency. These qualities colour to some extent all the styles of Australian building. They help to produce a background that is practical, unstylish, technically advanced, casual in detail and often hideously garish. And they produce the opposite: buildings that recognize the existence of a challenge, of an artistic emergency for a rich and lazy young nation which could quite easily be swamped entirely by imported mass-produced ideas.

Sensitive Australian laymen, aware of this general danger and searching architecture for a "National Style," look hopefully to the colonial building of the early nineteenth century. Here was a displaced, delayed, diminutive Georgian with all the charm of diminution and anachronism and just enough subtle peculiarities to mark it from other and earlier Georgian work. The domestic variant was quite distinctive: a low, hipped shingle roof, later corrugated iron, pulled down all round a white house like a wide hat brim shading the long evenly-spaced windows. Australians can see—though it is less perceptible to visitors—a continuing tradition based on this relaxed and random form. The uncrowded single-storey, wide sun-shading eaves, and extroversion, combined with the pecularities of the kiln-dried native timbers and the cheapness of Australian steel, still produce in unself-conscious construction a sort of indigenous character.

Australia has many things in common with Sweden and California, including a filial feeling for the twentieth century. Thus a fairly accurate idea of modern Australia may be gained by imagining an underpopulated California. It is hardly surprising that the buildings of both regions have been similar for more than a hundred years. The climate, colouring, and social background are similar, and both discovered gold and galvanized iron about the same time. On the other hand Australia may be pictured even better by thinking of Sweden and then imagining the extreme opposite. Australian taste is all peaks and valleys. No landscapes have been outraged more wantonly than the untidy olive and ochre sites of most Australian towns. The first move of the land exploiters still is to remove all trace of native growth. Fevered advertising, whether frank or subconscious, almost submerges architecture in the commercial areas and every sensitive building is all but smothered by

ROBIN BOYD

its neighbors. The one architectural vice Australia need not fear is monotony.

About five years ago Australia rose from the bed of a postwar trough suddenly to the crest of a building boom. The building industry became busier than at any time since it made the grotesque stucco palaces of the late nineteenth century. Expenditure on new building construction amounted to more than a quarter of the total investments in Australia. Lately the boom has become less exciting and more of a habit. The industry is now merely fully employed and expecting to participate with reasonable profit in the unlimited future which Australia nowadays pictures for herself (all going well in Asia).

The new confidence has concrete foundations in big public works, the most impressive of which is the enormous project in the Snowy Mountains where coastal rivers are being diverted through the range back into the dry interior. And it is ornamented with nonutilitarian buildings, like Sydney's Opera House and Melbourne's National Art Gallery and Cultural Center. Both these are giant projects in any language. They are now under construction, but a few years ago they would have been politically impossible. Then housing took priority to everything else. With the lifting of restrictions on "nonessential" buildings, the construction of houses now has dropped slightly, but the rate is still about 95,000 dwellings per year, and the number of separate houses under construction per head of population must still be close to a world record. The shortage cannot be estimated very scientifically. It is measured not by the number of homeless but by the number wanting more comfortable homes. The popular objective is a pretty, semicontemporary villa with venetian blinds and a lock-up garage for every family. The main obstacle to this amiable aspiration is not a shortage of builders, labour, or materials, nor of money in the weekly pay envelope. It is a shortage of capital, a chronic condition of Australia. There seems no limit to the dribs of money available for nondurable goods, but continually the flow of money for building investment strikes blockages. The optimism of the country is thus better reflected in the standard of refrigerators and the thickness of breakfast steaks than in the quality of new houses. However, the government, the insurance companies, and the banks do contribute their money to the building industry in another way: by commissioning some of the most elaborate of the new curtain-walled office blocks which are transforming the central areas of the capital cities.

The decline of housing to little more than half the total output of the building industry has reanimated the architectural profession, which was never greatly concerned with the cottages. It is not unusual for a man to be operating a satisfying little private practice five years or so after graduation. No fewer than 3,500 architects are registered in Australia. This is about 334 per million people—one of the highest proportions in the world, comparing with 76 per million in the U.S.A. Maybe this fact helps to explain (by the maxim of too many cooks) the characteristic inconstancy of Australian architecture. The drift from housing has also caused a reshuffling in the builders' ranks. The once-crowded field of "little" builders—the family teams and the random spec. builders—is thinning out. The only way to make a success of housing speculation now appears to be the big way: a hundred "young executive's villas" at a time, a package deal with finance arranged for the furniture as well, a multicoloured marquee, and the Minister for Housing flown to the site by helicopter to launch the parade.

In bread-and-butter building materials Australia has always been self-sufficient, if not opulent. Today the production of bricks, steel, cement, terra cotta, and hardwood is steadily if unevenly on the rise, keeping pace with the rapidly growing population. The most obvious deficiency of the land is in softwoods. For all practical purposes Australia has no native softwood. The ubiquitous eucalypt grows in hundreds of regional varieties of texture and colour, from the deep rust red of the western jarrah to the sun-bleached northern silver ash—an albino wood as light as an ocean beach. Some, like jarrah, is practically impervious to dampness and rot. Much of this is exported as railway sleepers. Other varieties, like the straight yellow mountain ash which climbs to three hundred feet in the southeastern highlands, do almost any indoor job beautifully and well: framing, flooring, or furniture. All of this wood is hard, and unstable while carrying any moisture, requiring diligent kiln-drying, which was early developed in Australia. It supplies about eighty percent of the timber requirements of the building industry. The remainder is made up of imports, mostly softwood. More than half of this is Douglas Fir (called "Oregon") from the U.S.A. and Canada. Some is "Baltic"—Scandinavian pine ready-milled into flooring and weatherboards, and some is Radiata Pine from New Zealand's plantations. About one quarter of the timber imports, to the value of some £3,000,000 ($7 million) annually, is spent on figured timbers from Borneo, Malaya, New Guinea.

While the local bread and butter of building materials has been wholesome, Australia developed a habit during a century and a half before 1950 of reaching abroad for the marmalade or peanut butter. For instance, while she made her own roof tiles and floor tiles, she imported the decorative tiles for the walls from the U.K., Italy, or Japan.

Since the early fifties a new concept of Australia as an industrial power and a factory for Asia has grown. Now there are, proportionately to population, more factory workers in Australia than in North America, and the ever-increasing load of refrigerators, power lawn mowers, television sets, room conditioners, and labour-saving devices which burden the working man is almost entirely made in Australia. The economy still rides on the sheep's back, but exports of industrial goods, including iron and steel products, aircraft, vehicles, and electrical equipment are rising continuously. Manufactured goods now amount to more than one fourth of the export trade. There is even the faintest hint of an architectural device emanating from Australia with these products. The adjustable glass-louvre window—which is one of the country's three contributions to domestic technology, along with the development of fibrous-plaster sheeting and stainless steel sinks—is being exported in sizable

Opposite: Model of National Art Gallery, Melbourne. *Architect* : Roy Grounds

Sydney Opera House. *Architect* : Jacob Utson

Sydney harbour and bridge

House at Palm Beach, N.S.W. *Architect* : P. Muller

House at Cronulla, N.S.W. *Architects* : Ancher, Mortlock & Murry

Home of Robin Boyd in Melbourne

Financial district of Melbourne. New office buildings; law courts at top right.

quantities from Queensland. Mainly these airy windows go to Asia, but others to the value of £70,000 annually are imported by the U.S.A., and double this quantity is bought by Great Britain. Galvanised iron sheeting worth some six million pounds is exported each year to New Zealand and Asia.

All the time the Australian content of building is rising. About three fourths of all hardware, light fittings, and sanitary ware used are Australian made. The remaining fourth is welcomed for variety rather than to make up a shortage. Most of the gas and electrical stoves and virtually all refrigerators and air conditioners are made in Australia, and quantities are exported. About ninety-seven per cent of the 140,000 tons of structural steel consumed yearly by the building industry is locally produced. The remainder is mostly giant sections which are not rolled because the manufacturers consider the demand is limited. A few prefabricated aluminum buildings are imported, and about the same quantity of steel prefabs is exported. Plastics of all kinds are made and used with an enthusiasm which suggests there might be a special appeal to Australians in the smooth, cheap, intricate precision of the colorful moulded product. On the other hand, no wallpaper is printed in Australia; the little that is used comes from England or Japan. More than making up for the comparative absence of wallpaper, Australia has a rapacious appetite for paint. An annual output worth $70 million from the local paint industry provides millions of gallons of vividly coloured paint for use on new buildings and in gingering up old buildings with "contemporary" fashion hues.

If this suggests a rather hideous mess on the surface of modern Australia, one must admit to a fair share of ugliness. Yet, of course, the vulgar colours and shapes of many busy commercial centers are not all there is to Australian architecture. Less obvious, there is a fair share of the individual soul-searching which accompanies a young nation trying earnestly to know its own mind. If the popular architectural mess is wilder than usual, so is the outcry against it. Protest and criticism are at least as lively as anywhere, and architecture is a popular art. It is popular because patronage of it is within reach of almost everyone sometime in his life, if not in his business then in the separate suburban cottage often shaped individually for him in defiance of technical advances or business efficiency. The design of big public projects is widely discussed, architectural criticism is given space in the daily press, and the intricacies of contemporary domestic architecture are a standard butt of television comedians. The people look to the architect for stimulation and excitement, and at the present time the architects are as uncertain as they are in any other country as to how they should respond. The younger architect still clings to the faith that there is rational justification for his modern eclecticism. He absorbs the influences of Europe and America separately through the magazines and in travel taken as soon as possible after graduation. His first trip usually takes him to Europe, concentrating on Italy, Scandinavia, and Great Britain. His second trip is to the U.S.A. He is looking for practice rather than theory, and on returning home he finds the American magazines more helpful than the English and European ones. Thus numerous curtain walls are rising in the bigger cities, twenty to thirty stories high, and as clean, conformist, noncommittal, and comfortable as anywhere else in the world. Then there are Australian versions of all the mid-century mannerisms, from European Brutalism to Edward Stone's grillwork, and eager young men who imitate Frank Lloyd Wright convinced that they are original, constructive humanists. There are also some quiet free-thinkers and those whose first trip overseas is to Japan and Australia's northern Asian neighbours. And there are, finally, those of the Annear spirit: the architectural bushrangers. It would be fun to think that these last are growing in number, strength and maturity, but the truth seems to be the contrary. The rebels are fading away as Australia gets more populous, prosperous, industralised, and confident. The exciting things in Australian modern architecture were until recently isolated experiments done with little more than sticks, wires, space, and unencouraged enthusiasm. But already the last continent is losing its innocence.

ROBIN BOYD

Fence must be looked at; fence is too much neglected;
Most ancient indeed is fence. But it is not merely
White ants' and weather's ravage must be inspected,
The broken paling where we can see too clearly
The neighbours at their affairs, that larger hole
Where Hogans' terrier ate it, or very nearly;
But fence most quintessential, fence in its soul.

For fence is defensa, Latin; fence is old Roman
And heaven knows what wild tribes, rude and unkown,
It sprang from first, when man took shelter with his woman.
Fence is no simple screen where Hogan may prune
His roses decently hidden by paling or lattice
Or sporting together some sunny afternoon
Be noticed with Mrs. Hogan at nymphs and satyrs;

But fence is earthwork, defensa; connected no doubt
With fossa, a moat; straight from the verb to defend,
Therefore ward off, repel, stand guard on the moat:
None climbs this fence but cat or Hogan's friend.
Fence is of spears and brambles; fence is defiance
To sabre-toothed tigers, to all the world in the end,
And there behind it the Hogans stand like lions.

It is not wise to meet the Hogans in quarrel,
They have a lawyer and he will issue writs;
Thieves and trespassers enter at deadly peril;
The brave dog bites the postman where he sits.
Just as they turn the hose against the summer's
Glare on the garden, so in far fiercer jets
Here they unleash the Hogans against all comers.

True it is not very often the need arises
And they are peaceable people behind their barrier;
But something is here that must be saved in a crisis,
They know it well and so does the sharp-toothed terrier.
They bring him bones, he worships them deeply and dankly,
He thinks Mrs. Hogan a queen and Hogan a warrior,
Most excellent people, and they agree with him, frankly.

The world has need of Hogans; they can contribute
To its dull pattern all their rich singularity;
And if, as is true, it pays them no proper tribute
Hogans from Hogans at least shall not lack charity.
Shielded by fences are they not free to cherish
Each bud, each shoot, each fine particularity
Which in the Hogans burgeons and must not perish?

It is not just that their mighty motor mower
Roars loudest for miles and chops up the insolent grass,
Nor that the Iceland poppies are dancing in flower
Nor the new car all shiny with chromium and glass
Nor the fridge and T.V., nor that, the bloom of their totem,
Their freckled children always come first in the class
Or sometimes at least, and never are seen at the bottom;

It is all this and so much more beside
Of Hogans down the ages in their proud carriage
And Hogan young and Mrs. Hogan a bride
And napkins washed and Babies fumbling their porridge,
Things which no prying stranger can know or feel
All locked in the strange intimacy of marriage:
Which by all means let decent fences conceal.

So let us to work, good neighbour, this Saturday morning,
Nail up the paling so Hogans are free to be Hogans
And Stewarts be Stewarts and no one to watch them scorning
And no one break in with bullets and bombs and slogans
Or we will stand guard at the fence and fight as we can.
World is against us, but world has had its warning;
Deep out of time is fence, and deep is man.

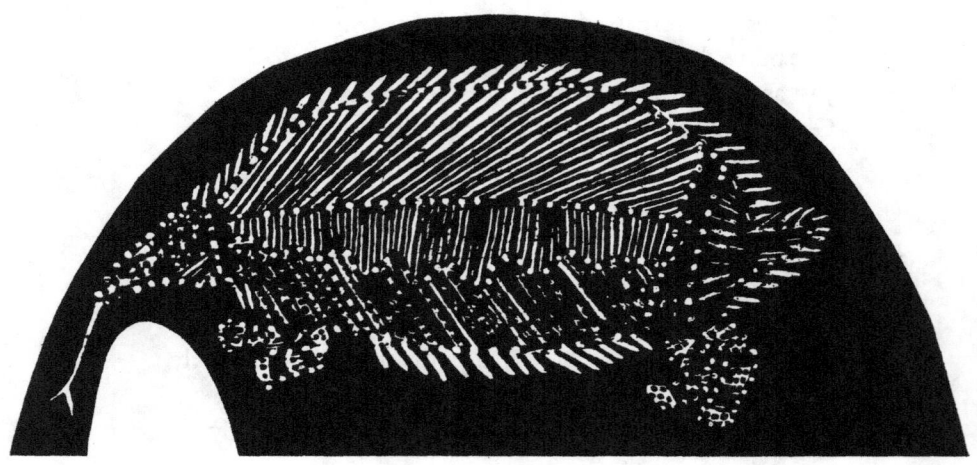

DOUGLAS STEWART

ANDREW FABINYI : *The Australian Book*

A MERE TEN AND A HALF MILLION AUSTRALIANS ARE, STATISTICALLY, AMONG the earth's most voracious readers and book consumers. They buy more than a quarter of all books exported from the United Kingdom, and are the U.S.' fourth largest book customer. In 1961 Australians spent $4 per head on books—in terms of local purchase value the highest book expenditure in the English-speaking world. Visitors to Australia, and indeed many Australians, find these figures surprising. Australian society does not, at first glance, present a bookish appearance. It is difficult to say where all these books are, what kind of books they are, and who are the people who read them. Bookshelves are not standard equipment in Australian homes, and books and literature are not staple topics in the Australian's normally clipped conversation.

Yet probing in any direction brings the same result. A recent Gallup Poll revealed that forty-nine out of one hundred persons were reading one or two books at a time. Wherever free libraries are available (admittedly there still are some districts without them) up to fifty per cent of the area's population enlist as borrowers. There are more than 4,000 recognized book outlets of which 500 come under the category of bookshop. There is one bookstore to every 20,000 of population, compared with one to every 40,000 in Britain, and one to every 90,000 in the United States. The estimated value of stock—mostly imported books—held by booksellers at the end of 1961 was $7 million. Bookshops still occupy central city positions, and economic factors such as basic unprofitability, and poor return on capital compared with other kinds of retailing and industry, are only just beginning to drive the Australian book trade towards the crisis to which booksellers in the United States have largely succumbed.

The articulate demand for books derives its strength in Australia, as elsewhere, from the needs of formal education for which the printed word is still the basic tool. The numbers of pupils at schools, of those who stay on for senior secondary classes, and of those who enter universities, increase year by year. Nevertheless Australia's spending on books is not merely a textbook bonanza, and certainly not the result of generous library budgets (public library book funds have been shrinking rather than expanding). Books of all kinds are being widely bought, and presumably read, by individuals as well as institutions. Here then is a rich book market to provide, at least theoretically, rewarding business for Australian book publishing—that is, the publishing of books by Australian authors, and printed and produced in Australia.

Practice, though, shows other trends. Australians, contrary to beliefs held in some parts of the world, speak, read and write in English. Whatever they achieve by way of publishing they have to do in the shadow of their growing, efficient, and prosperous competitors in Britain and the United States. Australia, again contrary to beliefs still held elsewhere, is no longer a British colony, but a truculently independent nation. Politically and economically she commands healthy respect in what is known as the Mother Country. She is no longer ruled from London *except* in book publishing where a core of British publishers regard her as their own colonial dependency— a market which can be deftly bargained with when buying American copyrights, a territory which, in the shape of original writing or (in the case of textbooks) practical local adaptation, provides splendid raw material, and which is then ready to receive the finished product: the London-produced book.

Consequently, indigenous Australian publishing appears as the one activity which has miraculously managed to stay out of the unprecedented world-wide change and development in publishing of the last fifteen years. Just after the war (in 1947) 1,178 different books were published in Australia. By 1960 the figure had dropped to 531, only to stage a phenomenal comeback of 1,840 in 1961.* This is an inflated indeed misleading figure as it includes for tht first time 1,027 government publications, commercial and semiofficial monographs and books by Australians and on Australia published overseas; none of these was listed in previous bibliographies. Nevertheless there is a net total increase which still suggests the turn of the tide.

Even throughout the period of decline there had been a constant, indeed spectacular, improvement in the contents and physical presentation of Australian books, and individual titles were printed and sold in much larger editions. However, it was only last year that Australian publishing found a healthy level of existence, if not yet prosperity, in a more sympathetic and expanding home market, and also in imaginative younger people entering the field. For the first time, in 1961, Australian books on Australian subjects dominated the scene. Today best-seller lists carry a special Australian section, and recently a monthly review has been successfully launched, devoted exclusively to critiques of Australian-published books. In the field of educational books the battle is swiftly being won. Twenty-five years ago most children at primary schools, and all students at high schools and universities learnt their lessons from British published books. Today almost all primary books are Australian, as also are most books used in junior and senior secondary classes. Australian books in the fields of history, economics, political science, and even languages and physics are now firmly entrenched in our expanding universities, even if tertiary education will, for another half century or so, continue to depend on British and American texts.

While Australian publishing is forging ahead to become a third force in English

---

* These are figures for the last fifteen years:

1947 : 1,178	1952 : 627	1957 : 661
1948 : 1,088	1953 : 516	1958 : 705
1949 : 666	1954 : 565	1959 : 765
1950 : 745	1955 : 612	1960 : 531
1951 : 688	1956 : 625	1961 : 1,840

The two largest publishers, in terms of title output, are Angus & Robertson of Sydney and F. W. Cheshire of Melbourne.

ANDREW FABINYI

language publishing its very existence is still being questioned, particularly abroad. In a world where techniques of mass production, mass advertising, and mass consumption are not only reaching perfection but seem to have become goals in themselves, is it really necessary to perpetuate in Australia a comparatively small pocket of English-language publishing? Should not Australians depend on the fine organization and global distribution facilities of British and American presses geared to pour out some 45,000 titles each year? Does Australian publishing bear any real relationship to economic laws and intellectual needs? Is it not significant that there is still not one firm which does or could function independently and that all Australian publishers are also either booksellers, or overseas firms' representatives, or printers, or appendages of newspaper interests? Is it not just pompous, misguided nationalism to want to edit, print, and publish books in Sydney, Melbourne, Brisbane, or Adelaide?

Book publishing still remains a creative and not merely commercial pursuit. A publisher and his editors are individuals who can, and do, make visible contributions to the intellectual landscapes of their communities. Many books (if we omit imaginative writing: most books) are born through a combination of a publisher's initiative and a writer's ability. A publisher who is alive, physically, mentally, financially, who can be abused or flattered in person, and is not just a signature coming from across the oceans, is, and must be, part of what we call modern democratic society. And indeed, if Australia had had to depend or were to depend solely on book publishing abroad, on the judgement of foreign editors, on publishing houses which are now run by capable accountants for watchful shareholders, if it did not have the dogged pioneering spirit of a handful of persons who have faced the difficulties and indifference of many lean years and who publish essentially because that is what they want to do—many books first published here, and some now part of world literature, would never have seen the light of day.

If one believes, as I do as an Australian, and as Americans did when during the last century they ceased to be importers of British books and built the American publishing colossus, that a genuine, distinctive, indigenous civilisation has emerged and must develop, that culture and literature are the effective means of national self-expression, and that it is through books that we can conquer worlds for pennies which we could not conquer physically for billions—then the argument against Australian book publishing, still bandied about, becomes meaningless.

For some time to come, Australian books will have to find their public primarily in Australia, but their survival—and the word is pertinent in spite of the upsurge experienced in 1961—will depend on whether or not they can find a market in other countries. There are many difficulties. The charge is often made that Australian writers are preoccupied with Australian material only and that this cuts them off from the export market and keeps the local scene at the level of a provincial literary society. This charge is basically true—and defensible. No writer, whether he is a novelist or a schoolteacher, a poet or a social scientist, lives in an abstract world, and no publisher will risk his money on the needs of an imaginary public. The body of

American writing brings with it the tang of the American way of life; English literature has always been "provincial" in this sense, whether it is the Brontës writing of Yorkshire, or C.P. Snow of a Cambridge college.

Australian literature is local only in the sense that all literature must have its roots in the native soil. All we desire to contribute to the world is our Australianism expressed in the characteristic shades of our English usage, the vividness of our urban and bush scene, and analyses of our social organisation, past, present, and future. Nevertheless, there are several harsh facts we have to face. People abroad are generally not interested in us, and their ignorance about us does not serve to whet their appetite for our literature. Our "down under" geography, basically unaltered by the jet age until and unless books go up by air at surface mail rates, makes it impossible to sell books in New York from Melbourne, or in London from Sydney. To get our books into the shops and institutions of other countries we must attempt to channel whole editions, small as they may be, through publishers more strategically placed than we are. There is a hunger for manuscripts, ideas, and even small editions, and American and British publishers keep on rushing between New York and London, with forays to the Continent, in search of material. But they show singular resistance when it comes to buying Australian-printed books, or even the rights of books already printed in Australia. The *first* right of Australian books, including Australian market rights, is, of course, a proposition London and New York are happier to talk about.

The breakthrough, then, is slow. But if one goes round the world as I did recently to talk to and learn from the friendly fraternity of bookmen, one knows that the pace is beginning to accelerate. Sales of Australian books in North America remains a problem not yet capable of solution. American overheads being what they are, there seem to be few firms or institutions willing to promote Australian books as such. (There is, of course, the occasional sheet deal or incidental sale of rights.) But in Britain, thanks to Angus & Robertson's London office, Australian-produced books are on the whole readily available and are capturing a handsome market. There are a few British publishers, too, who buy rights, and sometimes sheets of books initially published in Australia. The acceptance of Australian educational books, the best of which are good by any standards, for the first time in Britain is a matter of some historical significance, as is the attitude of some writers and agents who have recently offered Australian publishers rights independently from British and American publishers. There is a growing market for secondary and college-type books in South East Asia, particularly Singapore, Malaya, and Hong Kong, as well as in the South West Pacific. The great educational revolution which is changing maps and societies is no longer exclusively grist to the mill of British and American books. As well, there is a livening interest in translation rights mainly of novels and childen's books. A considerable increase in this traffic may be expected when, at the end of 1962, Australia presents for the first time a National Book Exhibition at the Frankfurt International Book Fair.

ANDREW FABINYI

The export of Australian books is complicated by the fact that many "Australian publishers" so-called do not represent Australian capital but are local branches of British and, more recently, American firms. Their activities—sometimes based on the idea: "if necessary, give the natives what they want"—are in themselves a form of capital export *to* Australia, and they seem to have no substantial interest in what, for them, would be reëxport. Many of their "Australian" books are printed abroad and local publication is often only a form of marketing. Some, if by no means all, have a tendency to publish in Australia only that which involves a minimum of risk: a textbook already approved by some syllabus committee, an overseas bestseller, a mass-produced children's book. The long view, the heavy investment needed for the small edition of a scholarly book, the selfless task of publishing first novels and poetry is often left to those Australian firms who can least afford it. The main, if natural, complication of exports and imports arises from the practice of many Australian writers of publishing their books outside Australia. I have always believed that an Australian author's first obligation is towards himself; he should publish his books in Australia or abroad according to his best interest. I am now beginning to think that Australian writers will increase their status and will find more economic and intellectual safety in publishing their books first *in Australia* now that Australian-owned firms are determined to enter world markets.

The years ahead promise further growth in the Australian book market, a corresponding development of Australian book publishing, and intensified competition between Australian firms and the overseas publishers with Australian branches. Australian books will, undoubtedly, find themselves rather more in an international context than they are today. There will be, there must be, more give-and-take and a better approach to Australian market rights; and, particularly, a closer relation with the emerging, indigenous publishing of South East Asia.

To be an Australian publisher is still something exciting and adventurous. Those of us who are in publishing, as owners or as professionals, are typical "nonorganization men." There is always the broad view, the consciously or unconsciously conceived obligation to nation and society, and the chip-on-the-shoulder ambition to catch up somehow, sometime soon, with the American and British giants who look at us more in amazement than in unfriendliness.

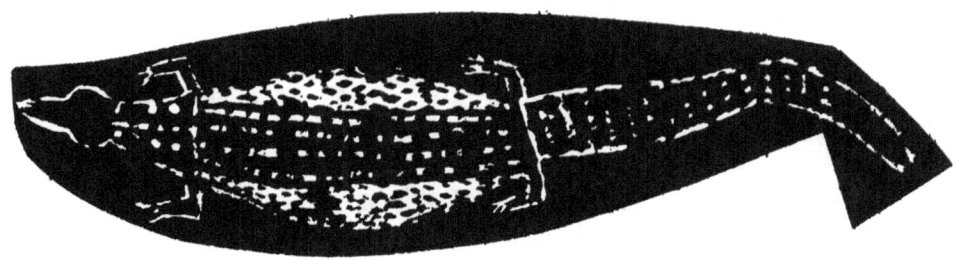

ROSEMARY DOBSON : *The Rabbiter*

Doubtless the river afforded him the conversation
Of water over stones, chattering reminiscences
Of flood and fire, contour and declivity.
Contentment and hazard, going to meet the Lachlan.

And doubtless his dog was an adequate companion,
Faithful and watchful, handy at a hollow
When the spade disclosed the mouth of the burrow,
And grateful for food by the fire at evening.

God knows it was cold in the house at nightfall
Yet they said he'd been seen at dusk near the she-oaks.
Is he, I thought, a legend out of Lawson,
Morley the rabbiter, camped by the river?

Crossed in love, lost to the girl by the sliprails,
Wronged, impoverished, shamed by a scandal,
Taking the guilt of a wild young brother;
Digging out rabbits, the poor old hatter.

From the slope of the hill I watched at morning
The vapour clearing away in the sunlight,
It might have been mist; or maybe, maybe,
The ghost of Morley over the river.

ROBERT D. FITZGERALD : *Tocsin*

And should that singing in your ears
be scythe-stone on the scythe,
cleaver and sickle, sword and shears,
have taken still their tithe
from green or yellow of the yield
and never scaled with rust
while harvest fluttered or there thrust
one stalk up from the field.

And you, alone here in your house,
believed you had in call
better company than the mouse
gnawing behind the wall,
not having learnt how walls fold in
narrowly where you dwell
until your self becomes your cell,
cut off from friends and kin.

Mostly, grey fellow, if you spared
a pause to think it through,
you saw the dark that must be dared
as no way meant for you,
nothing that need concern you much
with work or play on hand;
but there's a shadow where you stand
and at your wrist a touch.

No, it's no more than that a page
like one you turned on youth
flicks in your fingers now; and age
must read a further truth
hidden there in some word that gives
years yet or just an hour,
but suddenly shall speak with power
its cold imperatives.

What follows is for night to teach;
meanwhile this loudness bids
live hands and brain grasp all in reach
and eyes not shut their lids
on anything of earth that's found
intenser for threat's tone
shrilling, like locust-summer's own
which breaks off in mid-sound.

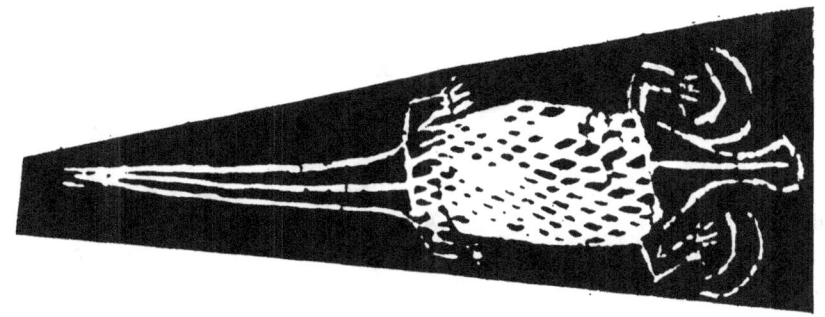

Tocsin

C. B. CHRISTESEN : *The Twenty-One Lives of* Meanjin Quarterly

"*Meanjin* is the first Australian literary magazine that can be regarded from a broader than a merely local point of view...no other Australian magazine has concerned itself so broadly with the world in general.... The essence of *Meanjin* is its stimulative quality; its awareness that Australia has a place in modern life with its problems and perplexities, and its literature a corresponding place in modern literature; and it attempts to define that place, raising questions that are important to the world in general and to Australia as part of that world .... *Meanjin* has now definitely a more than Australian importance."

> ...H. M. Green, *A History of Australian Literature* (1961)

AN EDITOR OF A LITERARY MAGAZINE IN A COUNTRY SUCH AS AUSTRALIA HAS the challenging task of helping to stimulate, guide, and foster a young and growing literature. He provides a forum for the beginner as well as for the established writer, and often it is an exciting experience to watch the flowering of young talent.

It is exciting, too, to help define standards of criticism, to make first assessments, to disseminate ideas—and to cultivate public taste, public response.[1] As Australia is still predominantly a pastoral and mercantile community, its main values and interests do not lean towards intellectual and artistic activities. Therefore the serious writer has had a particularly hard struggle to survive in such a climate of genial disinterest. If he did not physically die at an early age, he too often had an early death as an *artist*.[2] In general, and until fairly recently, only the most stubborn, the most tenacious, and resilient of our writers have managed to hold their ground and continue producing quality work into middle age.[3] So often there has been an abundance of early talent, but little continuous growth from decade to decade. And with few exceptions, the richness of nuance and tone, the texture of life characteristic of older nations has been inadequate to nourish and stimulate Australian writers to

---

[1] "The right standard for judging the intellectual work of any generation is supplied, not by the great minds that make their appearance in it, but the way in which contemporaries receive their work."—Schopenhauer: *Essays on the Art of Literature.*

[2] "The tragedy of Australian writing," F. J. Archibald said to George Black in 1893 after Francis Adams died by his own hand at thirty years of age, "is the low expectation of life of the average Australian writer. Take poor Francis Adams, for instance. His writing life was ten years. Last year Barcroft Boake slipped away before he was 27. Think of Marcus Clarke, Gordon, Kendall, Deniehy and Michael! Not one of them reached 45.... Writing is too fierce a way of living. It kills them young." Since those days the life expectancy of the Australian writer has somewhat increased!

[3] "...in their youth few writers are more brilliantly gifted than the Americans; few are more disappointing after the age of forty-five."—Henri Peyre: *Writers and their Critics.* "Something happens to our good writers at a certain age."—Ernest Hemingway: *The Green Hills of Africa.*

C. B. CHRISTESEN

produce a literature of more than local interest. Thus many of our writers—and painters, singers, musicians, dancers, scholars, scientists—oppressed by the limitations of Australian society, have felt impelled to migrate to countries with an older and richer culture.[4] (Often, alas, their roots were to wither in the alien soil.)

However, during the past quarter of a century increased 'social density' has been at least one important factor which has aided the Australian writer to produce work of a more varied and complex character, of higher quality, more perceptive of the human condition here. It is true to say that during this period more poetry of quality has been written, more plays, novels, stories, literary and art criticism, more painting, sculpture, and musical composition of genuine value have been produced than during any other period of our history. And all this has been achieved under conditions which (not to put too fine a point on it) have been far from propitious for a flourishing artistic and intellectual life. The contrast between the Australia of 1940, when the first issue of *Meanjin* appeared, and the Australia of today, is nothing short of amazing. And among the potent agencies which have helped change the cultural scene here are the literary magazines.

The largest and most influential of the Australian literary periodicals is *Meanjin Quarterly*.[5] Let me tell you something of its history.

Brisbane in the thirties was a deadly place for an aspiring writer to live in. For some years before a visit overseas I had tried to interest a number of local writers in the production of a literary review. Their response was profoundly discouraging, despite the preparation of an attractive 'dummy.' "It simply can't be done," they said. "Look at the number of literary magazines which have failed."

I was only too well aware of the deplorable history of similar ventures; but instead of striving to publish initially a fully developed journal, an expensive venture even in those days, I planned to work along different lines. It was obvious that unless adequate capital could be obtained to assure publication for a year or more, an unlikely event, then a more cautious approach should be made; and that from a very small local journal we should try to expand in easy stages and attract an interstate audience.

And so, after several further abortive efforts, I demanded manuscripts from three leading Queensland poets and critics, James Picot, Brian Vrepont, and Paul Grano. I offered to 'press the button' if they would feed me with samples of their work. Publication was to be irregular, for I did not then believe I could produce a monthly

[4] Australia's 'export of talent' in all the arts has been very substantial indeed. Few have returned home after making their reputations overseas. Among the writers Patrick White is a notable exception. The United Kingdom has usually been the goal of our writers and artists, whereas France and Italy attracted Americans.

[5] The title of the magazine was originally *Meanjin Papers*. In 1947 it was changed to *Meanjin*, and in 1961 to *Meanjin Quarterly*. For the sake of brevity the title *Meanjin* is often used.

or a quarterly. Estimates were received from local printers, but they were too high for my short pocket. Then I found a private suburban printer who had a small hand-press. His estimate for two hundred and fifty copies of an eight-page magazine, plus cover, was £4.10.0 (Today each issue of the magazine costs more than £3000 to print, produce, and distribute.) I promptly posted him copy and awaited proofs.

Have you ever tried to think of a suitable title for a literary magazine? We considered an endless list—all too stereotyped, or too esoteric. *Decision* seemed to be our best mark, until it was pointed out that no decision as to policy could possibly be made at such a time of war and uncertainty. Nor was *Direction* suitable—for little direction could be given to what was merely a tentative experiment, and when society, and all values, were in such a deliquescent state. And then one day I picked up a copy of the *Biglow Papers*. Alliteration: *Paroo Papers?* No. *Brisbane Papers?* Brisbane—what was the native name? I consulted files at the John Oxley Memorial Library. 'Mianjin,' 'Meanjin'—derived from *migan,* spike, and *chagun,* earth, place, land or country: the spike or finger of land on which the city proper was built. (I was convinced, even in those days, of Lawrence Durrell's claim that "the important determinant of any culture is after all the spirit of place").

And so, on December 11, 1940, the first issue of *Meanjin Papers* appeared, eight pages of hand-set type, with many misprints. The main heading was "Contemporary Queensland Verse," and as a purely hopeful gesture, "No. 1." It was called a "Traditionalist Number" and contained two poems each by Vrepont, Grano, Picot, and myself. The cover design, the footprints which for many years were to become well known, was by P. Stanhope Hobday.

A certain degree of symbolism here. There were four of us (each seemingly one-footed!); and for those politically inclined, the footprints were placed a little left of centre: editorial policy has never been party-political, though vigorously partisan on matters affecting civil liberties and academic freedom. Further, the footprints represented *mundowi,* or spirit-tracks of the traditional cult-hero of the aborigines: a symbol helping to reënact the past, to preënact the future, to gain moral and intellectual courage and life in the present and immediate future. (Professor A. P. Elkin's essay in an early issue, "Steps into the Dream-Time," discussed the symbolism.) In this way I tried to relate the magazine and its function to time and place. Lastly, we fervently hoped to use the journal to 'spike' local values in art and literature.

Well, it was all great fun at first. . . . The foreword reflected the state of affairs I found on my return to Brisbane from Europe after the outbreak of war. All cultural activities had ceased, and I promptly set about reviving them. For, as the first editorial declared:

". . . We believe it would be a grave error to suppose the nation should drop its mental life, its intellectual and aesthetic activities for three or five or more years, neglecting them and those trained to minister to them, and then try to pick everything up again after the war as though nothing had happened. Literature and art, poetry

C. B. CHRISTESEN

and drama do not spring into being at the word of command. Their life is a continuous process growing within itself, and its suppression means death. . . ."

No doubt an ingenuous, youthful statement. But while Brisbane's reaction to the first issue was disastrous, copies sent interstate met with a surprising response—so I decided to publish a second number, of twelve pages at a cost of £7.10.0. It contained a provocative essay by Picot on the state of Australian poetry, and was the first use of the 'spike'—which was thrust at a local critic, Firmin Mackinnon. This "Criticism Number" was also a financial failure (which is hard to conceive, considering the small outlay); and it contained so many printing errors that I decided to have the third issue set by Linotype—and hang the expense. The whole of that issue was inaccurately folded, and had to be returned to the printer; and the three-colour cover design, intended to represent a glowing hibiscus flower, was more suitable for a gardener's catalogue!

The irrepressible Randolph Bedford, author and parliamentarian, delivered a blast:

"Plucky for the time, but what a waste of good type and ink. If I tackle this ridiculous stuff I would have to make your paper a slaughter-house. Alleged to be new, it is as old as stupidity . . . as a youngster . . . I wrote of the soulful poem in derision. It began:

> In grim and lonely silence disarrayed,
> Fate turned a handspring on the closet roof.

I suppose this nonsense finds a recrudescence as a result of the last war—Gertrude Stein who wrote 'Tender Buttons' has even got an audience, and the other Stein, Ep, who makes an alleged statue like a swollen wardrobe trunk and labels it 'Pregnancy.' These alleged poets should be forced to do something useful, such as digging post-holes."

Bedford, an ebullient character, was most annoyed when I published his letter, and a stimulating exchange followed. I mention this incident now merely to show that any attempt in Brisbane in those days to take note of the trends of modern verse raised the ire of all worthy citizens.

But it would take far too long to recount the history of each succeeding issue. It was a crazy time to be publishing a literary magazine—we were even denied a permit to publish because, naturally, we could not establish a base year, and until I moved to Melbourne in 1945 I published the journal without authority from Paper Control. But in view of the responses, from Sydney to Perth, I decided to continue, always losing financially. Paul Grano, a lone brolga, pulled out early in the piece. Brian Vrepont went walkabout to Sydney and later to Perth. Signaller James Picot sailed with the A.I.F. for Malaya, later to die tragically in Thailand. And here I must confess it was always my dearest wish that my friend Picot would one day safely return to take over the editorship of *Meanjin*. Of all the young writers I've met, Jim Picot held the highest promise of really fine achievement.

I had met with a serious accident just before publication of the second issue. Soon after, I resigned my post as publicist for the Queensland Government and rejoined a metropolitan morning newspaper. It thus became increasingly difficult to publish the magazine, singlehanded, and in my so-called 'spare time.' Looking back, life in that 'frontier capital' during those war years takes on the quality of a nightmare. It was my wife Nina who kept me going, with her encouragement, her understanding, her practical assistance. The standard of printing, poor throughout Australia in those days, was surely at its worst in Brisbane. Apart from other problems, editorial and secretarial, the sheer physical effort needed to push through an edition every two months was unbelievable. I was even obliged to address and stamp envelopes by hand, and to deliver batch after batch to the G.P.O. for posting, a weary trudge from the printing office.

By the end of 1941 (No. 6) the magazine had begun to take shape. And then in 1942 I published the "Crisis Number," which was a fairly accurate reflection of what many people were thinking and feeling during those fateful years. Editorial comment pointed to the crisis of modern thought and knowledge, warned against some of our greatest intellectual evils, and of factors which were helping to strangle cultural life in this country. I know of no other literary journal, during those crisis years, that was striving to make articulate the mood of our 'thinkers and dreamers'. Vance Palmer's short article, "Battle," was the most important statement made by any Australian writer during those war years.

Not until the end of 1942 did I have a fairly clear idea of the kind of magazine I wanted to publish (that I have never fully achieved my ambition is irrelevant here). I sought to create an alive literary forum, a meeting place or clearing house for writers, for creative art in its various forms. I wanted *Meanjin* to present a 'portrait of its age,' of its Time and Place, a document of our aesthetic development. I visualised each successive issue as constituting a kind of literary laboratory, a workshop for experimental advance-guard writers—creative and critical work that defied settled conventions and perhaps shocked conventional sensibilities. And what an overlay of intellectual rock needed to be blasted! Now, with a quickening of national life and activity engendered by war and the threat of invasion—now was the time to eliminate the vestiges of our nineteenth-century cultural hangover. Now was the time to size up our needs, our liabilities, our resources, our possible ends and means —our whole cultural situation. And out of the ferment, the clash of ideas, would possibly come a new cultural flowering. To assist in that task, it seemed to me, was one of the chief functions of a literary magazine.

And there was in fact, during those war years, a remarkable increase of cultural activity. There was an excitement among writers and artists, a questing, a vast promise of better things to come. This alert and progressive spirit seemed to permeate the whole of society, finding expression in plans for community centres, among many other postwar projects. I believe aspects of that upsurge of national life and thought were reflected in the pages of *Meanjin*. Even today, those early numbers make stimulating reading. In other states there were similar literary ventures, born just before or just after the first appearance of *Meanjin*—each making its individual contribution and each in its own way complementing the other. And for the first time it seemed that an Australian book publishing industry would be firmly established.

In 1943 I began publishing a quarterly instead of a bimonthly. The journal had by now become established, and the circulation rose to 4000 copies an issue. But as *Meanjin* developed, editorial and administrative burdens increased proportionately; and the monetary losses mounted.[6] Judith Wright, then an unknown poet, came to Brisbane as honorary secretary. Business affairs were placed in the hands of a firm of accountants. The very success of the magazine now promised to be its undoing, for it could no longer be run efficiently on a part-time, unpaid basis. Correspondence alone, throughout Australia and overseas, was very considerable indeed.

For some time I had been publishing a proportion of work by non-Australian writers—Aragon, Theodore Spencer, Henry Treece, Oscar Williams, and Karl Shapiro, among others.[7] A large number of U.S. servicemen, passing through Brisbane on their way North, visited my Brisbane home; and many of them were, or were to become, writers. And with an eye to the future, I was endeavouring to foster a kind of literary lend-lease, particularly regarding postwar British Commonwealth relations, when I hoped Australian writings would receive warmer hospitality in the United Kingdom. A forlorn hope, alas.

Then late in 1944, when publishing and production problems seemed well-nigh unsurmountable, and when I was on sick leave, I received first a letter from Mr. Colin Badger, at that time Director of the Extension Board at the University of Melbourne, and later an invitation from the then Vice-Chancellor (Sir John Medley) to transfer the magazine to Melbourne. I flew down for a conference, and early in 1945 Melbourne University Press took over production and distribution. The edi-

---

[6] I might be pardoned for revealing here that I have over the years contributed more than £10,000 out of my own earnings. I have never received a salary for editing and managing the journal, though during recent years I have recovered some out-of-pocket expenses.

[7] In later issues overseas contributors included: James Aldridge, Walter Allen, Rewi Alley, Michael Ayrton, Max Born (physicist and Nobel Prize winner), Bertolt Brecht, Alex Comfort, Caston Criel, Basil Davidson, Charles Edward Eaton, Paul Eluard, James T. Farrell, Waldo Frank, Robert Greacen, Sir W. K. C. Guthrie, Nazin Hikmet, Howard Mumford Jones, Joseph Jones, Albert E. Kahn, Arthur Koestler, Jack Lindsay, Christopher Logue, Georges Lukács, Arnost Lustig, Helen M. Lynd, Archibald MacLeish, Saadat Hasan Manto, Colin McInnes, Arthur Miller, Pablo Neruda, Anaïs Nin, Kathleen Nott, Sean O'Casey, K. M. Panikkar, Alan Paton, William Plomer, Ezra Pound, Victor Purcell, Kathleen Raine, C. Rajagopalochari, Sir Herbert Read, Elmer Rice, Paul Rotha, Sir Charles Snow, Derek Stanford, Montagu Slater, Jean-Paul Sartre, Hugh Trevor-Roper, Bruce Sutherland, Dylan Thomas, Charles Vereker, Alexander Werth, Jiří Weil, H. H. Wilson, Karl Wolfskehl, Basil Willey, Arnold Zweig . . .

torial office was at the University, and has remained there to this day. This gesture on the part of the University of Melbourne is unique in Australia.

However, those first few years in Melbourne, as they affected *Meanjin*, were better left undescribed in any detail. Although the University was providing accommodation, part-time secretarial help, and £100 a quarter, my yearly losses mounted alarmingly. Just before my departure from Brisbane a leading Melbourne bookseller had broken an agreement and caused serious financial loss. Melbourne University Press, hampered by wartime restrictions, was unable to handle the journal successfully, and I had to rescind the agreement. A Commonwealth Literary Fund grant of £100 in 1946 was not renewed the following year because a member of the Parliamentary Committee objected to an editorial comment.[8] When the British Board of Trade in 1947 placed an embargo on imports of Australian books and periodicals—acting under Article 9 of the American Loan Agreement—our United Kingdom market for about a thousand copies a quarter was lost, never to be regained. Repeated applications for CLF aid, supported by the Advisory Board, were rejected by the Parliamentary Committee. Gradually the circulation again increased, however, and the Department of Information helped by placing an order for a thousand copies of each issue for distribution abroad. But when a new government came into office the Department of Information was disbanded and the order was abruptly cancelled, causing further heavy loss.

Production costs had now become more than I could possibly cope with, and in 1949 I successfully appealed to the University for aid through the Lockie Bequest. Again I applied for a CLF grant, and personally discussed the matter with the Prime Minister (Mr. R. G. Menzies). My proposal was adopted, and a grant of £400 a year was made to the University of Melbourne to assist publication of the journal.

Since those days, the CLF and University subventions have gradually been increased, and recently we received help from The Myer Foundation. Unfortunately our increased revenue, from subscriptions, trade sales, and grants, has never been able to keep pace with the inflationary spiral. It is not generally realized, to give only one example, that the Australian printing industry's costs have risen more than six hundred percent since 1940.[9]

Well, there are the bare bones of *Meanjin's* story over the twenty-one years. To attempt to place flesh and living tissue on the framework is a task perhaps for someone other than myself. No reference can be made here to the personalities of the many writers, Australian and foreign, with whom I have had dealings. An editor certainly has a special function, but he is essentially in the hands of his contributors. Thus any

[8] No details of political attacks on *Meanjin* have been given in this article. These have been fairly considerable on occasions, particularly during the 1951 Referendum and the "Petrov case" during 1954–55, ranging from attacks in the Federal Parliament to 'outside' pressures on the University.

[9] Australian printing costs are today about double United Kingdom costs.

C. B. CHRISTESEN

success *Meanjin* may claim is basically due to those writers who have responded to the editor's requests.

Eighty-eight issues have been published, comprising so many millions of words, equivalent to so many average-size novels. But statistical computation is of little importance. What matters is whether the magazine has been of value to Australian letters. I can only hope that the contribution has in fact been worthwhile.

Now, upon its coming of age, *Meanjin Quarterly* has entered a new stage of its development—and at a time when Australian cultural life is entering a new period of maturity.[10] I am convinced our writers and artists are on the verge of making a major breakthrough. Five years, ten years perhaps; but something exciting and vastly important to the whole of the country is in the offing.

For instance, until fairly recently criticism of our native literature was invariably ephemeral, thin, lacking in substance.[11] There were two main reasons for this: 1) suitable periodicals were lacking; 2) most of the earlier critics, while often vigorous and incisive, were ill equipped in learning and in the techniques of scholarship. When *Meanjin* first began publication, scarcely any university teachers were devoting serious attention to Australian literature. Several of our leading critics were graduates, but members of teaching staffs were notoriously in the minority. Indeed, the attitude of most academics toward our literature was indifferent, if not overly antagonistic. Now the situation has been almost entirely reversed: Australian Literature has become respectable enough for serious academic study!

On balance, the contributions of critics trained in scholarly disciplines have been vastly beneficial. The trend is increasingly toward concentration, continuity, articulate precision, and self-awareness. There is danger here only if the scholar and the critic fail to fuse into the humane man of letters. But for the first time in our history, we now have a group of discerning young (and not so young) academics who are directing a steady penetrating gaze at our literature and history, and at the ambiguities in our country and its people. Valuable reassessments are being made, and new critical ground broken. Improved library holdings and access to archival material are aiding research; and while no appointment has yet been made to the first Chair of Australian Literature (at the University of Sydney), Australian literature courses are now available at most of our universities. "The posture of criticism," which according to Marjorie Barnard "is still unpretty," is no longer downright deplorable.

[10] 'An advance guard of Australians are feeling their way towards a new culture—which involves also a new view of their weird [sic] continent and its possibilities.'—*The Observer* (London, 1961).

[11] Literary criticism long remained 'the most inactive aspect of American literature,' wrote Morton D. Zabel in his introduction to *Literary Opinion in America*. Van Wyck Brooks points out in *The Writer in America* that when Thackeray visited America he urged his hosts to think better of their writers. Up to about the beginning of the first world war, Brooks claims, Americans scarcely believed their writers were doing, or could do, anything important; or at least important in comparison with writers in Europe. Australian-American literary parallels abound.

The changed situation might be attributed, in the main, to the (painfully slow but fruitful) activities of the Commonwealth Literary Fund, which among other services helps to finance lectures on Australian literature at the universities; to publication of reliable critical texts, literary histories, and bibliographies—and to the regular appearance of one or two responsible periodicals large enough to publish the full-dress critical essay sufficiently informed in depth, energy, and imaginative intensity. (Book reviewing in the daily press is for the most part elementary, though one or two weekly or fortnightly journals of opinion occasionally carry skilfully written reviews.) And an increasing knowledge of our past is also aiding higher standards of criticism. The development of our own publishing industry, so vital to the growth and well-being of an indigenous literature, is discussed elsewhere in this issue.

Looking back over the twenty-one years, I feel justified in making the following observations:

I was invited to transfer *Meanjin* from Brisbane to the University of Melbourne to enable specialists in the various disciplines of the humanities to communicate with an intelligent reading public. Efforts over several years to publish a 'general-purpose,' academic (but nonlearned) journal having failed, it was decided to give support to a potentially useful literary magazine already in existence. The intention behind the invitation to Melbourne was laudable; but the practical support given to me, financially and by contributions from staff members (particularly in the English department) was grossly inadequate. I had to rely mainly on contributions from members of other universities. Melbourne provided me with office space, telephone and lighting facilities (but not furnishings or stationery), and eventually a grant from the Lockie Bequest ("to aid literature in Australia") which now, after seventeen years, amounts to £1500 a year. But the grant from the General Fund still remains at £50 a year. As I look at a large filing cabinet jam-packed with correspondence and memoranda testifying to my long and gruelling battle to gain increased support from the University of Melbourne, I often recall an extract from a letter Hugo von Hofmannsthal wrote to Richard Strauss:

". . . these people have no immediate relation to art whatever, but perpetually confuse art with education, i.e., with learnedness, two things which have nothing whatever in common."

I offer that quotation with malice toward none. But as editor of this particular kind of periodical (literary and academic, but not a learned journal), I am more interested in the creative process than in scholarly exegesis or explication. I am of course personally interested in textual scholarship, but my main interest is in finding and publishing the first-rate poem and short story, in disseminating new ideas and in breaking new critical ground, rather than in publishing orthodox writings about writings. I mention this matter here only because I have often been urged to confine

C. B. CHRISTESEN

the journal to literary criticism. Such a policy, I have contended, would invalidate the very reason for *Meanjin's* continued existence. An outsider such as myself—a kind of literary juvenile delinquent, I suppose—has had extraordinary difficulty in gaining a proper understanding of the rôle or function of a magazine of this kind. . . .

And yet without the University's financial contribution, and without the grant from the Commonwealth Literary Fund, which is now £1000 a year, I could not have continued publishing a journal of this size and scope. Thus these two agencies—and since last year The Myer Foundation (£500)—have (almost unwittingly) helped to provide a singularly useful service to Australian literature, and to our writers and readers. I make bold to suggest that the work recorded in *Meanjin's* eighty-eight issues will in years to come prove to be of the utmost value.[12]

Meanjin today is searching for a new manner in which to make articulate a national condition with universal applications. Our main critics are displaying a steady commitment to extending a vision of their antipodean world, noting with clinical precision the changes that are taking place in Australian cultural and social life, rejecting certain attitudes and assumptions that have long been part of our intellectual and emotional baggage.

Earlier I said it was exciting to be involved in these pursuits, and I repeat it. The humus out of which new talents grow is in fact richer in Australia today: recent literary and art developments might lead in all kinds of directions, though—as with Gogol's celebrated Troika—it is impossible for anyone to say precisely where the road will end.

Which reminds me that I at least must reach an end! I have given an account of the origin and development of this journal, and pointed to some of our problems and aspirations. But because so much has been left unsaid, perhaps the significance of the following quotation from Lytton Strachey might not be lost upon discerning readers: "This is all that is known to men, and indeed more than is known, of the life of the blessed Saint Neot. But not more than is known to the angels in heaven"! And if I have given an impression that I have not enjoyed the long-drawn purgatorial experience of guiding *Meanjin* through its twenty-one lives, I have been guilty of the grossest deception. Most Australian writers, I suspect, suffer from a love-hate relationship toward their country. So perhaps it is true, as Hemingway once said: "To write well about some place, you've got to hate it . . . the way a man hates his wife."

---

[12] 'The cultural historian of the future will be anxious to exercise his imaginative, interpretative powers on this period, to try to chart the invisible tidal currents that underrun it, to understand the real meaning of its germinations. In that interpretative task what single source of material will he find, to help him to understand, more rich than the files of *Meanjin?*'— A. A. Phillips speaking at *Meanjin's* 21st anniversary dinner on December 11, 1961.

JUDITH WRIGHT : *Two Poems*

The Other Half

The self that night undrowns when I'm asleep
travels beneath the dumb days that I give,
within the limits set that I may live,
and beats in anger on the things I love.
I am the cross it bears, and it the tears I weep.

Under the eyes of light my work is brief.
Day sets on me the burdens that I carry.
I face the light, the dark of me I bury.
My silent answer and my other half,
we meet at midnight and by music only.

Yet there's a word that I would give to you.
The truth you tell in your dumb images
my daylight self goes stumbling after, too.
So we may meet at last, and meeting bless,
and turn into one truth in singleness.

Brush-Turkey

Right to the edge of the forest
the tourists come.
He learns the scavenger's habits
with scrap and crumb—
his forests gone, he lives
on what the moment gives;
pretends, in mockery,
to beg our charity.

Cunning and shy one must be
to snatch one's bread
from oafs whose hands are quicker
with stones instead.
He apes the backyard bird.
Half-proud and half-absurd,
sheltered by his quick wit
he sees and takes his bit.

Ash-black, wattles of scarlet,
and careful eye,
he hoaxes the ape, the ogre
with mimicry.
Scornfully, he will eat
thrown crust and broken meat
till suddenly—"See, oh see!
The turkey's in the tree."

The backyard bird is stupid,
he trusts and takes;
but this one's wiles are wary
to guard against the axe:
escaping, neat and pat,
into his habitat.
Charred log and shade and stone
accept him. He is gone.

And here's a bird the poet
may ponder over,
whose ancient forest-meanings
no longer grant him cover;
who, circumspect yet proud,
like yet unlike the crowd,
must cheat its chucklehead
to throw, not stones but bread.

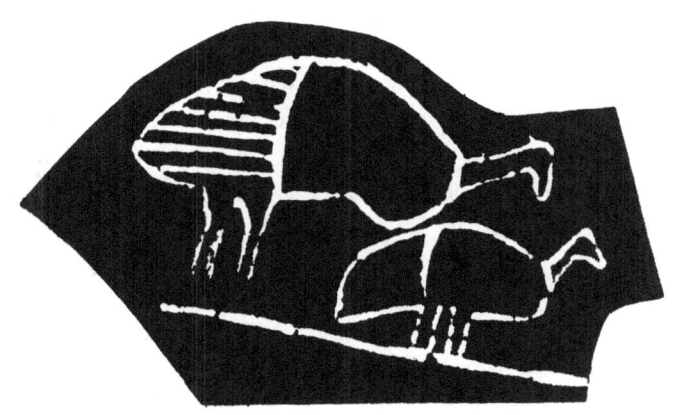

Brush-Turkey

T HE DEVELOPMENT OF AUSTRALIAN LITERATURE OWES MUCH TO A FEW
outstanding figures. J. F. Archibald gave a tremendous stimulus to indigenous
writing as the cofounder and moving spirit of the Sydney *Bulletin,* the
weekly magazine which expressed the nationalist ebullience of the nineties, gave
writers a national forum, and created a strong literary tradition with a democratic
and radical flavour. That tradition was expounded so strongly by Henry Lawson in
his short stories and verse that he became Australia's most representative writer, and
his influence still endures. A. B. "Banjo" Paterson linked the bush ballads with the
old bush songs, the rude but vigorous voice of the people, and promoted the popu-
larity of the ballad. George Robertson was influential as publisher, and the leading
firm of Angus & Robertson has given most valuable service to the literary cause.
Many of the national legends and aspirations are embodied in the work and personality of that remarkable veteran Dame Mary Gilmore. Contemporary writers, especially the poets, owe much to the encouragement and the critical standards of
Douglas Stewart as editor of the *Bulletin's* Red Page, its literary section devoted to
criticism and poetry.

It was the founder of the Red Page, however, Alfred George Stephens, who enjoys
the honour of being the strongest single force in the shaping of Australia's literature.
He was not only its greatest critic but he was the Johnsonian arbiter whose judgment
made and unmade the reputations of writers in his day. He exercised his power in
several different forms. Firstly, he gave a new status and prestige to writing, both as
an important art and as an articulation of the national scene, character, and spirit.
"The great names of Australia and of Literature," he proclaimed roundly, "must
not be taken lightly." Secondly, he raised literary criticism to such a high level that it
became a decisive influence in the growth of the new literature that was then finding
its own distinctive voice. Thirdly, he was personally responsible in a vital manner
for encouraging and recognising the merits of such significant writers as Steele Rudd,
Furphy, and Shaw Neilson. Finally, it was he who gave the decision in many cases as
to what writers should become part of the literary canon. He did this not only as
editor of the *Bulletin* Red Page from 1896 to 1906 by means of his critical judgments but also by his selection of what authors and books should be published by the
Bulletin as a publishing company. Between 1897 and 1906 he was responsible for
the *Bulletin's* publishing twenty-three books, including anthologies and art books as
well as the volumes of fourteen individual writers. Later he also published three
books of Shaw Neilson's poetry. Australian publishing was then on such a small
scale that his election often decided the shape of Australian literature.

In all these various ways A.G.S., as he signed himself and as he was generally
known, exercised a critical dominance for which it would be hard to find a parallel in

English and American literatures. There was, of course, the power wielded by Dr. Johnson in his day, but it was modified by the influence of other English critics, whereas A.G.S. possessed an authority that was not seriously challenged in his *Bulletin* hegemony. So, too, Emerson and Poe, Whitman and Mark Twain, however influential in many ways, were never in the position to determine in such a single-handed fashion what American literature was to be as Stephens was able, as critic, editor, and publisher combined, to determine the shape of Australian literature. He represents, I think, a singular case of critical dominance in literary history.

Australian writers themselves freely acknowledged their debt to A. G. Stephens. Will Ogilvie said to him: "Yours was the verdict of the Yea or Nay." Mary Gilmore declared: "Whatever has any grace or graciousness in my verse is owed to you." Shaw Neilson said of his champion, editor, and publisher: "I owe him so much that I cannot bear to criticise him. . . . A.G.S. under all his bluff was a wonderfully tender-hearted man. I found him exceedingly generous in every way. He put in a lot of time on my verse, and lost money on it too." Joseph Furphy appreciated the efforts made by A.G.S. to persuade the *Bulletin* to publish the mammoth manuscript of *Such is Life,* and wrote to him on the 24th August 1899: "I thank you for the thoughtfulness which prompted your letter of 17th last, as well as for the solicitude which has always marked your connection with *Such is Life.*" Later Furphy told Stephens that he was well content with the *Bulletin's* terms of publication of his novel, and added: "Honestly, I am conscious of a sort of subterrananean conviction that there is a deus ex the *Bulletin* Co. moving in a mysterious way toward an Australian literature."

The authority of Stephens and the value of his work have been recognised by the literary historians no less than by the writers of his day. Thus Vance Palmer has stressed the excellence of his critical writing and the tremendous stimulus it gave to the writers: "It was a more penetrating criticism than any that had been known in Australia; it broke down walls and let in air and light. . . . Undoubtedly it stimulated the writers of the day and gave them a feeling that they had an audience, that they were not talking into the void. There was the lively, challenging presence of the Grand Inquisitor himself . . . and there was the community of readers he had gathered around him. . . . His influence on the writers of his day was immense. . . . While A.G.S. was there on the Red Page it seemed worth while to write, and a compulsion to write well." And on his selection of authors for publication in the *Bulletin* Library, Palmer comments: "It was left to Stephens to say what writer had original virtue, to distinguish him from his fellow—Victor Daley from a dozen other songsters about wine and roses, Will Ogilvie from a crowd of galloping rhymesters, Bernard O'Dowd from the dealers in rhetoric and political invective.

"After a space of forty years [Palmer was writing in 1941] his judgments remain valid. The writers he singled out really were significant. And no important work has emerged from the files of those days to accuse him of neglect."

A. G. Stephens, H. M. Green has written in his recent monumental *History of*

Australian Literature, "was in his day much more than the most notable of Australian critics: throughout the greater part of his life he *was* Australian literary criticism, so far as current writers were concerned: there were some other critics of some importance, but they mattered only in a secondary way and to a comparatively small circle. . . . It was not merely that he made the Red Page the focus in Australia of criticism of current literature, overseas as well as Australian; in the space that Archibald gave him, and in which he was left almost absolutely free Stephens made himself a pulpit, almost a throne: he might perhaps be regarded as a trusted Grand Vizier deputizing for his Sultan. For a decade he was philosopher, teacher, lawgiver to his subjects, whom he told what to read and how to write and why; and for the most part they obeyed him without question, even with enthusiasm: there was a general recognition that 'old A.G.' if a despot was a benevolent despot; that he exercised his power in what he believed to be and what almost always was the interest of his contributors."

The most striking tribute to A.G.S., however, was a genial caricature written by his friend the poet Victor Daley, who had a neat turn of epigrammatic wit in his satires. In a piece entitled "Narcissus and Some Tadpoles" he pictures the Red Page Editor "lilting loudly" at his desk:

> I am the Blender of the pure
> Australian Brand of Literature.
> No verse, however fine, can be
> The radiant thing called Poetry
> Unless it is approved by me.
> I am the Critic set on high,
> The Red Page Rhadamanthus I.
> The Master, too, of the Event
> Am I on this weird Continent . . .
>
> I make or mar. My daring hand
> Explores the entrails of the land,
> And finds, beneath a greasy hat,
> An Austral Homer at Cow Flat.

Daley then gets in a couple of shrewd hits at two occasional faults in Stephens: his overrating of his favourite writers and his pride in 'discovering' new talent. Thus the monologue of the Red Page Rhadamanthus is supplemented by voices from Proof-Sheets and the Waste-Paper Basket commenting as a brief Greek chorus:

> Voice from Proof-Sheets.
> A primrose by the river's brim
> A splendid sunflower is to him.
>
> Voice from W.P.B.
> But he himself—bear this in mind!—
> Must be the first that flower to find.

T. INGLIS MOORE

However seriously A.G.S. took his critical task and however solemnly he could pontificate at times, he had a robust sense of humour, and it is characteristic of him that he printed Daley's satire in his own magazine, *The Bookfellow*.

Like many Australian writers, A.G.S. was Celtic in origin, since his father was a Welshman and his mother was born in Scotland. He himself was born in Toowomba, Queensland, in 1865, and died in Sydney in 1933, at the age of sixty-seven years, still working vigorously as a journalist and critic. He was educated at the Toowomba Grammar School, where he did so well that he passed his Senior University Examination at the unusually early age of fourteen. After that he was self-educated. His father was part owner of the *Darling Downs Gazette* newspaper, so that he had "ink in his veins." He soon had ink on his fingers, too, for at fifteen he became a printer's devil. He served his apprenticeship in the printing trade first in Toowomba, and then in Sydney, and became a journeyman printer. This technical training was valuable to him later as a journalist and editor-publisher. He knew how copy should be prepared and how to see a book through the press. Whilst working in Sydney he furthered his education by studying at the Sydney Technical College and gaining certificates in proficiency, especially in French and German. His later reading in French and German literatures helped to give an international breadth to his criticism.

Turning to journalism, he was only twenty-three when he became editor of *The Gympie Miner,* and became an active force in the intellectual life of this vigorous mining township in Queensland. The first writing of his we have on record is the series of nine papers he read to the Gympie Literary Circle, preserved in the Mitchell Library, Sydney, and written in the purple ink he affected right through his lifetime in an old exercise book. These papers make interesting reading, since they discuss a broad variety of subjects ranging from history and literary forms to writers in Australian, English, French, and American literatures—Adam Lindsay Gordon, Dickens and Sheridan, Molière and Longfellow. Already A.G.S. was writing vigorously and independently, aggressively nationalist in temper, yet also witty and irreverent in phrasing. His parody of Longfellow's "Evangeline," for instance, is racy and pungent.

A.G.S. then joined the staff of *The Boomerang,* a Brisbane paper founded by William Lane in 1887 as a radical, democratic, and nationalist organ of opinion. No other paper in Australia outside the *Bulletin* at its height gathered together such a galaxy of talent. It had, however, a precarious financial life, and in 1891 A.G.S. went north to settle in Cairns as editor and part owner of *The Cairns Argus,* marrying there and making a wide reputation by some original and forceful pamphlets on Queensland politics.

He was twenty-seven when in 1893 he set out to see the world, and spent nine months visiting America, France, England, Wales, and Scotland. The next year he published in Sydney his first book *A Queenslander's Travel Notes.* It was a characteristic joke when the frontispiece showed the photograph of a bearded and grinning full-blooded aboriginal entitled "A Queenslander." On the last page the author inserted his own photograph. The *Travel Notes* still make entertaining reading, for they contain incisive observations on America, Britain, and Europe, as well as A.G.S.'s democratic convictions. The critical, often debunking, note struck is strongly reminiscent of Mark Twain's similar reactions to Europe.

A.G.S. was about to settle down in London as a journalist when J. F. Archibald, always scouting for original talent, "leg-roped" him for the *Bulletin* staff, so that A.G.S. in 1894 began his fruitful run of twelve years on the *Bulletin,* first as a junior subeditor and then, from August 1896 to 1906 as editor of The Red Page, which he launched aptly by a review article on Henry Lawson's famous collection of short stories *While the Billy Boils.* That decade of his editorship of The Red Page was epoch-making in the development of Australian literature. It came when the *Bulletin* had grown from its small and uncertain beginnings in 1880 to be a political, literary, and cultural power in the land as a national paper, read throughout all the colonies, and expressing the exuberant nationalism of the times. Stephens reigned as its literary dictator, since Archibald as editor gave him complete freedom on the literary side of the paper. It was a happy meeting of the moment and the man, since the literature, hitherto largely colonial in character, was entering upon a stage of indigenous growth, flowering as writing which was deeply Australian in subject, outlook, and idiom. Indeed, Australian literature falls broadly into three periods: the colonial period from 1788 to 1880, when writing was done by emigrés from Great Britain or by native-born writers influenced by English models; the nationalist period from 1880 to 1914, the outbreak of the first world war, when writers were almost all sons of the soil and intent upon expressing Australian themes in an Australian way; and thirdly, the modern period from 1914 to the present day when the ardour of the nationalist "nineties" was replaced by either individualist writers or those affected by various internationalist influences, but growing in maturity and diversity.

Australia was extremely fortunate to have A. G. Stephens as the dominant critical voice during its efflorescence to stimulate and guide the new indigenous writing. Too often Australian literary criticism has fallen into one of the two extremes of colonial inferiority complex and uncritical nationalism. With the first extreme the critic can find nothing good in the local Nazareth, the shadow of the great English literature bears oppressively upon him, he looks askance at anything Australian and even, as with a recent critic, praises a friend because his poetry has no wallabies in it, i.e. it has nothing distinctively Australian about it. With the other extreme the patriotic critic tends to confuse patriotism with criticism, and wants everything aggressively Australian. Now A. G. Stephens preserved a salutary balance. On the one hand, he shared the fervent patriotism of the times, and was as ardently Australian as could be. He looked for writing which had its roots in the soil, which had a distinctive national relish in it. Thus he saw that Steele Rudd (A. H. Davis) had created a kind of popular folklore in his tales of farming life in *On Our Selection.* It was he who helped materially to "make" Rudd's book by suggesting that the dis-

T. INGLIS MOORE

parate short stories contributed by Rudd to the *Bulletin* be given fresh force and significance by being unified as stories of the one family. So, too, he saw the earthy merit of the bullock-drivers in Furphy's novel *Such is Life,* and fought to get the book published. Without A.G.'s penetrating judgment and editorial tenacity the manuscript would almost certainly never have been published—to become an Australian classic.

On the other hand, A.G.S. insisted that Australian writing be judged by international standards. He was no narrow nationalist but constantly referred local work to English or European or American literature, instituting sharp comparisons. He was remarkably catholic in his taste, and opened The Red Page to a diversity of talents, to the intellectual O'Dowd and the symbolist Brennan no less than to bush balladists such as Lawson, Paterson, and Ogilvie. He published articles on French symbolist poetry and European writers. His outlook was international as well as national. As a critic he brought balance and maturity into his assessments, and thus fought against the parochialism to which an isolated country like Australia, remote from the world's cultural centres, often succumbed. He ridiculed the cult of local colour when Douglas Sladen, editing A. L. Gordon's poetry, complained that Gordon had not written adequately about the local fauna. A.G. quoted Sladen to damaging effect: " 'He has very little to say about any lizards!' Now, by the nine-headed Muse, why should a poet say things about lizards? Surely never before in the history of literature was there a preface-writer who complained of his poet's lack of lizards. . . . 'And nothing about the enormous iguana!' 'Impossible!' you say. Alas! it is true; we have Mr. Sladen's boundless assurance for it. Deaf to the call of conscience, blind to the beacon of duty, Gordon says 'Nothing about the enormous iguana!' . . . In the name of lizards and the enormous iguana, what are poets for?"

A.G.S. had his limitations, of course, like any other critic. His own original writing in prose and verse was undistinguished. He was often egotistic and dogmatic. Occasionally, as Daley commented, he inflated the value of his latest discovery. He also had his whims and crotchets, such as his theory that genius was "a disease of the pustule . . . resulting from an abnormal series of cerebral vibrations." He preferred the lyric to the epic, demanding that poetry be "sung, not stated." At times his fondness for verse-music and sentiment led him astray, so that he overrated minor songsters like Louise Mack and M.A. Robertson whilst underrating intellectual poets such as Brennan and O'Dowd. As an editor he took wide liberties in "subbing" his copy, rewriting whole lines or even stanzas. In my collection of Stephens material, for instance, I have manuscripts of Robertson verses in which the original writing is indecipherable under the emendations of A.G., penned in his invariable purple ink. His taste went awry when he tried to alter the subtle cadences of Shaw Neilson, and he eventually confessed of Neilson and his poems: "He feels better than I know —as a rule."

It must be recognised, too, that A.G.'s power in his heyday came largely from the felicitous combination of his talent and the *Bulletin's* power. When he left the *Bulle-*

tin in 1906 "in a huff and a hurry" both suffered from the divorce. The Red Page declined in the hands of his successors, whilst his later criticism, if as good as ever, lost its power when shorn of the *Bulletin's* backing. His own magazine, *The Bookfellow,* despite its brilliance, led the precarious existence of all purely literary magazines. He had a hard struggle to keep his family by means of the magazine and by journalism, book-selling, and book-reviewing. His daughter told me that the great day in the Stephens regime at one stage was the arrival of books from England for review, since A.G. would read and review them quickly, then sell them to the secondhand bookshops, so that the Stephens family would enjoy a good square meal. Yet he never complained, remained robust in his manliness, and maintained his high critical standards to the last. He published short monographs on Daley, Kendall, and Brennan and one collection of critical articles punningly entitled *The Red Pagan.* P. R. Stephensen paid a vigorous tribute to him in a reprinted lecture delivered in 1940, whilst in 1941 Vance Palmer edited his valuable *A. G. Stephens: His Life and Work,* which contained judiciously selected extracts from the critical writings and an excellent biographical introduction. Most of A.G.'s criticism still lies buried, however, in the files of the *Bulletin* and the *Bookfellow.* There is need for a collected Stephens and a full biography.

Reading over the whole field of A.G.'s critical production, one is struck by its fine quality and wide range. The errors and blind spots are minor besides the major achievement. The judgments on Australian writers can only be fully appreciated, of course, when one keeps in mind the fact that they were usually pioneering evaluations made on new writers. The critic had to break virgin ground. He had to establish standards and signposts in uncharted territory, pushing the literary frontier forward. A.G.S. did this job magnificently. His judgments on the whole are penetrating and illuminating. They get to the root of the matter. They light up the subject in a luminous sentence, a terse phrase, or a pithy metaphor.

What could be better, for instance, than A.G.'s comment on Louis Stone's novel *Jonah?* "Structurally *Jonah* is equivalent to 'two rooms and a skillion', and the skillion is only a 'lean-to'. The hunchback Jonah, greatly conceived, remains misshapen in fiction as in fact; he typifies the book he entitles."

Of Kendall: "He is poet of Nature and himself—not poet of Humanity."

Of Gordon: "His poetry is intellectually obvious. Often crossed with a personal warp, commonplace wisdom is its typical woof. Everyman's wisdom makes Everyman's prophet . . . . In the end we love him for transfusing life: his poetry is a man's heart beating."

Of Henry Kingsley's pastoral novel: " 'Geoffry Hamlyn' is a pleasant, rambling story of the old school, patchy in interest and very patchy in merit. It is never quite dull enough to bore, and rarely bright enough to excite. You put it down without difficulty, and take it up without anticipation."

Of Douglas Sladen: "Mr. Sladen's work in relation to this country has been characterized by energy and incompetence."

T. INGLIS MOORE

A.G.S. was not quite right in his verdict on Brennan: "Brennan's is a bush of poetry that smoulders and never really burns." Yet it remains true of much of Brennan's work, and the word 'smoulders' is extraordinarily acute and apt. Nor could there be a more fitting or striking summary of Brennan's poetry than "his didactic sonorous spectacular commentary on I, Mine, Me."

Such examples of critical acumen and incisive prose could be multiplied, since they occur on almost every page of A.G.S.'s criticism. They come with the verve of a Hazlitt. They follow the injunction A.G. laid down to Neilson: "Meat off the blade at every cut." To read such critiques is a delight as well as an illumination.

IT SEEMS A PITY THAT JOE TISHLER IS NOT KNOWN OUTSIDE AUSTRALIA, FOR HE had much to please the world or, at any rate, the English-speaking countries. Like Shakespeare, because of his strongly personal and idiomatic style, he might be difficult to translate into foreign languages. But consider the warmth, the depth, the broad, universal humanity of such a piece as, say, "The Drink Maniac":

> He raised a chair and he's eyes did glare,
> Heavy drinking had drove him insane.
> "Serpents of hell," he did fiercely yell,
> "Hence or I'll rent thee atwain."
> He's terrified wife did fly for her life,
> From the grasp of the maniac,
> Who whirled the chair in frantic despair,
> And cried "Demon's, I'll drive yous back."
> He gnashed he's teeth, did laugh and weep,
> When two constable's bold broke in;
> He did struggle and writh in their iron grip,
> And shrieked "Free me ye fiends of sin."
> Under lock and key he grew calm as could be,
> Into a reverie of gloom he did sink.
> Untainted by crime, stricken mad in he's prime.
> From the fatal influence of drink.

Then, too, of universal interest were his historical pieces. If you could not, perhaps, exactly describe "An Austrian Spy" as "a European Event" it did at least describe—and in memorable terms—an historic event in Europe:

> A group of cossacks were
> Huddled in a village Inn
> During an halt on the route
> To the battle din,
> When they were aroused
> By a comrade's frenzied cry—
> By god the waiter's
> An Austrian spy.
> From the cossacks rang out
> A diabolical cheer
> When his throat was severed
> From ear to ear.

Tishler—or "Bellerive" as we all knew him: the nom de plume was taken from a town in Tasmania where he once lived—did not often write on American themes. I hardly think it is fair to count "The Eskimo's" as such (If Eskimos are an American theme) because he tells us in his "Poetic Dairy" that that graphic piece of description of the far frozen North

> Where the white bear's prowleth
> Amidst the ice and snow

arose from a memory of his schooldays "when I'd pay serious attention to my teacher's interesting accounts of the Arctic regions." Nevertheless, at the time when Bellerive was at his peak, in the early nineteen hundreds, the Australian writers with whose outlook he had most in common—the balladists, and such short story writers as Henry Lawson—were considerably influenced by Bret Harte and Mark Twain, and one of Bellerive's pithiest little narratives, "Indian Duel," clearly derives from the same source:

> Two Indians with knives
> Did feint and bend low,
> As they endeavoured to
> Strike a fatal blow;
> They circled around—
> And with bated breath,
> Clinked knives in their
> Horrid duel to death;
> Snakelike the elder at
> He's foe did dart,
> Missed he's aim and
> Was stabbed to the heart;
> Realising he's victim's
> Soul had sped,
> The vanquisher grimly
> Scalped the Dead.

While his peculiar talent waits for the wider recognition which it obviously deserves, Bellerive is pretty well known in Australia: at least I hope so, for I have recently edited *The Book of Bellerive,* a selection of his masterpieces—but I doubt if he enjoys quite the fame now that he did when he and the newspaper he wrote for, the *Bulletin,* were both in their heyday.

I hope it is not necessary to introduce the *Bulletin,* as well as Bellerive, to an American audience. It would be like trying to explain what the Statue of Liberty is. But, briefly, the *Bulletin* was a weekly newspaper started by J. F. Archibald and John Haynes in 1880. It was intended to be, and at first was, a bright, breezy, irreverent, faintly scandalous commentary on Australian affairs; but it quickly grew to be a kind of Voice of the Nation for which everybody wrote who could write well and which everybody read. "The Bushman's Bible" they used to call it because of the hundreds of paragraphists who filled its pages with observations of the birds, beasts, bugs, and bushmen they had seen Outback and because of the great short story writers, Lawson, Dyson, and Steele Rudd, who described the life of the land for all the people who were living it but had never seen it put in words. But it was a city man's Bible, too; and, when A. G. Stephens became its literary editor, published the lyric writers, Hugh McCrae and Shaw Neilson. Politically, nationally, and culturally, things were stirring in Australia at the turn of the century, and the best place to see them stirring was in the *Bulletin*. As Bellerive himself summed it up—not in his best style, though the piece has indeed a remarkable flatness—in his memorial to J. F. Archibald:

> Firm and competent for
> The literary strain
> His position as chief he
> Did successfully retain.
> Young writers of promise
> Who faced the brunt
> During his period
> Did reach the front.
> Varied sheets of verse
> In details in prose
> Passed through his hands till
> His editorship's close.

Where Bellerive faced the brunt and unquestionably reached the front was in the *Bulletin's* "Answers to Correspondents" column. It was a place where contributions were acknowledged with scathing criticism and where the worst of them, for the general delight, were printed. "I rizzle, I sizzle, I sing!" wrote one aspiring poet. "Are you, by any chance," asked the Answers column, "a sausage?" Bellerive was the Answers' star contributor. At once humble and proud—for he knew his place, yet felt it to be a place of honour—he shone there regularly for forty years.

What did he write about? Very often, like most poets, about himself. His "Poetic Dairy" tells how he was born in Dunedin, New Zealand, in 1871; how, his parents having emigrated to Australia in his infancy, he "was sent to a State school at an early age and, although slow at learning, I evinced poetic signs and would often visit the melbourne Cemetery to witness a pathetic burial"; how, in the bush and in the cities, he led a wandering life, selling brooms from door to door or traveling the outback as a hawker. It was on one of his hawking ventures that he was "Charged by a Bull":

> Charged by a bull
> With fierce bowed head,

DOUGLAS STEWART

For a solitary tree
In terror I sped.
When aloft among
The branches high,
I realised I was
Too young to die.
I watched the bull
Make off in rage—
Foiled like a villain
Upon the stage.

But he wrote on public themes, too. The first world war, as we have already seen in "The Austrian Spy," inspired him mightily. "Upon their city buildings," he wrote in celebration of "The Downfall of the Belgian,"

Huge shells did fall and burst,
Their noble heroes slaughtered
Poor Belgian was accurst;
The german wolves of battle
Had dealt a fearful Blow,
And thousands grimly yearneth
For the downfall of the foe.

He was a great chronicler of famous cricketers, actors, writers, and race horses. I have always particularly liked his tribute to a cyclist named Plugger Bill Martin—

Plugger Bill Martin of
The distant past
On the old push bike
Was remarkable fast,

but perhaps for its American interest, as well as an illustration of his gift for stating the plain facts of a situation with no superfluous adornment whatever, I should also quote here his lines to the actress Maggie Moore:

In the United States
At a elderly age
Died Maggie Moore
Of the brilliant stage.
Back in the eighties
In the drama struck oil,
She cleverly starred
At the Melbourne Royal.

He was fascinated—as today a poet might be inspired by the spacemen—by the early balloonists and celebrated their exploits in many an exciting narrative, sometimes realistic, sometimes, as in "A Balloon Tragedy," giving free rein to his vivid imagination:

> As a balloon sailed thro' space
> An Aeronaut star
> Attacked a student friend in
> The swaying car
> While above the clouds the
> Huge balloon sailed
> A fearful struggle between
> The aeronauts prevailed
> You've robbed me hissed the assailant
> Of the woman I love
> And I'll hurl you to eternity
> By the saints above
> Overpowered by the student
> Was the aeronaut star
> And hurled into space
> From the swaying car.

But, above all, it was the life he lived and saw in the Melbourne slums that moved him to take up his pen and, snug by the fire with his Italian wife in the cottage that eventually blew down in a storm, jot down, while she knitted, yet another moving and humane, if distinctly odd, poem for the *Bulletin*'s Answers. Witness "An Aged Man's Hideous Escapade, at the Victorian Home for the Aged and the Poor, Royal Park, April 8, 1909":

> A veteran sailor climbed up
> On the garbled roof of the Home,
> And along the parapets and tiles
> Like a cat did roam.
> The warders endeavoured to capture
> The daring climber bold,
> Clad only in his nightshirt—
> Upon the roof in the cold.
> Letting forth a loud yell, like
> A wild animal in pain,
> The eccentric old joker
> Scrambled down again.
> He had not forgotten
> His rough dare devil ways
> When afloat on the deep
> In his hardy younger days.

Bellerive was published, of course, as a joke; and he was very funny; but it takes some unique quality for a man to be a joke for forty years. I have myself read miles of bad verse for the *Bulletin* but never came across another Bellerive. Most of the people who laughed at him could not, in fact, have written as well themselves. He had a style; he had a personality. Disregard his obvious weaknesses, and he did have pithiness; he could look beyond himself and write of the world at large; he did have imagination, even if of an extremely lurid kind; he did have humanity; and sometimes, in his nature poems on seagulls and snails and pigs and roosters and cheesejumpers and fleas and bedbugs, he wrote both amusingly and charmingly. He is a "natural" in words as Grandma Moses and the Douanier Rousseau are naturals in paint. In another age he would have been a writer of street songs and ballads.

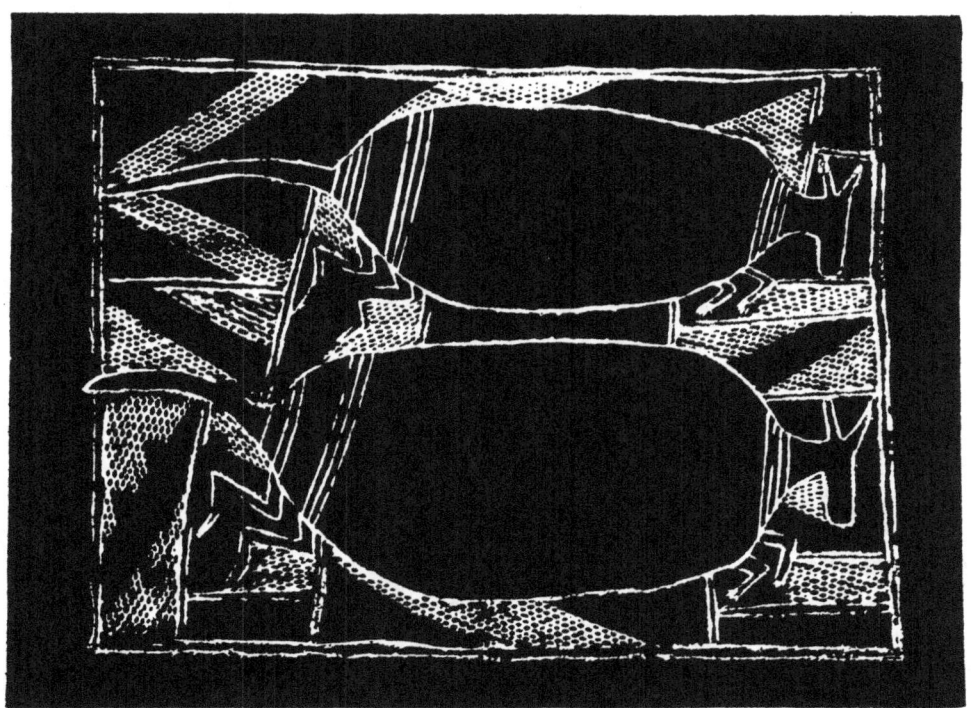

Words For Wyatt's Lute

When she loves me
I love her least,
I'm sure to lose
When I love most,
My best of love
She turns to scorn
Yet swears she loves me
When I yawn.

Look on another
Man, and I
Will break my heart
From jealousy,
But let me kiss
Her sister, then
My darling is
My own again.

So praise with me
The moments when
We find in bed
This golden mean
Lest cheated by
A paradox
We die for love
Or from the pox.

Mothers and Daughters

The cruel girls we loved
Are over forty;
Their subtle daughters
Have stolen their beauty,

And with a blue stare
Of cool surprise
They mock their anxious mothers
With their mothers' eyes.

ELWYN LYNN : *Australian Painting and Sculpture Today*

I T TOOK A LONG TIME FOR THE AUSTRALIAN ARTIST EVEN TO RECORD HIS NEW and strange environment; in the nineteenth century he did it in a variety of modes ranging from English topographical water colour to romanticism. By the end of that century (and still widely practised in the twenties of this) was developed Australia's own type of impressionism: a broken touch without vibrancy, but an evenness of effect without formlessness, because the harsh shapes of tree and landscape ever intruded.

In the twenties, however, in Sydney, under the influence of Cézanne and the post-impressionists there did develop a group interested in flat-patterned abstraction and colour harmonies: its influence was not great and had no causative role in the efflorescence of abstraction that sprang up in Sydney after 1955.

Landscape painting retarded the growth of Melbourne's social commentators and mythmakers; charm and good taste hindered the progress of vigorous abstraction in Sydney after World War II; yet we have passed through a decade that may be the most important in the history of Australian art.

Lest one be accused of looking with the eyes of a Texan temporarily full of Australian patriotism, one had best look with those of out-of-town critics. Indeed, in San Francisco and in England, Australian art made a more favourable impact than it does at home.

In December 1959, a cross section of Australian painting was shown in San Francisco at the Palace of the Legion of Honour; of it Alfred Frankenstein, in the San Francisco *Chronicle*, remarked that it was "full of life, vitality and invention," that there were parallels with European and American art, but that all works were highly individual. In the San Francisco *News-Call Bulletin*, A. J. Bloomfield hastened to remove misconceptions: "People Down Under are not buried in a cultural wastebin. . . . There are a few examples of provincial landscape work, but they are thankfully at a minimum. In short, there are stacks of paintings that are good-looking, sophisticated and 1959-ish."

The exhibition of Recent Australian Painting at London's Whitechapel in July 1961, was personally selected by its director, Bryan Robertson, on a visit to Australia. In the catalogue introduction he noted the lively and direct sense of touch, the urgency, even self-conscious bravado, and the high-pitched colour. He felt that there was an attempt to grapple with an unhumanized landscape which still holds for artists that shock of recognition long gone in Europe. In being challengers rather than interpreters of their landscape, and, indeed, in all their art, artists loaded their canvases with individual experience that went deeper than mere subjectivism, for: "A pull towards a metaphysical abstraction now informs nearly all Australian art, in common with America," wrote Robertson.

The Exhibition held surprises for some twenty-five critics and even raised some questions in aesthetics: Sir Kenneth Clark felt that the isolation was a refutation of historical determinism in arts, while Edward Lucie-Smith considered the attempts to evolve a native Australian mythology rather self-conscious. The *Daily Telegraph's* Terence Mullaly said it made London art "look wearily academic," and the *Times* saw a toughness, boldness, and lyrical response even in the use of paint; "There is a strong continual interplay between lyrical feeling and dramatic incident"; a feeling so strange that Eric Newton declared that Australian art had to be studied "as we studied Oriental or Mexican or African art before it could be enjoyed." Behind it, he said, was "something with a meaning."

While the *Daily Mail* wrote: "The fearsome loneliness of the outback, the presence in immense territories of extraordinary fauna, the legends of pioneer settlers have been vigorously felt and translated no less vigorously on big canvases" and the *Evening Standard* added of the abstractions: "They retain the toughness, the spaciousness, and I imagine, the sunbaked textures and colours of their native land," John Nash of the *Yorkshire Post* saw no parasitism on the environment, but, "It is the intensity which unites these pictures and provides the national flavour. Whatever the style, they have a grandeur of imagination that is unique."

As selections from the exhibitions toured England Anthony Tucker of the *Guardian* in April this year has the latest word: "Its impact was not simply that of rawness or freshness, but, above all, that of urgency. This was painting stripped of European graces; stripped of aesthetic refinements; and deeply concerned with purpose and meaning."

The story of Australian art is the tale of two cities, Melbourne and Sydney, six hundred miles apart by rail and having a population of about four million between them. What the *Times* said in July 1960, of the painter (he also makes rather baroque ceramic sculpture), Arthur Boyd, when he showed—in true Melbourne tradition—a *series* of paintings on one theme, that of the tribulations of a Chagallian half-caste bride, could be said of most Melbourne figurative painting where the greatest impact has been sought with the minimum of immediate means: "They assault the eye and the mind sometimes to an uncomfortable degree, but they speak in that vigorous Australian tone of voice, harsh and lyrical at the same time, and that haunting language of Australian myth, which have brought us something new, strange and fascinating in figurative painting."

Most fascinating and most internationally known has been Sidney Nolan who would have shared the feelings that recently prompted a Manifesto of the Antipodeans who deplored the trivia of abstraction and restated the belief that the interpretative image of the objective world was the basis of art. Nolan and Albert Tucker had already won recognition for legends of the bushranger, Ned Kelly, and explorers of the inland. Tucker is represented in both New York's Guggenheim and Museum of Modern Art and recently returned to show harsh, eroded landscapes almost submerging bushrangers and explorers who grappled with it, landscapes, as pervasively

ELWYN LYNN

ELWYN LYNN, "Across the Black Soil Plains," 1961.
Mixed media and P.V.A. on masonite, 36 x 48". The
title is both satirical and appreciative of a traditional
painting by Lambert in the Gallery of N.S.W. Through
textures and non-art materials he aims to achieve a
pervasive mood unobtainable by other modes. Collection: The Artist.

Right: PETER UPWARD, "January Seventh," 1961. P.V.A. and pigment, 79 x 54". The swathe here varies from the thinnest vibration of paint to thick, clogged masses like furnace clinkers; yet there is no sense of fumbling or awkwardness. Pictorial presence is in the gesture itself rather than in its relation to its background. Collection: The Artist.

Below: LEONARD HESSING, "Middlecove Charcoal," 1961. Charcoal on paper, 25 x 20". Primordial forms rendered with the tense elegance of a Watteau depicting bristling banditti, but with surreal overtones often characterizing Hessing's drawings. Collection: The Artist.

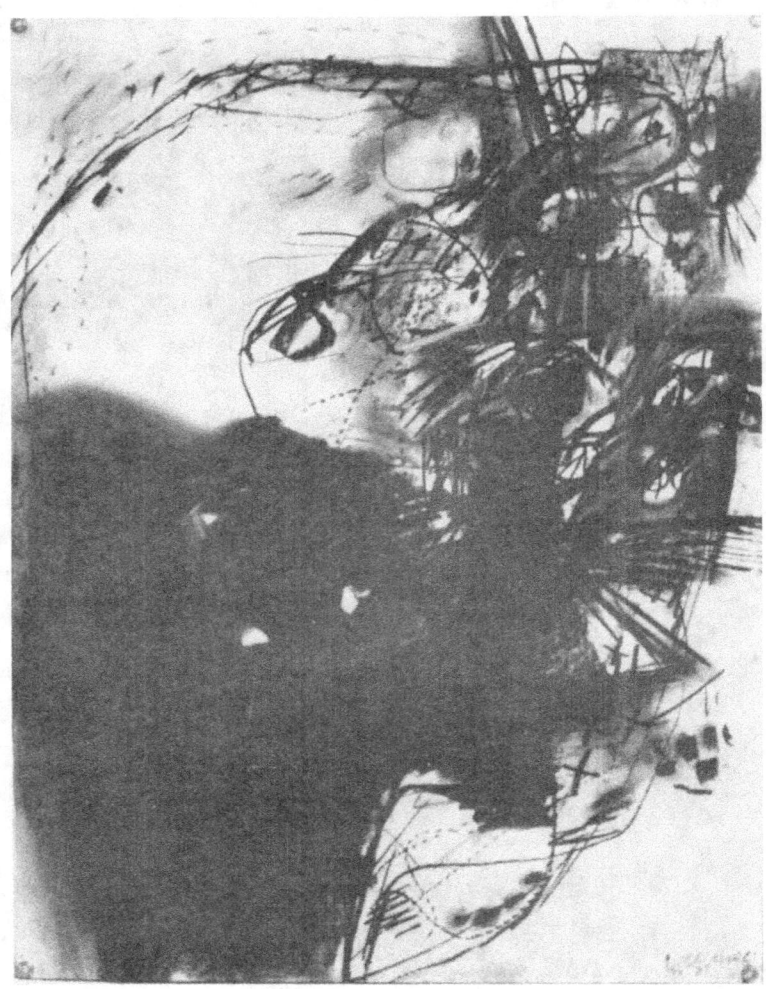

Above: MICHAEL BROWN, "Mirg's Migration Into Heaven," 1961. Hand drawn and printed on newspaper, 10 x 30". An arbitrary mythology for the literary section of any advertiser's audience. It is well to note that "Mirg is a beaut. He is friendly and never morose." Possession: The Artist.

Left: MICHAEL BROWN, "Bush Carpenter's Girl-Friend," 1961. Wood, bottle tops, tinfoil, and kettle whistle, 20" high. This is one of the first of Brown's assemblage works. He was in New Guinea in 1960 and was impressed by the way natives incorporated *objets trouvé* into their sculpture and ornaments. The consolations of lonely bush carpenters obviously have their dangers. Possession: The Artist.

Right: ROSS CROTHALL, "Mad Woman," 1961.
Enamel on masonite with plastic roses, 24″ high.
Not everyone can grow his own plastic roses.
Possession: The Artist.

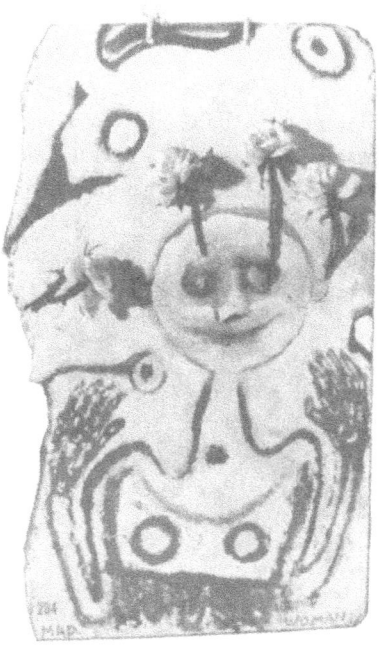

Below: JOHN OLSEN, "Journey into Yon Beaut Country No. 2," 1961. Oil on masonite,
48 x 72″. Olsen often goes for a walk with Klee's line, crosses Corneille's tracks, notes the
erotica in landscape, and finds his own inventive path through it all. If Dubuffet is around,
then he's enjoying the landscape, too. Collection: Art Gallery of Queensland.

Right: JUDY CASSAB, "Evening," 1961. Oil on canvas, 36 x 28". Judy Cassab is deeply impressed by the Centre, to which she has made several trips, and she has held two successful one-man exhibitions in London of abstract interpretations of the dry inland in the blaze of noon or at nightfall. Collection: The Artist.

Below: GODFREY MILLER, "Unity in Blue." Oil on canvas, 36 x 48". One of the fathers of abstraction, Miller's ecstatic alliance between pointillism and an architectural structure has produced infinitely graduated mosaics of pulsating colour. Collection: The Art Gallery of N.S.W.

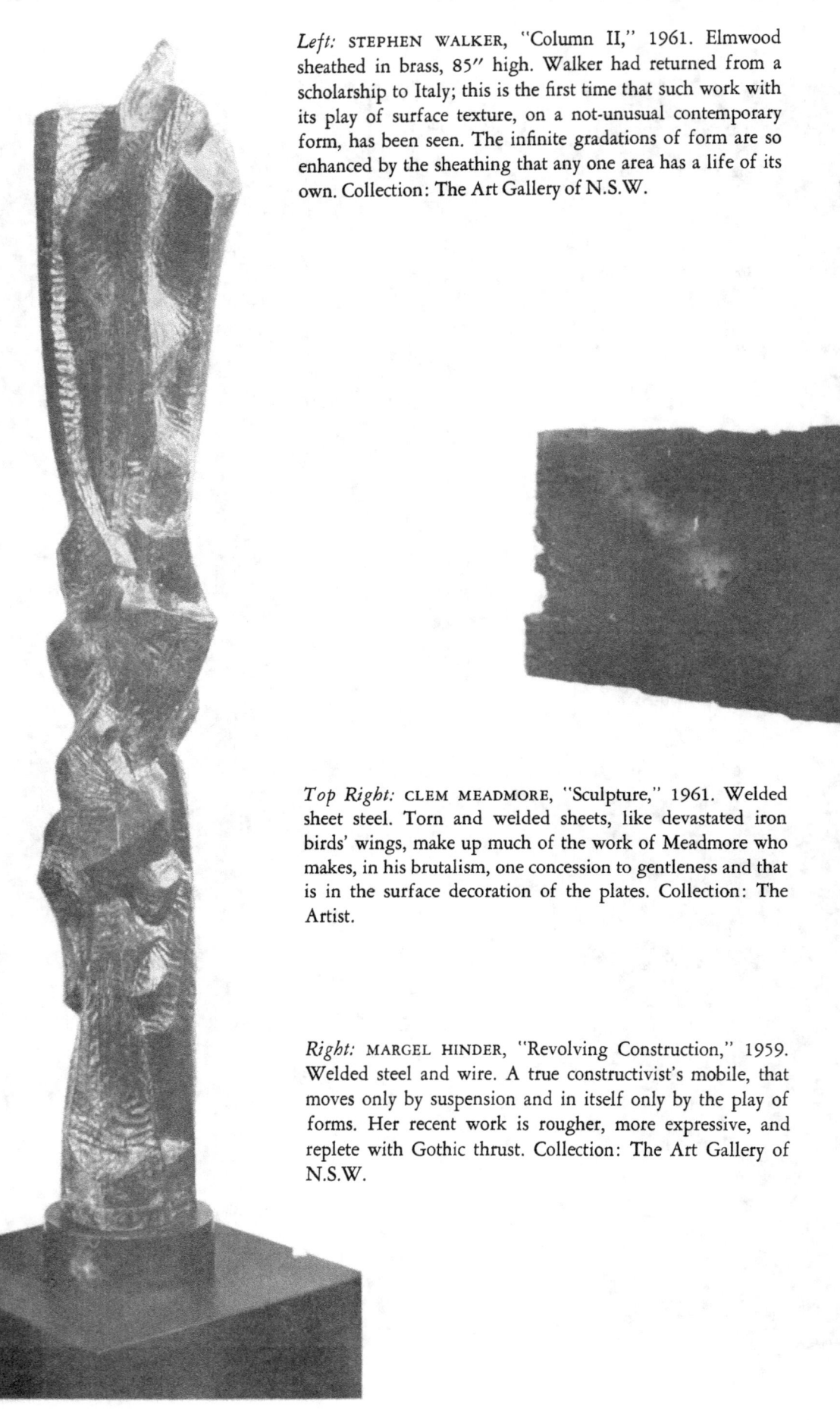

Left: STEPHEN WALKER, "Column II," 1961. Elmwood sheathed in brass, 85″ high. Walker had returned from a scholarship to Italy; this is the first time that such work with its play of surface texture, on a not-unusual contemporary form, has been seen. The infinite gradations of form are so enhanced by the sheathing that any one area has a life of its own. Collection: The Art Gallery of N.S.W.

Top Right: CLEM MEADMORE, "Sculpture," 1961. Welded sheet steel. Torn and welded sheets, like devastated iron birds' wings, make up much of the work of Meadmore who makes, in his brutalism, one concession to gentleness and that is in the surface decoration of the plates. Collection: The Artist.

Right: MARGEL HINDER, "Revolving Construction," 1959. Welded steel and wire. A true constructivist's mobile, that moves only by suspension and in itself only by the play of forms. Her recent work is rougher, more expressive, and replete with Gothic thrust. Collection: The Art Gallery of N.S.W.

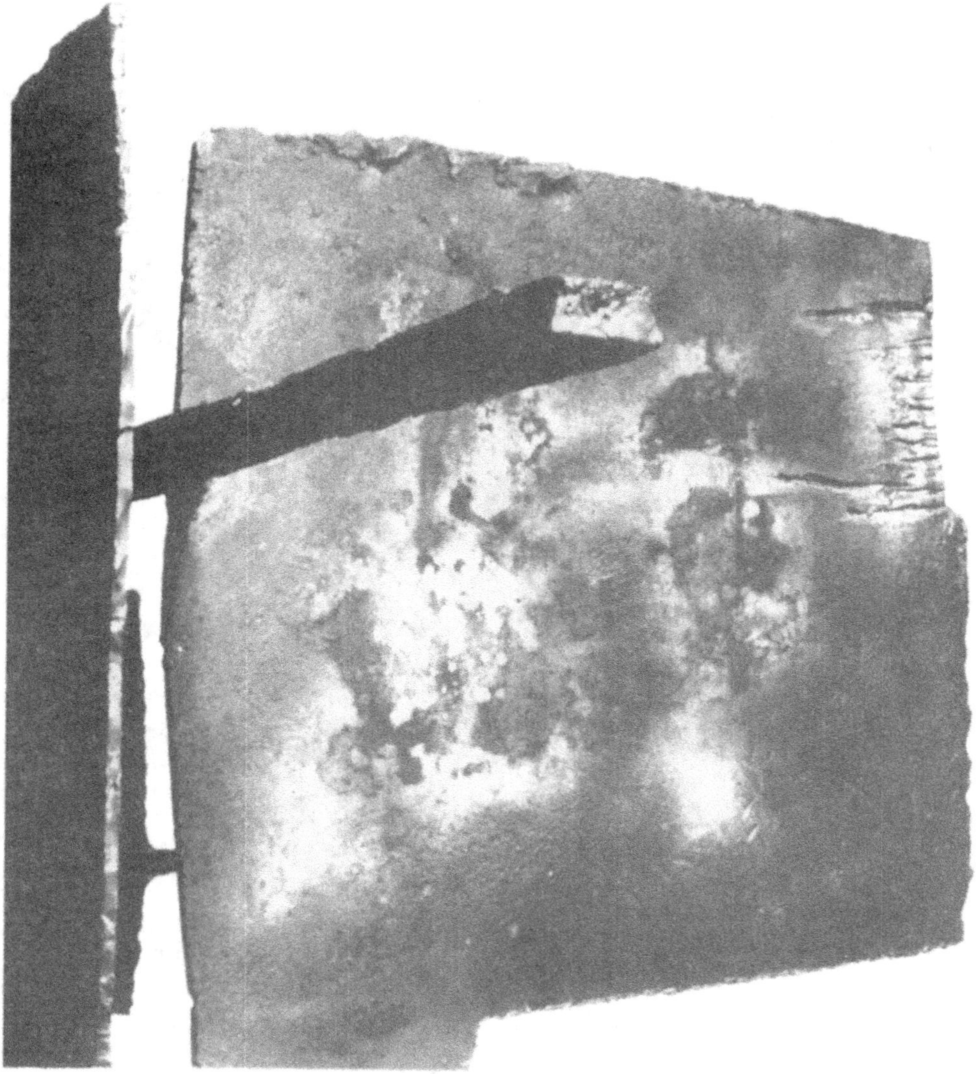

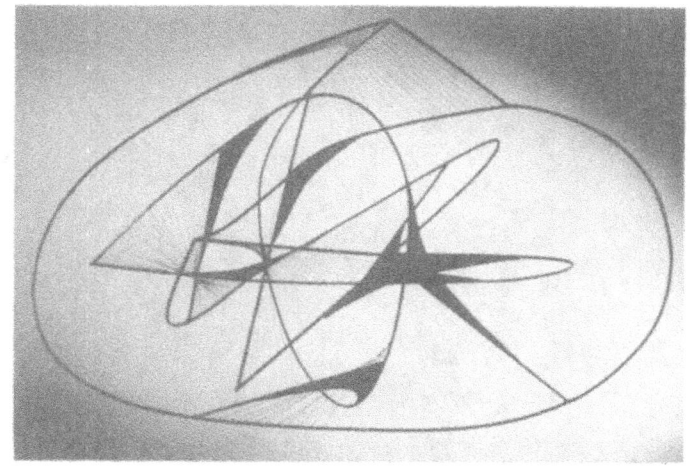

Right: WILLIAM ROSE, "Metropolis."
Oils on masonite, 66 x 42". A kaleido-
scope, almost of scaffoldings and cubist
skirmishes scattered over a monochro-
matic background. "You make one
stroke," says Rose, "and you are out
there on your own." Collection: Mr.
Robert Shaw.

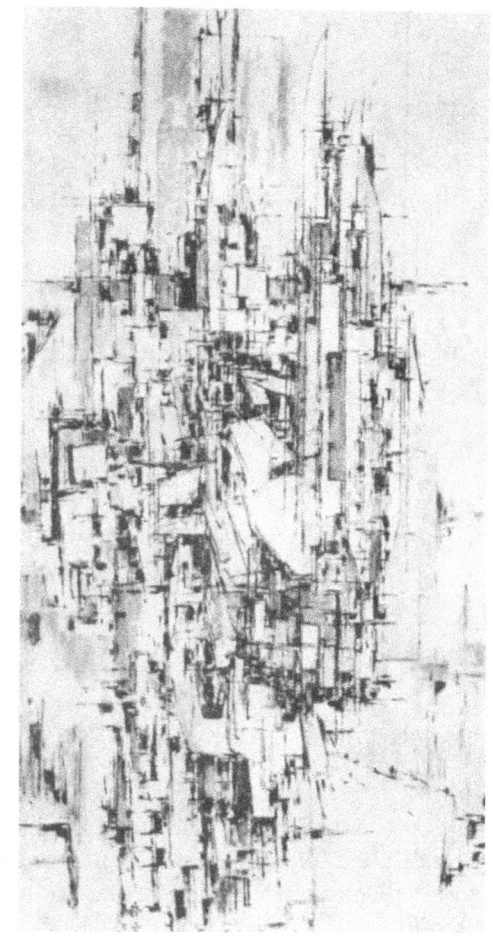

Left: CARL PLATE, "Destructive Paragon No. 1, Permanence," 1959. Oil on canvas,
30 x 28". Plate believes that painting is like the iceberg: The important part lies below the
surface. His surfaces, usually in subdued colours, are almost imperceptible in their move-
ments: lines traverse the surface in tentative gropings. Collection: The Artist.

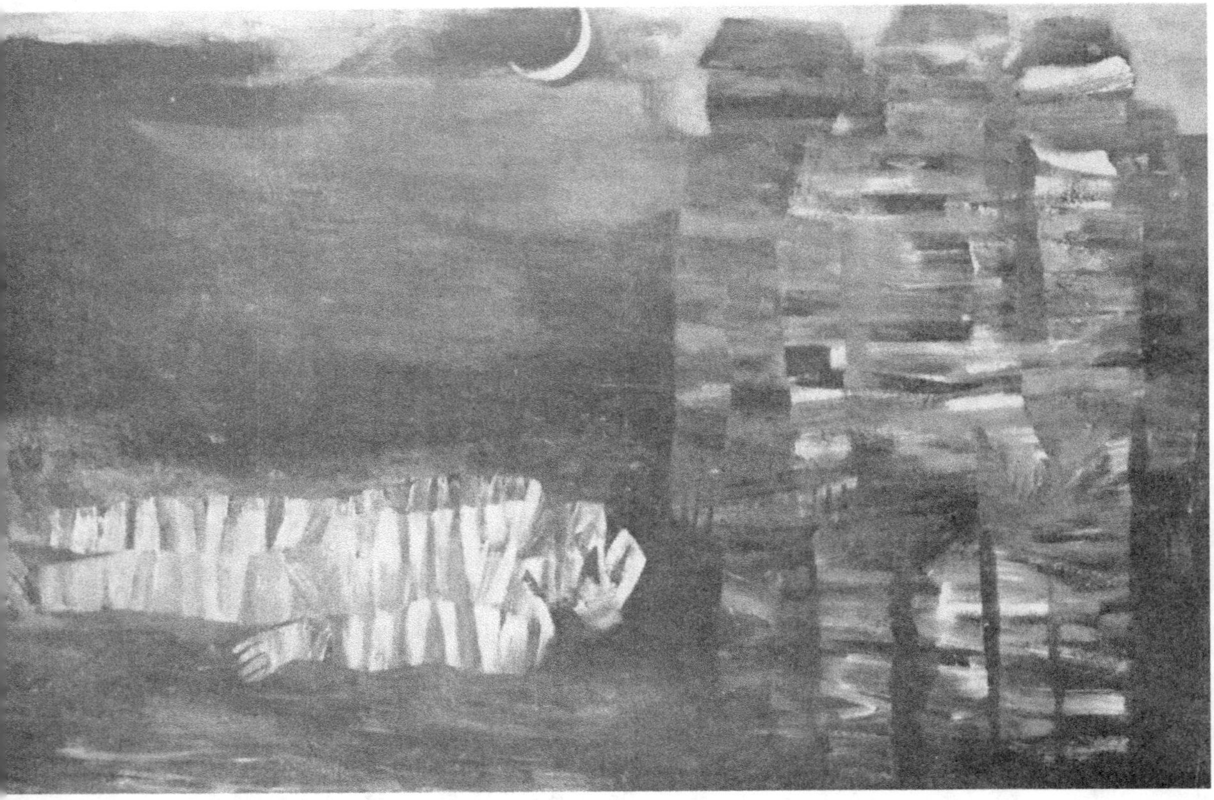

Above: JON MOLVIG, "Ballad of the Dead Stockman II," 1959. Oil on masonite, 48 x 78". This dark and foreboding work involves the bush ballad, Australia's partial convict ancestry, and the incredible loneliness of the life of a stockman. Collection: The Art Gallery of N.S.W.

Left: JOHN COBURN, "Totem," 1960. Oil on masonite, 48 x 32". Coburn is concerned with legends, signs, icons of great simplicity, and glowing colour; one is always more impressed by the hidden geometer than the overt geometry. Collection: Private.

Right: LEONARD FRENCH, 1961. Oil and mixed media. After being influenced by Leger, French has developed a style that involves encrustation of raised surfaces with gold leaf and strong colour. The mediaeval and Byzantine brilliance is so heavily contained in varnish that much of his work is like jewellery in amber. Collection: The Rudy Komon Gallery.

Below: CHARLES BLACKMAN, "Reverie in the Street," 1960. Oil and enamel on masonite, 48 x 60". One of a number of pictures done during recent years where, in colours from the lurid to the sombre, Blackman explores the uncomfortably revealed and the dark side of the soul. Collection: National Gallery of Victoria.

Below: BRETT WHITELEY, "Dark Painting," 1961. Tempera and oil on board, 55 x 76". Little has been seen of Whiteley's work in Australia; he was most successful in London after going there on a scholarship. He sold to the Tate, won a prize at the Young Painters' Biennale in Paris in 1961. Critics commented on the erotic nature of his work at a one-man show at Mathieson's Gallery (London), 1962. Collection: The Artist.

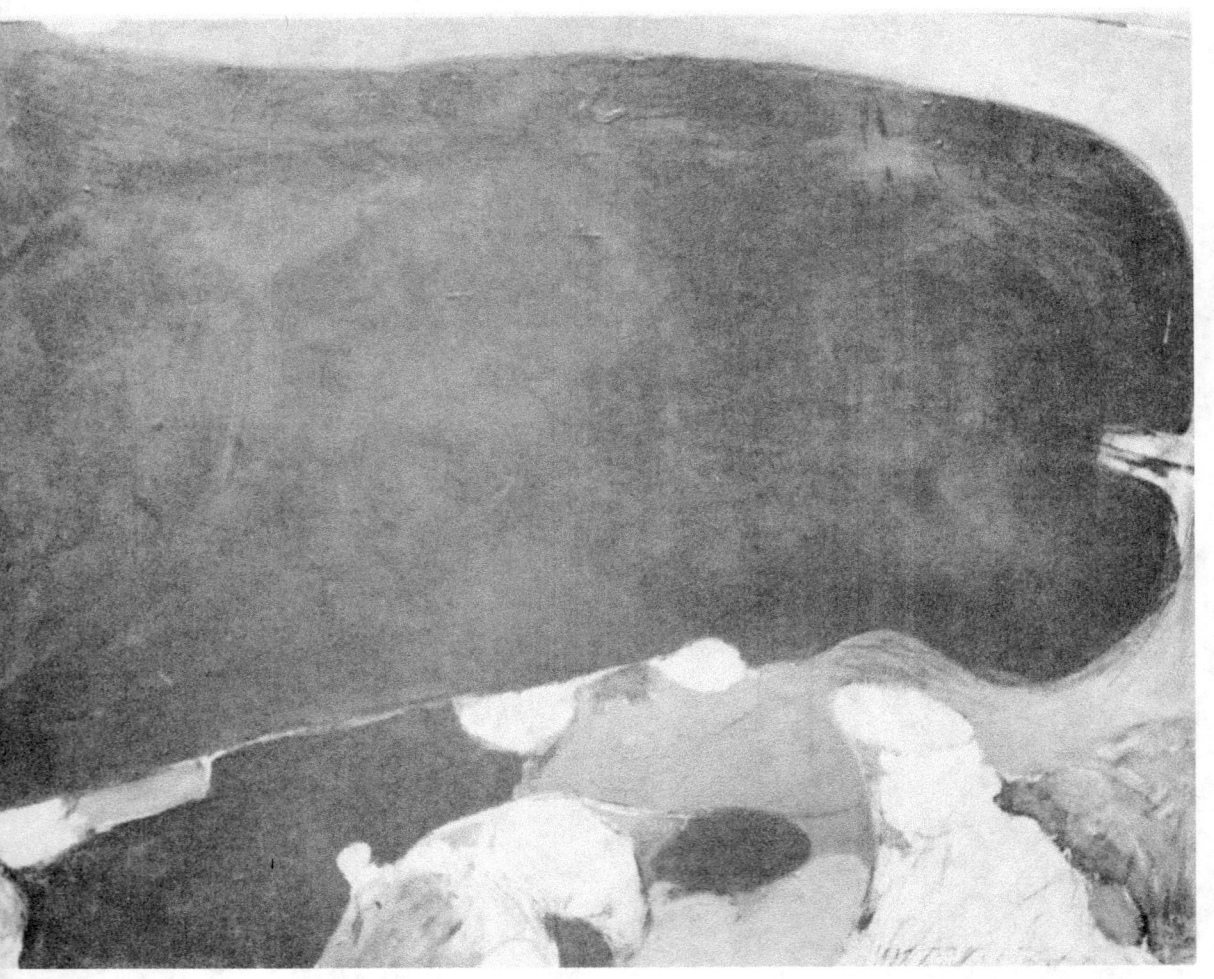

Right: STANISLAUS RAPOTEC, "Tension 51," 1960. Oil on masonite, 48 x 36". One of a large number of thunderously emphatic works, in abstract expressionist gesture, called "Tension." All have an air of intensely vigorous gloom. Collection: The Artist.

LAWRENCE DAWS, "Sungazer," 1961. Oil on canvas, 72 x 64". Lawrence Daws was one of the three Australians shown at the Young Painters' Biennale in Paris in 1961. He lives in London, and under the influence of such Italians as Afro and Vaglieri, he has abandoned his flat-patterned cubism for a more ephemeral world. Collection: The Artist.

ELWYN LYNN

sad, blighted, angry, and tender as the cluttered gum forests of Boyd.

Nolan's Kelly had not been so iconological as Tucker's; the story he told with un-surpassed pictorial invention and primitive flatness was witty and even awkwardly elegant. He followed these with a series on the brown residual ranges of the Centre and, then, a series on the animal scarecrows produced by the inland droughts. Recently the primitive immediacy of Ripolin enamel and subject has given way to a more surface-conscious series in polyvinyl acetate on Leda and the Swan, and on Gallipoli where Anzacs (Australians and New Zealanders) first fought in an European war.

The range of feeling in Charles Blackman's fiercely poetic and tenderly satirical works is wide; from a whimsical set of works on Alice in Wonderland and Picasso-esque heads, he has recently painted works of great tonal contrasts, elegies of light and darkness, of persons blinded by glare or turned away from the light; an almost mediaeval contrast between the pit and the halo.

Other Melbourne figurative painters of note are: John Perceval with his loosely painted wharf scenes and his lush coastal forests; John Brack, who has turned from his Buffet-like nudes and interiors to quaintly patterned persons from way out, via, it seems the East Indies; and Clifton Pugh who has combined expressionism and the staccato rhythms of cubism to present crows, wildcats, decayed animals in landscapes full of enmity.

Sydney has a lone figurative painter of importance: even when Robert Dickerson's people wander in the bush they are haunted by the loneliness and monotony of the city; detribalised, psychotic, uprooted, they band together to be never so much apart. In flat colours and areas, they are cardboard people of deep commitments. Farther north, some six hundred miles, in Brisbane, Jon Molvig has been deeply influenced by German expressionism and the pessimistic ballads of the Australian bush.

There *are* some abstract painters in Melbourne: George Johnston deploys Capo-grossian cogwheels; Asher Bilu gently evokes the opposite world of fantasy; Robert Juniper, some seventeen hundred miles farther west, in Perth, too, creates a Klee-like world of abstraction.

Abstraction dominates Sydney art: sculpture may fluctuate in both cities between figuration and abstraction, but in Sydney abstraction is the subject of discussion, the winner of prizes (which play an important part in this isolated enclave in the Pacific), and, finally, the victor over a genteel charm that long plagued the city. The influence of almost every form of international abstraction, except the hard-edge school, is felt. The belated change did not gather force until 1955; since then the pace has been bewildering.

A New York sense of space and thrust informs the work of Nancy Borlase and Herbert Kemble: French finish and prettiness are far from their aims. The influence of cubism is strong in thelarge flat areas of John Coburn, with their stylised, enig-matic presences; Godfrey Miller arranges his prismatic fragmentation rigorously, yet creates a pulsating cubism; William Rose's works are like detailed plans for the scaffoldings of buildings: his matchlike strokes are scattered like small Mondrian colonies on monocrome backgrounds.

Geometrical incisiveness is alien to the work of an acknowledged leader, John Passmore, and to Judy Cassab, Robert Hughes, and Margo Lewers; their surfaces may be rough or feathery, fragmented or controlled by unobtrusive structure, yet they are fused in a free-floating pulsation that recalls Cezanne, Afro, Stamos, and Guston. Cassab is more concerned with taming the harsh landscape; Hughes bathes man and landscape in a hard dry light. Ross Morrow lies between these painters and the linear abstractionists in his attempt to render the solid infinity of the outback in a few simple strokes across wide areas.

The most exciting group at present is that of the linear abstractionists: gesture, line, graffiti, untrammelled movement of heavy forms are their means. The line of Stanislaus Rapotec (migrants have played an important role in Australian painting) amalgamates contour and mass as it moves slowly in sombre colours, or whiplashes its way through Kafkaesque swamplands. For Rapotec, painting must flow unimpeded by academic preoccupations; Leonard Hessing would agree, but where Rapotec emphasises carelessness and speed, Hessing is more calculated in his enticing romantic abstraction where gloomy areas project tense and energetic lines. John Olsen, the leader of the younger abstractionists, employs lines that, far from being tense, wander like innocently gleeful scrawls as whimsical as Klee's and more erotic than Dubuffet's. Much is based on renditions of landscape, where one is involved with the contours, which are not simply objects of contemplation.

A much more jagged calligraphy is presented by Daryl Hill and Thos. Gleghorn who erupts the surface in a chaos of gesture, squiggles, and frustrated thrusts: both have obvious references to landscape and its atmosphere. But none is so unequivocal in his attitude or closer to de Kooning, Pollock, and Kline than Peter Upward, who regards his great swathes of thick pigment and P.V.A. not as seismographs of the emotions, but simply as homages to their own self-sufficiency.

In an article such as this there is little room for nonconformists like the surrealists or Leonard French with his raised, gold-leaf encrusted surfaces, richly decorative and somewhat like a mediaeval Leger, and the vegetative abstractionists derived from influences like Sutherland's.

Collage is emerging; Elwyn Lynn has undeviatingly practised texture painting since his return from Europe and the U.S.A., in 1959. In early 1962, however, there burst upon the scene a trio—Ross Crothall, Colin Lanceley, and Michael Brown— called the Subterranean Imitation Realists, who are Australia's authentic Junk and Pop-Art School, assemblers of savage "pictures" and whimsical statues.

In general, sculpture has not been so exciting; it has had a fairly consistent history of figuration (Lyndon Dadswell and Tom Bass are still vital practitioners) and constructivism (the earlier work of Marget Hinder, Robert Klippel, and Gerald Lewers); few have been the expressionists like Danila Vassilieff, but recently there has emerged a more expressive brutalism, a roughness, a Gothic thrust and a return to archaic forms in Marget Hinder, Clem Meadmore, Frank Lamb, and Lenton Parr, whereas sculptors like Stephen Walker and Owen Broughton produce a constructivism modified by evocative, even surreal, overtones. Too often, however, Australian sculpture is unimaginatively derived from the English school of Chadwick, Butler, Armitage, and Moore.

An article such as this can hardly outline the whole scene: our reliance on magazines, our need to travel, our lack of market that has driven Nolan, Whiteley, Arthur and David Boyd, French, Gleghorn, and others abroad, and such facts that no state gallery has a painting from the New York school or from the West Coast, though we do see plenty of English abstraction which is often like seeing American work secondhand. We have a large number of conservative painters akin to those of London's Royal Academy and middle-of-the road painters still producing a repetitive impressionism.

Perhaps it is the isolation, the strange land, the artistically philistine environment, the variety in art itself, that help create the urgency and impact; we agree with Robert Hughes that art in Australia is no mere "cultural activity"; it is "exorcism, a ritual in the dark."

ON AND OFF THROUGH THE YEARS, BY OTTERWELLS ALIVE AND KICKING AS well as by Otterwells tucked away in the family graveyard, the scandal of Great-aunt Fanny had been mulled over with conscious dispassion, and repeatedly put aside like a tricky crossword. There was, anyway, always happening, in this or that Otterwell-dominated part of Tasmania, another Otterwell wedding, birth, or birthday. Or Lent began or school holidays or shearing or a vice-regal visit or the racing season or war or . . . well, tedious external things. No one alive seemed sure how Fanny's prolonged sojourn in foreign territory had started: she herself divulged nothing, but a tattered rumour inclined to some necessary patriotic gesture during the 1914–1918 War. Aunt Ann, being Aunt Ann, had other ideas—unpleasant ones, suggestive of hanky-panky, and diplomatically disregarded. Great-aunt's legendary predicament was a subject as engaging as a pet tortoise; it often came out, like a snail, at night. But it withdrew, pronto, at the merest squeak of new christenings, courtships, or tonsillectomies. Finally, however, explosively out of the blue, Uncle Eustace pronounced a decision: he—he himself—would fetch her back.

In the family, Uncle Eustace was famed and feared for this nineteenth-century forcefulness, this taking-the-bull-by-the-horns Chinese Gordon resolution, as much as he was renowned for being the one Otterwell bachelor, not only for his period but for as far back as records were known. The probity of his bachelordom, with no heart-of-gold barmaid kept in a Battery of Point love nest, and certainly no one or nothing else more dubious kept anywhere, added a dignifying halo to the eccentricity of wifelessness. Who knew what forces galore, untapped by wife, child, hidden sorrow, poverty, or unmentionable vice, still occupied him? For example, at seventy-three, he had just given up Royal Tennis.

On Christmas Eve 1960, after performing a Father Christmas as terrifying as Lear, and while reviving himself with Courvoisier, he czarishly shouted them all . . . even Uncle Hereward who always fidgeted whether to take an umbrella or not, blazing or pouring . . . into believing that they had inclemently abandoned Great-aunt Fanny "among who knows whom," Eustace blared Ezekielly, "among tradespeople, shepherds, mercer's counter-jumpers, journalists! And *exactly* where, who knows, eh? Forty years! A disgrace to us all. While Fergus was alive it was wise to keep mum, eh? But he's been dead for twelve years. Best leave it to me, eh? Pour me another, Varley. Leave't to me, eh?"

"Yes, oh yes, Eustace," they heard themselves cravenly pipe, and would have crossed themselves had they been one of *those*. Eustace was an alarming not-to-be-denied Pied Piper once he got going. They all quickly had another drink. After all, it was Christmas too.

By Candlemas, Uncle Eustace, in Isle of Butte tweeds, point-to-point cap, and pelargonium buttonhole, face pink as sporting paper or baby's, had dominated, sniffling rather and headachy, Fanny's uprooting. It was a chilly day, miles from anywhere respectable. Trees dripped on him as though he were a postman. Her nearest neighbour was a politician with a scruffy Socialist past. She should never, of course, have spent all those years there. She should have been with the family. With the family she would be. Reluctantly, he had to leave her, at the railway station, to travel on, poor lady, with a man with a suspect accent, to Campbell Town where Uncle Eustace proposed to catch up with her next day.

The next day he was unable to keep his appointment because of what he savagely called a summer cold. This so swiftly galloped into danger that on St Valentine's Day he nearly died.

"Completely dying would, in the circumstances, have been absolutely killing," said Gwendoline, young Mrs Ian Otterwell, who concealed a marshmallow heart under a shocker's exterior.

"*And needlessly* ironic," said Aunt Ann, fingering her cameo as though she'd said nothing at all.

Not until Whitsunday was he finally out of bath chairs and his knees out from under afghans, and he fit and pink and loud enough to ask about Great-aunt Fanny. Silence fell. Time dropped a number of stitches. He asked again, more loudly. Evasion was tried: Hereward offered a cigar. Evasion and cigar were roared at. "But . . ." they all began chattering at the same time, disobedient children botching justification, "but Eustace *dear,* but old boy, but Uncle, while you were so very, *very . . .*"

In listening to the dangerous wind keening around Eustace, in listening to the wind that never stopped flowing through the garden of Otterwells, tugging off a leaf, a branch, a heart, a life, they had, one and all, utterly forgotten to keep an eye on Great-aunt Fanny's move.

Not saying they were but unmistakably considering them ninnies, he next day drove fifty-odd miles to see if Fanny were settled in her proper place.

While everybody was telephoning everybody else, there he was, in the family graveyard with its own century-old chapel, peering and poking about, getting cemetery mud on his brogues, trouser cuffs and knees. He returned to the car with the ominous stride of Alexander the Great. He drove back as recklessly as a joy-riding hot-rodder, and held the floor.

The billiard-table-sized Welsh slate slabs roofing the vault, in which Fanny should long ago have circumspectly been, seemed not, he thought, *to have been recently moved.* She'd certainly—he'd seen to that, eh?—been got out of that other wretched cemetery. Perhaps . . . per-*h-a-p-s* . . . he further thought . . . moss in the crevices *could* have been recently disturbed, could indeed have been replaced with a species of commercial piety. But he'd forgotten to take his spectacles; autumn leaves and a Scotch mist had made pure decision difficult. Curse that summer cold!

A telephone call to the undertaker's revealed that he of odd accent, who had been in charge of Fanny's digging-up, train trip and reinterment, had been a short-time employee since returned to Australia. A Mainlander! Eustace gave a terrible shout, and crashed down the receiver. The earth, that great globe, winced. Varley dropped a sugar bowl, fortunately silver. A Mainlander! . . . someone from . . . Carlton was it, eh? Wooloomoloo?

Swiftly as a Terrytoon vegetable, suspicion put on buds, leaves, dire flowers. Uncle Eustace became taller than Abraham Lincoln, and noisier: "The fellow's a jackanapes. Mortician he calls himself. An employer of criminals. Dabbling in cremation like a blasted Hindu, the silly ass. Phonograph music and foam-rubber lilies! Coffins of xylonite . . . plastic . . . whatever the muck is, I suppose, eh? Mortician! Right from the jump I was against his joining the Club. He's like the barber's cat: all . . ."

"Eustace!" snapped Aunt Ann, "There are gentlemen present." She had been a maidenly suffragette with, nevertheless, ears.

In the next few days Eustace occupied himself Napoleonically, very much head-of-the-family, with the minutiae of a grandiose plan. He wrote fiats to everyone, each succinct sentence brutally clear, too specific, too personal to be misunderstood or fobbed off. Intimations of excommunication glittered so ferociously between the lines of his old man's virile copperplate that newer Otterwell wives, the just-read command on Spicer's Deckle still between their fingertips, switched off spin driers or forsook semi-built Constance Spry flower arrangements, and sped in M.G.s to buy trowels or whatever they were. Otterwell telephones were rung, and rang, constantly. Who, my God, last had the crowbar from the potting shed of the old Sandy Bay place? What the hell *was* a mattock? Listen, dear, Varley says we'll be expected to picnic. . . . If you do a double lot of your divine little scones with Gentlemen's Relish, I'll do a double of my special Melting Moments, and we'll interfeed . . .

No one cared to let the side down; no one dared scamp Uncle Eustace's mandates.

On the selected Sunday, from every part of Tasmania, cars packed with tools, food, wicker-clad thermos flasks, children, and their Otterwell parents and relations, moved towards the graveyard. Wound up like a clock, generations ago, the family ethos was so well-oiled, had ticked so surely and sturdily for so long, that it would have been useless as well as traitorous for any member to suggest *I should like to be otherwise, someone else,* or *elsewhere today,* as useless as saying *I should like to be an echidna* or *called Dostoevski.* From faith and habit, non-Otterwells seemed to them as eels must to eagles, however glossy and silver-plated the eel, however like fractured sunshade the eagle. Sheer lunacy this plan of Eustace's, they might think, but ratifiable Otterwell lunacy. We're all in it. So, by ten o'clock, everyone punctual, from Melton Mowbray, St Helen's, Westbury, Huonville, Oatlands, New Norfolk, everywhere, everyone had arrived. It was an autumn day, exquisite for any outing, perfection for one of this nature: nowhere are sunshine, birds, breezes, weeds, more subtly exhilarating to the senses and conceit of the living, than in a graveyard.

HAL PORTER

Fecundity was the first impression—children everywhere; their knowingly unin-habited ink-blue, dead-still Otterwell eyes spotted the air. There seemed double the actual children, for each child had accompanied its own Sunday-go-graveyard self as one extra child simmering unseen to be barbaric and crazed, to flash diabolically aflame past the corner of adult consciousnesses. But, the time early and the occasion touchy, they discreetly simulated severe charm and, speechlessly as nursery rhyme characters on kindergarten friezes, carried buckets, rakes, and Dutch hoes. With their tweedy aunts, with wavering aunts, champagne-bottle-legged golfing aunts, tituping aunts, and Burne-Jones aunts, they advanced towards and grouped themselves below Uncle Eustace who had disposed himself, civic statuelike, on top of the vault to which, in an orderliness obscured by gorse, periwinkle, and pre-Raphaelite Austrian Copper briers, other Otterwell graves lined up.

Even Aunt Ann, inclined to perpetual fractiousness, was momentarily decorous in the group which, standing quietly as waxworks, chins uplifted, listened to Uncle Eustace. Only the oldest aunt, Aunt Beatrice, sat. She sat in a camp chair, centrally front, her bone fingers burdened with diamonds and rubies. The crowd, accidentally dramatic, of overlapping generations had the impermanent coherence of a combina-tion in whose each mind, as much as in the corporate one, lay no mental reservation like a segment of decaying trevally. At least, on this occasion. First of all, beneath their soles lay the boxed scraps of their own dead. Second, many of their houses had once been these dead's, or contained objects wherein the grimaces or half smiles of the dead still lingered—in Wainewright portraits, darkening looking-glasses, on the bumlike curves of silver rose-bowls, in photograph albums containing pressed pansies picked last century by fingers that, then, could write *Otterwell* on a will or a love letter. Third, Great-aunt Fanny, so long a sherry-party joke, now claimed by right of blood this protective picnic, this family prying into her gothic contretemps. Was she here, *now,* below, in her destined niche, filed for reference on the Last Day? That is what the family, through Uncle Eustace, hoped and had jolly well paid for. Or had the Mainland ghoul, obviously with a face caddish as a monkey's, done some-thing too nasty to think of but nevertheless thought of . . . a council rubbish-tip? a lake bed? a stinky fire in a Midland's gully once lair for convict bushrangers?

As they listened to Uncle Eustace avoid putting these outraging possibilities into words, they stared remorselessly at him, their thoughts sprinkling salty glints of anger in their eyes. He, too, began to glint—but he was rebuking *them.* "Moreover," he was saying, "moreover, the graveyard, our graveyard, the *Otterwell* graveyard . . ." He was rubbing it in. ". . . is in a shocking state. Eh? As you can see." As they could see. "Our own people! We are to blame. We! *We!*" They were to blame. "That's why I wrote you all to come prepared to clean up while the vault is investigated. Except, of course, Aunt Beatrice." Aunt Beatrice lifted an ancient jewel-knobbed hand with queenly deprecation. Everyone looked at her as at an unbelievable idol but with sufficient affectionate respect. "There are," continued Uncle Eustace, "enough of us, God knows—eh? In my letters you were each allotted a certain task in a certain section. It took some planning." He paused. He stopped pausing, and made a dangerous remark: "Any questions?"

Before Aunt Ann could uncurl—he knew his danger—he sidestepped quickly, sidestepped authoritively: "*Good*—no questions. Charles, you have the crowbars? Mattock, Greg? Pickaxe? Billhook? Mallet? Bamboo rakes . . . Grace? Varley? Ah, I see you've a trowel, Young Christopher!" Everyone had brought everything asked for, and held them up: *sans-culottes* preparing to march on the Tuileries. Everyone except . . . and Uncle Eustace's eyes narrowed . . . "Your secateurs, Ann?" Aunt Ann's German secateurs were famous. She had not brought them. She tossed her head; no angel, she did not fear treading. *Her* little indigo eyes also narrowed, and flashed wickedly. Level-toned yet sharp, she said, "I have brought Fanny's own silver teapot. I felt it fitting."

To everyone's surprise, Aunt Beatrice said, almost cried as loudly as someone younger, "*No!*" What could she mean? Her old mind wandering, off and away?

Aunt Ann stuck out her chin, whiskery as an as-yet-unshaved youth's at Eustace. It was a mutinous gesture. Uncle Eustace clenched a fist.

"An unseemly disturbance is imminent," whispered twelve-year-old Young Christopher who was wicked, sophisticated, and far too handsome. His cousins sycophantically giggled. "Fie! So early in the day. And before us innocent innocents. Oh, *fie!*"

But Grace, lanky gentle Grace, said gently, "Aunt Ann asked me to bring *our* secateurs, Eustace," and she held them up, high, at the end of her long long long arm, like a symbolic Communist. There secateurs were. Uncle Eustace laughed—oh, quickly and fruitily as a prime minister. "To work!" he shouted, semaphoring mean-inglessly. "To your posts! To work!"

In a geyser of released conversation, of greetings, of hullabaloo and movement, children bursting like grenades from between adults, the group milled and crumbled and scattered. To work all the women went except old Aunt Beatrice whose lilac coloured chiffon scarf was rearranged, one after another by five women. To work all the children seemed to go except the youngest twins with silkworm silk hair who ran about clutching their flies, and squealing, "*We* are to blame. We! We! Wee-wee. Pee-wee. Wee-pee. We pee. We poo. We poo-poo!" Their stately Labrador, its severe head like an heraldic profile or one from an old walking-stick handle, lumbered woodenly as a rocking horse between them. A surfeit of forbidden things to do had lashed them to exaltation.

While the women, garden-gloved or gloveless, worked on paths, headstones, urns, broken columns, sandstone scrolls, granite tombs and cast-iron railings, their un-fettered, faultless voices called in the sunlight above the buried, tongueless skulls.

"My dear, how very kind of Eustace to put me on Digby's grave—I shouldn't admit it with his age so clearly stated, but we were childhood sweethearts. Though he once stole my agate marbles."

"This rose bush must be a cutting from the big *Maman Cochet* at The Grange."

"Shall I scrape all this moss away? It looks so fitting and darling. Or just leave aesthetic enough, like the Japanese?"

"I wish I'd brought my old steel kitchen knife. Men don't *know* about steel kitchen knives."

"What *did* James Frederick *really* die of?"

"I," said Aunt Ann, "shall not pretend that I am at all surprised, but Eustace has allotted me the prickliest grave."

Although these statements seemed merely the trite ones of feckless humans, and utterable by anyone with a tongue, they revealed that the speakers had preserved, throughout their own vicissitudes and those of the world they had been born into, viewpoints and moralities as much of their class as their accents were, and their children. These creatures, in constant motion, had seemingly much multiplied, separating themselves from themselves as amoebae do. They mafficked about with the alacrity of vandals to whom no vandalism was that day permissible. Some, for a while, browbeatenly scratched lichen from headstones, or permitted themselves to be hectored into carrying off pruned brier suckers and Evening Primrose stalks. Otherwise they roamed restlessly outside the cage of adult duty, hampered by miles of undulating paddocks and the obvious infinity of a cloudless sky. Aunt Ann kept on capturing some of them with her fishhook eye and, as other aunts did, mistaking them for their siblings or cousins. Were they, she asked, street arabs or swineherd's waifs crept in through the may hedge? This was surely cryptic humour on her part. Yet, even to aunts and uncles less whimsical than Aunt Ann, there appeared more of these youngsters, who no longer wore sailor suits and knew of *The Windsor Magazine*, than seemed reasonable. The gold-mopped twins, for example, had become a sextuplet, banshee-shrieking by with attendant Cerberus.

Meantime, ponderously and sonorously and warily, the men confronted the paramount mystery of Great-aunt Fanny. Dedicated and daylight Burkes and Hares, they assessed the vault covering. Under their offhand dandyism and leather-patched sports coats was the muscular and maternal brutishness of those who worked with animals and their neuroses and needs, and who fought into submission, just as their women in labour fought necessary pain into submission, the seasons and the earth. These Otterwell males, or males chosen as sires by Otterwell women, had weathered youth, injudicious passions, disillusion, the whims of weather, scandals, and boils on the backside, with concealed and tenderized arrogance. Their manners were perfect, and would have remained so while they killed an enemy or stopped a crucifixion. Tenderly their huge hands and shrewd eyes examined the tomb; tenderly they prodded crevices with crowbars and pickaxes, inviting each other's suggestions to poo-hoo them, before attacking like convinced burglars the vault slabs. With vigour and precision they made the first attempts at prising. These failed. Swearing began. Those who did not smoke pipes offered each other cigarettes, saying, "Christ, eh! She's going to be bloody tougher than we thought. Christ!"

Young Christopher was, of course, in earshot. He possessed a special sense.

"They are blaspheming," he said to his entourage of underling cousins.

"They are blaspheming," echoed the myrmidons and, giggling from trying not to giggle, held dirty hands over their mouths, and stuck out their round bellies farther, and rolled inky eyes.

"They are corrupting influences," Young Christopher continued, "They are immoral fiends and wick-ed monsters. We must inform the sheriff! Yippee!" And he galloped off, being, centaurlike, horse and rider; and the smaller centaurs galloped at his pace after him, caracoling like a posse of goodies behind him, and shrilling like Comanches around the church.

The men made a scarecrow of marble angel with their coats and, thus coatlessly defiant, attacked the slabs again.

Presently, for Otterwell women were deft, most of them had fulfilled Uncle Eustace's behests. On the other side of a raffish rosemary hedge was a handful of humbler graves, not Otterwell. Gwendoline, forthrightly why-notting and dammit-all-let's-do-the-decent-thinging, persuaded others less forthright and more dubious, but amenable to sentimental platitude disguised as decisiveness, to work with her on these alien plots.

With less intensity of feeling they idly toiled, as at an inferior charity, and were so toiling, and placidly deep in obstetrical legend, when a shadow they immediately knew was monitory fell upon their bowed backs, and a fluting astounded voice said:

"Those graves are not *ours!*"

It was Varley, intellectual and perfectionist (her rose garden was a miracle, so were her potted shrimps; she read Elizabeth Bowen), who had just restored Edwin Otterwell's grave almost to the condition it was in 1863 when he had died under a runaway barouche.

"What the hell does it matter, Varley?" said Gwendoline in a contemporary way, softish but boldish, from her kneeling pad. She pushed back a lock of hair to stress barefacedness. "Dammit, let's be decent!"

"Need you swear?" said Varley who really didn't mind a scrap. "I don't think we should interfere."

"With the *dead?*" said Gwendoline lighting a suave cigarette.

Varley was not to be caught. She too lit a cigarette—slowly—and blew out—slowly—an actressy cone of smoke.

"With the dead of others. The dead do not belong to themselves. Graves belong to *others*. Those others should tend them with love. They are not *ours*. Your work, however worthy, is . . . is municipal. There is no love."

"Bosh!" said Gwendoline and, to show unabashment, "*Dammit*, Varley!" Young Christopher would have cherished this but was being immaculately vile elsewhere. All the children were. The twins and their dog, because they had been forbidden the road, were on the road terrifying a rustic Teddy Boy passerby who had intended terrifying them.

Gwendoline spoke again: "Oh, *double* bosh, Varley!" for Varley, towering, had fixed her with a navy-blue look.

Varley said, "Be that as it may. Gwendoline, you've laddered your stocking—left leg."

Gwendoline said, "Damn and *blast!*"

Women said, "Spit, dear."

Who said, "Surely, Varley," yanking out a thistle belonging to an unloved non-Otterwell, "*surely* it's easy to love humanity when it isn't there?"

It sounded a Brontë-ish remark but came, naturally, from Aunt Ann whose magnanimities even had always a dash of vinegar. Varley, who had once published at her own expense a book of poems (*Roses of Silence and Solitude*), looked away, mysteriously as a poetess vouchsafing nothing, and walked away thinking something nicer.

Nearby aunts, older, some, finding it time to suggest to themselves starting a headache as reason for luncheon but mainly cups of tea, drew from their pockets noon-showing enamelled watches they had had since black *moiré* butterfly bows tied back their then-thick-and-coloured hair.

Varley, drifting, saw in the distance, fraily royal under the big Cedar of Lebanon, Aunt Beatrice. Old old aunt, time-shrivelled aunt, had long ago, restless and fretful, left her camp chair. With a trailing totter, she had moved from group to group in her Queen Alexandra manner—the painted and thickly powdered face also; the gracious word dropped vaguely here and there. Yet she seemed touched by the wing of an intangible bitterness, to be seeking wearily, seeking and seeking. Now that the vault was full—or would soon, they hoped, be proved to be, for Great-aunt Fanny had been destined for the last unoccupied niche—perhaps Aunt Beatrice, long the widow of a husband buried at sea, sought a place for herself. She tacked; she contemplated spaces; she tacked again. Certainly, certainly, when next the family gathered she would be underground, bereft of her far too many wonderful old-fashioned rings, of her paint, of her Arabian nimbus of scent, even of her scant flesh. Underground where? Oh, where? She had entered the blue shadows of the cedar, uninterested in the housewifely kneeling, the trowelling and grating and hacking and snipping, the chattering, the bonfire the children were prodding into smoke a paler blue than the cedar shadows. "Joffre Blue," she whispered. It was a colour of her middle years. Tears suggested themselves to her. "Joffre Blue," she was whispering when Varley arrived. "Fanny spilt Indian ink on my Joffre Blue blouse with the pearl buttons."

Using a handkerchief almost all lace she blotted a shallow tear before it furrowed her powder.

"Why, Aunt *Beatrice* . . ." said Varley, coming into the shadow. "Darling, why not come and sit down again? Or should you like to be in the car? Luncheon'll be soon."

Old Aunt Beatrice looked haggard above her chiffon pussy-cat bow of scarf. She spoke with querulous wildness:

"I don't want to be buried *outside*. It's too noisy. Grasshoppers. Omnibuses going past to Hobart. And too much light." Varley knew that she sat always with her back to it, the blinds three-quarter-down. "I want to be in the *vault*. With grandmother and mama and Alexander and Galamiel. Fanny always grabbed everything. She spilt ink on my blouse. She gave my lovely scrapbook to the Orphan's Home. *Without* permission. *She's* in the vault. It's not fair. She doesn't care. Look where she got herself buried the first time. . . ."

Varley was becoming horrified when there was a great calling-out and waving from the men: "It's open! It's open! We've opened the vault!"

Varley looked *Come on, Aunt Beatrice* and held out a hand.

"Leave me here," said the ravaged old woman in the cold shadow. "**Leave me.** I don't want to see . . ." She did not say *Fanny* but grew infinitely fragile.

Varley did not know what to do, and felt larger than a land girl.

"Go away," said Aunt Beatrice, waspish. "Go away and leave me, mean selfish Fanny," said the old woman to Varley.

Within minutes, all of them, husbands, wives, aunts, uncles, children, twins and dog, cynical Young Christopher, flushed Varley, were at the vault.

What ultimately and most and for years impressed the adults was that the name plates on the coffins were completely untarnished, as though they'd been done with Goddard's Plate Powder the day before; this despite the fact that six inches of strange still water that seemed depthless covered the floor.

What impressed the children first was a frog sitting on Galamiel Otterwell's coffin. But that was explicable: water, frog, place for frog to sit when not in water.

What impressed the children most, and nightmarishly until they themselves approached death, were the metallic-green blowflies, fat and important, sulkily muttering as though drunk. Why? Whence? The boys scratched their necks, and did not want to ask questions.

Great-aunt Fanny was not at home.

As, they all said, they had all along all known.

The last niche was empty.

Rage (quite savage) and horror (sickening) overtook the Otterwells, and they edged more closely together. The rage was clear cut at good money paid for what amounted to profanation, at being gypped—the *Otterwells!*—by a Mainland spiv. The horror was an atavistic and family horror that, somewhere—and they were responsible, which increased the horror—a section of their heritage and own lives had been lost as carelessly as a tennis racquet. Otterwells had been sunk in oceans, blown to bits in currently fashionable wars, buried in China, in Père Lachaise near Sarah Bernhardt, in dozens of places, and even Ireland. Those were seemly enough; there was evidence; if tears were to fall they knew which quarter to splash towards. The losing of Great-aunt Fanny was . . . was . . .

HAL PORTER

The men swore vilely, even Uncle Hereward who could rarely make up his mind. Uncle Eustace seemed to be planning something in the nature of a Royal Commission. The sun grew hotter. One aunt, foreseeing endlessness without tea, considered a half faint on a suitably low tomb.

Meantime, where *was* Great-aunt Fanny?

Varley, as always, came first to her senses. Precise and romantic and fervid, with her Otterwell-ink-dark but un-Otterwell-protruding eyes, she twined among them and conspiratorially revealed another truth to them. Presently, in silence, they had all turned their eyes towards the Cedar of Lebanon.

Without a word to each other the women started to move, to subtract themselves from the mingled group, to begin walking towards the cedar.

The men, dividing themselves from the children, moved a few paces after the women, and then stopped. The path to the cedar was not for them. They lit pipes and cigarettes, and turned inwards to each other, backs to the women, backs to the children. Life is not for men.

The children looked down their noses: they had been made to feel like children. They got smaller, starved-looking, even world-weary Young Christopher; they drew together and retreated. There was an impression of walking backwards from an insane world.

The women now began, young and old, to hasten, almost to run stumbling, towards Old Aunt. They had no manly or childish embarrassments; they were female, and of earth. Some began to weep as they hurried but without wiping away the great sweet tears, the soft soft tears, the tears coloured with life and death.

Old Aunt saw them coming, a pack with some appalling information to reveal, and some outrageous deed to do—it must have seemed so to her faded eyes. Yet, for she had been a woman too, she touched her scarf and moved into the sunlight that was less kind to her painted wrinkles, and advanced towards them, fantastic and beautifully hideous. They were upon her; they surrounded her.

"Oh, Beatrice!" they cried, tears streaming down. "Oh, Aunt Beatrice, Great-aunt isn't there! She's not there! Fanny isn't there! Oh, Aunt Beatrice, where *is* Aunt Fanny? Lost! Gone! Not there! Empty! The niche is *empty!*"

Aunt Beatrice knew what they were telling, what gift they had run to bring her in their hands stained with graves. She closed her eyes happily against their happiness for her, yet two old tears, and two more, and another two, ran refreshingly as creeks through the drought of powder.

"*Poor* Fanny!" she said in her ecstasy.

ALAN MARSHALL : *Work in Progress.*
From an Autobiography

I SAT FACING A MAN ACROSS A POLISHED TABLE. HE WAS A HEAVY MAN WHO filled his padded, swivel chair as if moulded into it.

His face was loose and full and revealed no bone structure beneath the flesh of his cheeks and chin. His blue eyes had the steadiness they had acquired from their constant use as instruments of observation. They had lost their power of friendly communication. They had been used too long to look at men and women as parts of a machine dedicated to his advancement to retain what I was seeking.

He wore a tailored, grey suit and a white shirt, washed and starched in some exclusive, suburban laundry. The cuffs of the shirt, fastened by gold links, extended just the right distance beyond the sleeves of his coat.

The skin of his pale hands was as thin as tissue paper. Across the backs of his hands it had loosened into a multitude of wrinkles though his palms were young.

For six months I had been meeting men like him.

He was looking at a letter he held in his hands. He was not reading it; he had already done so. He was searching his mind for words to say to me, words he found distasteful but which his conditioned mind demanded.

I knew the contents of the letter he held; I had written it. It was dated December 5th, 1920.

"Dear Sir," it said, "I see by this morning's 'Age' that you are advertising for a Junior Clerk to fill a vacancy in your office and I hereby apply for the position.

"I am 18 years of age and am an accountantcy student studying for the final examination. I have already passed the Intermediate.

"I enclose copies of four character references. I have no references as to my clerical ability since I have not yet held a position in an office.

"I would appreciate an interview with you when I could furnish further particulars.

Yours sincerely, Alan Marshall."

A year before, when I had begun sending this letter to business men advertising for a clerk, I had included another paragraph:

"Unfortunately, through having contracted Infantile Paralysis in my childhood, I am forced to walk on crutches. This in no way impairs my ability as a clerk, nor does it prevent me carrying heavy ledgers."

I did not receive replies to this letter with its revealing paragraph but failed to understand the reason until my father, worried over this lack of response, read one of my applications.

He held the letter in his hands for a long time then turned it over and looked at the back as if this blank side, too, was important. He returned it to the table and stood looking out the kitchen window to where, beyond the sloping orchard that surrounded the house, the blue dividing range walled the horizon.

He had come to a home in these timbered foothills twenty miles from Melbourne in order that I might study accountantcy. I had won a scholarship at a Melbourne Business College when we lived in the bush and this achievement seemed to my father evidence of a future in which important businessmen would clamour for my services.

Now he was experiencing the reality, a state he had reached with disbelief and shrinking reluctance since it had been forced upon him without preparation from past experience. The outback values of equality and mateship upon which he had been nurtured and which he regarded as permanent aspects of human relationships were being threatened by the attitude of people towards his son. He had missed little of the implications inherent in the stories I told him of my experiences.

He turned to me now and said, "I'd leave out that bit about your crutches if I were you. You see . . . Well . . . If you get an interview you'd be set, I think."

It seemed dishonest to me and I told him so.

"They'll have to find out sooner or later," I argued. "Why shouldn't I tell them at the start so they'll know. If I went to see a chap and I hadn't told him I'd feel crook."

"You shouldn't," he said. "What have you done! You're all right; you tell him in the letter you'll give him all the particulars about yourself when you see him. What's wrong with that? If a bloke wants me to get him a horse that can pull, I'll get him one that can pull. Say it's blind now. Well, I tell him that after he has a look at the horse. One of the best horses I ever had was blind. You don't have to tell them everything till you see them."

"All right," I said.

I began to get answers to my letters. Men wrote asking me to come to their office for an interview. I became familiar with the quick look of surprise that came upon their face when I entered the office, the lowering of the head to my letter which they studied while adjusting their mind to this unexpected development. Then the indrawn breath of decision that lifted their shoulders a little, the meeting of our eyes. . . .

"So you are on crutches, eh?"

"Yes."

I explain why.

"Hm! Yes . . . Unfortunate . . ."

The reasons they gave for rejecting my application were generally clothed in expressions of sympathy, softened by platitudes or unconsciously directed to feeding their admiration for themselves.

So there were some who gained happiness and a feeling of pride in their excuses and some who avoided my eyes as I rose to go.

There was the breezy man with the watchful secretary:

"I know how it is. You can't tell me anything about crutches. I spent three months on them—skiing accident. I had to get driven to work for months."

He looked down at his hands that for three months had grasped the wood of crutches, and he was smiling.

"Don't you get sore under the arms." He was proffering information, not asking a question. "Very few people realize that about walking on crutches. I was red-raw under the arms."

Years, before so far back it seemed like an unpleasant dream, I had been "red-raw" under the arms. Now my armpits were as tough as the soles of feet.

"Yes. That is one of the problems," I said.

The tall man with the military bearing and the grey moustache was more direct:

"I know you won't mind me mentioning your—er—well, physical disadvantages. They are obvious and it would be foolish of me and unfair to you to gloss over them. What is important is that they render you unfit for office work of the type that is demanded today and there is nothing I can do about it. If I may offer a word of advice I think you should learn to make baskets—something like that. I understand there are institutions that teach such things. They are organized to help people like you and they do a lot of good."

My father was standing beneath an apple tree when I told him what this man had said. He heard my story through then clenched his eyes and twisted his face as if suddenly seized by some internal violence he sought to suppress. He raised his face to the sky, brought his two fists up beside it then jerked them downwards as two explosive words burst from him.

"Baskets! Jesus!!"

I found it was useless to argue with the men interviewing me. They resented my efforts to persuade them I could do the job.

"It is very difficult for me to be frank in a case like this," pronounced one man gazing at the fingernails his thumb was testing on the hand curled in front of him, "but I know you would be a person who appreciates both frankness and honesty."

He turned from his nails a moment to look intently at me over his glasses as if a sudden doubt of my right to the claim demanded a still and merciless warning.

I felt an answer was expected of me, a plea for mercy, maybe; a wringing of the hands . . .

"Yes." I said.

"Being crippled, of course, is the trouble." His nails again engaged his attention. "The work here involves carrying heavy account books from the strong room to the desks."

"I can carry ledgers."

"Yes, yes . . . That's all right. But there are stairs."

"I can climb stairs."

He was becoming irritated. Loud and angry words were his method of strengthening a cause weakened by argument but he controlled the impulsion to shout at me and said slowly and distinctly, "You don't understand. The work here demands a strong, healthy body in those I employ. I'm sorry."

He rose and opened the door.

The door . . . The door . . . Doors that were held open and closed behind me—a long parade of doors like shields, held by men barring the way to independence, fulfilment. . . .

Though the attitude of these men towards me varied according to their characters they were bound by a common object—the preservation of their business. Their business was profit, their means of attaining it, efficiency. My crutches suggested inefficiency, a burden that profits would have to carry rather than a promise of their increase.

But the words they said to me gave different reasons.

I wondered what reasons this man would give for dismissing me, this man with the polished table upon which rested an onyx penholder with its two upright pens like horns protecting him. On one corner, framed in polished wood, was a photograph of a woman and two little girls. The woman was dressed in white and she sat on the stone wall of a sunken garden with the little girls leaning on her shoulders, their arms around her neck. It would be difficult to walk to that spot from the big house, a portion of which one could see towards the top of the picture. Crutches would slip in that steep garden.

The man behind the table was finding it difficult to formulate suitable excuses. He returned my letter to the pile beside him. He riffled the letters with his thumb, his head bent sideways to watch as if the height of the pile interested him.

"Yes," he said slowly as if encouraging a decision rising reluctantly from uncertainty. "Yes . . ."

He suddenly patted the pile of letters as if dismissing them then turned to me and said crisply, while resolve was still strong, "I'm afraid you are not suitable for this job."

Having delivered himself of this judgment the need to continue in such a tone must have seemed to him unnecessary. The axe had fallen; why continue to strike!

"I wish I could employ you," he said in more normal tones, "but you just couldn't stand up to the work."

I could usually face these men, observe them almost in a detached way fumbling for the right phrases, but I hung my head before this man.

My father once told me about a horsebreaker he knew who sought to break the spirit of his horses. When he was breaking in a spirited horse he would say, "I'll take him for a long run to get the fight out of him."

I felt like such a horse. A score of men sitting at tables had taken the fight out of me. A tired man on the street had said to me, "When a bloke's got a job he owns a bit of everyone he sees; when he's out of work they've all got the knock on him and all he wants to do is to get away from them."

I wanted to get out on to the street, away from this man paying lip service to generosity. He was waiting for me to speak but I had nothing I wished to say to him. But I spoke. As if to myself I expressed the thought then beating in my mind, "I need the money."

I think he was suddenly pleased that he could now reveal the generosity and kindliness he felt marked his character.

"Oh!" he exclaimed. "Yes . . ."

He put his hand into his pocket and pulled out two shillings but I had raised my head and he put it back when he saw my face.

I could have told him I already had two shillings in my pocket.

An hour before, while waiting to keep this appointment, I had been standing in Bourke Street, my back against the concrete of The Myer Emporium. I was tired and drooped upon my crutches in what was to me an attitude of rest. I watched the people pass—the girls with cloche hats, bobbed hair, and short, formless dresses; the blue-suited men with their starched collars and Borsalino hats. On the roadway, cable trams clanged warnings and strong horses pulled brewer's waggons laden with barrels. Everything that moved had purpose.

Some people looked at me then glanced away. The glance of one stooped old woman was arrested by my appearance and she stepped out of the stream of people and stood in front of me fumbling with her black bag. It was fastened by the grip of two little nickel knobs and these she clicked apart.

While her thin, mottled hand searched within the bag she looked at me with eyes that age had not quite robbed of a youthful candour. Her face was no longer firm but had shrunken into folds and lines of character.

She smiled and said gently, "It's sad that you have come to this but I had a son once and he was crippled and I know all about it."

She placed two shillings in my hand. "It's not much but it will help."

I felt the hot blood in my face. Some people had paused to watch us. I wanted to dissolve into nothingness, to remain hidden forever from people. I put the two shillings into my pocket then took her hand.

"Thank you," I said. "Maybe you will never realise how much your kindness has helped me. I wish everyone was like you."

"God bless you!" she said and she went away.

I stood up. The man behind the table was suddenly relieved that the interview was over and he assumed a friendly manner. He rose quickly to his feet and hurried round to my side of the table with outstretched hand.

"Can I help you?"

"No, thank you. I can manage."

ALAN MARSHALL

CHAPTER 2

I RECEIVED A LETTER FROM THE SECRETARY OF THE DONVALE SHIRE COUNCIL IN answer to one of my applications.

The shire office was in Wallaby Creek, an isolated settlement twenty-eight miles from Melbourne. The hub of the settlement consisted of a general store, a blacksmith's shop, a hotel, and the shire office. This group of buildings were huddled together on the top of a hill, one of the many forming the foothills of the dividing range which lay a few miles to the north.

Around the settlement the cleared paddocks of farms were open to the sun. Beyond them the untouched bush stood guarding the mountains, a barrier of brooding messmate, ironbark, and red box trees awaiting the advancing axe.

The shire office wanted a junior clerk at 25/- a week. The difficulty of getting board in such a place, of living on the wages offered, was all in my favour, I thought. Not many would apply for such a job.

"Is it possible for you to call at the shire office for an interview?" asked the secretary in his letter.

Our house was eight miles away across the hills from the shire office. Father drove me over in the gig. We rocked together over rough dirt roads and talked about the job I felt sure I would get. Father was not so sure.

"Take care you face him in the right way," he advised me. "You can tell how long a man's been out of work by the way he asks for a job. A man just out of work holds his head up. He's confident. The horse hasn't kicked him yet. The bloke that's been out for months is licked before he starts. He walks in like a cattle pup that's been knocked about. Don't do that. You're just as good as he is. Walk in smiling. If he thinks you've been out for a long while he'll just think there's something wrong with you. What's his name, by the way?"

I took the secretary's letter from my pocket and unfolded it.

"Mr. R. J. Crowther," I said, reading the signature.

"Hell!" exclaimed father looking suddenly gloomy.

Mr. R. J. Crowther was a thickset, powerful man with round shoulders and a jutting neck that held his head in advance of his body. He was the only man employed in the office, a brick building with two rooms, and I gathered the impression he disliked his job, was soured by it, and would like to leave. He spoke gruffly but I could see it was a gruffness born of his own discontent and not directed against me.

"You can have the job if you want it," he said shortly. "There's no future in it. It's temporary. We're behind in our rate notices and I need help."

His eyes were not registering details of my appearance. He was concerned with his own problems and I was an interruption.

"You can start in the morning," he said looking at the table as if pondering on the effects of such promptness on himself.

In a moment he raised his head and studied me. His eyes became interested and he asked, "Where will you board? Do you live near here?"

"I am going to find out if I can board at the pub," I said. "Our home is too far away for me to come over every day."

He shook his head and compressed his lips. "It's not a very nice place."

I thought he meant the meals were bad.

"I don't mind what I eat," I assured him.

"No." He had smiled. "I suppose you'll be all right. They might be stiff in their board though. I don't know."

"I'll go in now and find out." The hotel was next door.

"All right. Let me know how you get on before you leave." He changed his tone. "That's your father outside, isn't it?"

"Yes."

"Let him deal with the pub. It would be just as well for you to remain outside, I think."

There were three men in the bar when father entered. He shouted for them. I watched him through the open doorway from where I sat holding the horse.

After a while he began talking to a woman wiping glasses behind the bar counter. She listened a moment then glanced out at me and nodded her head in some confirmation. She began talking to him at length and I felt sure she was telling the usual story of a woman she knew who had a crippled son and how this woman had "tried everything" and how she began feeding him on yeast or something and it "worked wonders."

Or maybe she rubbed him down with a dry towel stiffened through soaking in brine and this "worked wonders." Or maybe the son took sea baths each day and in six months he was walking. Father had heard many such stories.

When he came out he climbed in to the gig beside me and said, "Well, you're set. She'll let you board there for 22/6 a week. She wanted the twenty-five bob you're getting but I broke her down on that. I think she's all right. We'll give it a go anyway. What we'll do—we'll drive home now and get your things and come back this afternoon. You'll have a clean start in the morning then."

We drove home along a road of trees and stony creek beds and birds that I had not seen on my way over. I felt elated, secure, and the world was full of enchantment. It did not matter that the job was temporary, had no future. It was a stepping stone to becoming a writer.

Though I was studying accountantcy I never regarded it as my life work. It was a way of earning a living while I learnt to write. The pieces of paper I carried in my pocket did not bear definitions of bills of lading or promissory notes; they contained descriptions of people, scraps of dialogue, and ideas for short stories I would one day write.

I saw myself sitting in my spacious hotel room writing when all others were asleep. It was this picture that was beautifying the world for me.

The room, when I saw it, was like a box. Father had carried in my bag on our return in the afternoon and left me with a pat on the shoulder. I sat on the iron bedstead with its sagging mesh and thin, worn blankets and looked around me.

The single bed almost filled the entire room. It stood against a side wall, its head beneath a dirty window. Through the window I could see a back verandah littered with an old stretcher, cases of empty beer bottles, barrels, a rusty meat safe, and untidy heaps of straw.

A stained, pine wardrobe beside the bed partly obscured the window and filled the space between the head of the bed and the far wall. At the other end of the room a washstand was jambed against the end of the bed. A kerosene lamp with a smoked glass stood on the washstand beside a porcelain basin decorated with red roses.

A tattered scrap of rug lay on the linoleum-covered floor. In front of the doorway the linoleum had worn away, uncovering a half moon of splintered floorboards to menace bare feet. The room was filled with the damp, mouldy smell of confinement and disuse.

I could never write here. I felt depressed and stepped out into the passageway confronting my door and running the full length of the hotel. A number of doors opened off this passage. Those to the left led into bedrooms; those to the right, to the hotel's public rooms.

The first one to the right opened into the kitchen from where I heard the sound of voices. A man and a woman were talking together.

"If I'd known that before he'd never have touched me," the woman was saying.

As I walked past the doorway the man hailed me. "Gooday," he called.

I turned and went into the room. A huge wood stove upon which rested a number of saucepans threw out heat from a brick-lined recess let into the wall. A table in the centre was covered with cooking utensils and vegetables awaiting attention. Upon the ceiling, dust and fluff sealed by smoke and steam formed a thin, dark fur that a finger could have grooved with a stroke. The air was heavy with the breath of a stockpot steaming on the stove. High on one of the walls a picture of Carbine pleaded against obscurity behind a film of oily grime.

"How're ya goin'?" I greeted the man.

"Not bad," he grinned. "Can't complain."

He was standing at the table peeling potatoes. He was a short, swarthy man with bright, interested eyes and would have been about twenty-five years of age. His black hair was unbrushed. He had no teeth and his lips sloped back into his mouth. His nose hung down over his upper lip forming with his jutting chin a pair of soft mandibles.

The striped, cotton shirt he wore was opened to the waist revealing a hairy, brown chest beaded with sweat. He didn't wear a singlet. His trousers hung precariously from the loose, leather belt around his waist. Their tattered cuffs had slipped over the backs of his boots to the floor so that he trod on them with his heels every step he took.

In the months that followed I got to know him well. His name was "Gunner"

Harris. He was a petty thief from Melbourne, a pickpocket, who between periods in the hands of the police worked on a piecart that stood on the corner of Elizabeth and Flinders Streets.

"The coppers picked me up and gave me twenty-four hours to get out," he explained to me once. "That's why I've buried myself in this joint."

He had lost his false teeth a few weeks before my arrival.

"I was a couple of days on the grog and I threw them up on the grass somewhere out in the paddock at the back. Now I can't find the place. Funny! You'd think a bloke could go straight to them."

This first meeting with him gave me the impression of a different type of man. The picture I had of a pickpocket presented a well-dressed, sharp-faced man with the hands of a pianist. Gunner's hands were not slender; they were square, the fingers wide apart.

I concluded as I looked at him he was a simple, kindly fellow born in some poor Melbourne suburb and driven out here through lack of work.

The woman had been watching me with eyes that must have looked with such appraisal at scores of men. They missed nothing, understood everything.

She was about forty with a full, rich figure that provocatively resisted the confinement of her tight cotton frock. Her eyes were steady and speculative. They contained no warmth. How many betrayals had hardened them! What had they seen in the faces of men that gave them the wariness of a creature about to pounce on food!

Yet, she was pretty. Her smile was attractive.

She was the cook and her name was Rose Buckman. Her husband had left her. ("You can't hold a man in his forties unless he's frightened of you.")

"You're the chap that's going to work next door, aren't you?"

"Yes," I said.

"Born in the bush?"

"Yes." I smiled at that.

"Well, I suppose you've got to come out sometime." She cut the pastry hanging over the edge of the pie dish with quick hands and put the dish in to the oven.

"What's your name?" asked Gunner.

I told him.

"How are you on the grog?" he asked, grinning at me. He threw back his head, raised his hand, and emptied an imaginary glass of beer down his throat.

"I don't come at it," I said.

"We'll soon fix that here," he said. He lifted a dish of peeled potatoes and walked over to the sink to wash them. He turned on the tap and looked back at me while he waited. "We'll soon fix that here, lad."

"What about girls?" asked Rose returning to the table. "Have you got a girl?'"

The question confused me. My cheecks grew hot and I looked away from her.

"No," I said.

"I think, we'll put him on to Maisie," she said to Gunner. They laughed together in some secret enjoyment.

Their interest turned to the girl. "When is she coming up again, do you know?" she asked Gunner.

"On Friday, she told me. Another bunny this time."

"That's Maisie. . . . She never knows when she's on a good thing."

I left them and walked down the passage towards the front, passing the dining room, the lounge with its voices and laughter, and finally the bar. The floor of the passage was uneven and in places gave to my tread as if the supports below had long rotted away.

Outside, a verandah extended the width of the wooden building and here, too, the floor boards were uneven and decayed. The verandah windows were painted green with the word "Bar" upon them in gold. Men were sitting on the two benches beneath the windows. They were resting between drinks while waiting for the arrival of someone who would shout for them. A couple of dogs lay at their feet. Through the doorway of the bar came a babble of men's voices.

A couple of gigs, some wood drays and waggons, and a buggy stood on the gravelled area in front of the hotel. The horses in their shafts stood with drooping heads and half-closed eyes in the summer sun. Some cars had nosed in amongst them and came to rest with their radiators facing the verandah. Beside one of the cars a saddled horse was tethered to a post.

To the side of the verandah was a gateway into the hotel yard. The gate, weather-beaten and broken, had been pushed open and was lying half on its side, one hinge still leg-roping it to the post. Long, dry grass concealed its bottom rail, leaning over and covering it protectively from the sun and rain.

A number of Muscovy ducks lived in the yard. They watched me walk through the gateway, thrusting their heads forward and back in a jerking fashion as they moved away from me. Fowls pecked at the straw and the dry cow dung littering the yard.

A long, thatched stable barred the way to the paddocks beyond. It was built of upright slabs hewn with a broadaxe from the huge trees that once had grown where it now stood. The squared supporting beams rested in the forks of thick, sapling trunks sunk into the ground. Time had weakened their grip on the earth so that they all leaned drunkenly to one side away from the prevailing winds. The whole structure seemed about to collapse with the weight of its thatch from which grass had grown, seeded, and died. A cow stood chewing its cud in front of the divided stable door, the top half of which was open. From inside I could hear the munching of horses.

Beside the stable an enclosure of rusty, galvanised iron bore the word "Gentlemen" painted in white on its side.

All that I was seeing was strange and new. It was intensely interesting like the opening pages of a history book that hinted at adventure in unexplored country.

And yet, the bush in which I spent my childhood was to me the natural beginning of a future; here was the unworthy end of a past.

The people in the hotel had reached an end, too, I thought, just as unworthy as these neglected, decaying buildings. Yet it was the setting that had the voice I wished to hear, not the people to whom I was still an alien. The conversation in the kitchen had been held across a fence and I had no desire to cross it and enter their bare, muddy paddock.

I felt happy out here with the ducks and the horses that had always been part of my life. I felt a reluctance to return to the hotel.

I took out my notebook and pencil and sat on the ground to write but I became lost in mind-created stories I couldn't put down, and when I rose to go in to tea there were only two sentences added to my notes.

"The Muscovy ducks were white like snow. Dirt never clings to the wings of birds."

ALAN MARSHALL

DONALD R. STUART : *Up from the Dust*

One Aspect of the Question of the Aboriginal

How to start? No, not how to start this article. There is an editorial wastepaper basket for articles that start wrongly and continue so. How to start a journey up from the dust, a journey of a small segment of a broken people, a people whose land has been taken over by an all-powerful alien conqueror, a hardfaced, clever conqueror with waves of people, wonderful tools, strange new skills, new wealths, and no respect, no slightest regard, for the age-old customs of the land. How to start? A difficult question, but it had to be answered, or the ancient people would go the way of so many of their race, into the outer darkness of extinction. All over the continent of Australia, since the first European permanent settlers arrived in 1788, the Europeans had pushed the aboriginal people aside, and in the island state of Tasmania the nineteenth century saw the complete extinction, or extermination, of the Tasmanoids who were, for all practical purposes, the same people as the mainland Australoids.

The whitefellers of the late eighteenth, the nineteenth, and the early twentieth centuries had made tremendous material progress, but even their earliest muskets had been more than a match for the spears and boomerangs of the blackfellers. They brought with them from Europe something much deadlier than firearms, however, in the form of diseases against which the blackfeller, isolated for who knows how long from the rest of humanity, had no defence. Measles, the common cold, mumps, scarlet fever, chicken pox, were hideous plagues for the blackfeller, and deaths were numbered in hundreds, among a people whose small tribal communities rarely averaged more than a thousand souls. Was it a lack of defence against the new diseases, or was it the blackfeller's habit of lying out, hardly, in almost all weathers, so that the fevers of the whitefeller abed and warmed, wrought havoc on the chilled and weakened blackfeller? It is a point of interest, but the blackfellers died.

As the explorers, the pioneer sheep and cattle men, the prospectors, moved ever farther on from the fertile coast towards the arid interior there were skirmishes, but always the European settlement progressed, always the blackfeller, no match for the whitefeller, fell back from his once proud position of custodian of the land to the position of ill-used agricultural and pastoral labourer. Perhaps nowhere in the world, at any stage of mankind's ceaseless travelling and venturing forth, has such a clash of very advanced and very backward cultures taken place. We know, roughly, the social and economic organization of the whitefeller, 1788 to today. Let's see some faint glimpse of how the blackfeller had organized his affairs, before the great invasion.

First, it must be noted that Australia has no indigenous plants from which harvest can be taken sufficient to carry a farmer through to the next harvest, and it has no indigenous animal capable of draught or saddle work. Secondly, the continent had been entirely unconnected with the ancient massive civilisations of Asia, Africa, Europe, and the Americas. These factors, understandably, had led to the preservation intact of the oldest way of life, the way of the parasitic food gatherer. What the earth brought forth of animal and vegetable, the blackfeller gathered, and moved on. He had the spearthrower, the boomerang, the spear, the digging stick, the oval wooden dish, and little else of material things. He went naked, he made no house except a lean-to or at best, in a few areas, a wattle and daub structure, hemispherical and not big enough to stand in, he roved his tribal territory in small hunting parties, and was seemingly as primitive in his ways as the emus and kangaroos that were his largest game. To almost all Europeans he was, and to most he still is, the most backward of all humanity's many backward peoples. But beneath the terrible austerity and frightening poverty of his material life there flowed, and among some segments there still flows, a hidden river of immense wealth of social organisation, of philosophy, of deep and beautiful thinking about Man and his relationship with the rest of the Universe. The blackfeller did not regard himself as master of the environment in which he found himself, but he did not go to the other extreme and regard himself as a miserable worm too sinful for anything but woes and tribulations here and eternal hellfire later. He placed himself somewhere not at the centre of the vast plain, but somewhere off centre, and as he could regard all other manifestations of Life, so those manifestations could regard him. His creation myths, illogical and unscientific as are all the creation myths of mankind, were full of the idea that life is of itself good, strong, beautiful, meant to endure forever. The heroic figures who laid down the world that is were men of greater than life size, they were Kangaroo Men, Emu Men, men of many kinds; and the ceremonial reënactment by the blackfeller of the great journeyings and wondrous creation feats of those old, ever-present, all powerful heroes was sufficient, in the blackfeller philosophy, to ensure that all the natural species, vegetable and animal, would continue to thrive and be available as food. The generation of offspring, human offspring, was the result of spirit children, who were waiting to be born, taking up their abode in a woman, there to be grown and brought forth. There were localities that were frequented by these spirit children, and a pregnant woman knew from which locality her child had come. In her journeyings she had passed near some such locality and she or her man had "dreamed" the child into her womb. Though it is unlikely that the blackfeller was unaware of the biological facts of life, his myths concerning pregnancy are perhaps more beautiful than the European cabbages or stork illogicalities and no more illogical.

Being part of the natural world, with no means of influencing his environment other than magico-religious means, the blackfeller was not arrogant. Being poor in all material things, and richer than most other humans in things of the nonmaterial world, he had no need of any form of money. Being dependent on his status as a member of a group for his share of the esoteric, spiritual life, and for his very exist-

DONALD R. STUART

ence as a living being, he made for himself a kinship system that made every man, woman, and child a relative. His system had no orphans where all a man's father's brothers were his father. (Rather, there was—is—one word for all such men, though every man knew his own biological father.) Mother's sisters were Mother, Father's sisters, aunts, Mother's brothers, uncles, and so throughout all the community. Every man was tied with indissoluble bonds to all his fellow humans, his privileges and obligations were laid down and changed as he grew from childhood to adolescence and the varying degrees of manhood, and never were his privileges more than the others could perform, never were his obligations greater than he could bear. His life was hard, the social code was strict, his position always sure and such as a true man could accept with pride. It was a static organisation, formalised, stylised. No man could rise to power over his fellow men, no man could accumulate wealth in a land that gave just enough for each day, no man could set himself apart. All men had access to the heritage of myth and ritual and ceremonial. It was a brittle organisation of a people who had come to terms, to a perfect balance, with a harsh environment. It was a logical and most beautiful organisation, unchanging, and as brittle as spun glass. At the first contact with the whitefeller's competitive, materialistic system, it shattered. There could be no middle ground; the blackfeller could not move from his immemorial position without a major severing of all the finely tied bonds that held him to his land and his people, and the whitefeller had a mandate from his God to bring to the savage *all* that he brought. That the blackfeller should lose and the whitefeller should win was inevitable.

By the fourth decade of the present century, the position in the Pilbarra district, in the North West Division of Western Australia, was that the blackfellers were station hands, musterers, and general roustabouts on the sheep and cattle stations, at an average wage for adult males of £1 to £1.10.0 and sustenance, with their women employed as domestics, unpaid. Many of them were prospectors for alluvial tin and alluvial gold, but none had achieved the financial status of even the poorest grade of unskilled whitefeller, and all were illiterate. Many families of part-blackfeller, part-whitefeller descent had managed to pull themselves up to a position of semiacceptance, on the fringe of the whitefeller's world, and living on the fringes of his townships.

By 1945 a few, a handful, of blackfeller men, knowing that the position of their people was intolerable and was growing worse, planned a strike, a withdrawal of their labour from the sheep and cattle stations. They were aided in their planning by a whitefeller, Donald McLeod, a man who had tried hard to bring the part-aboriginal people to protest against their lot but had failed. In the fullblood black-fellers he found men who would believe in him and in his grand visions of a black-feller cooperative venture that would dominate the entire North West Division. The strike, which was a serious blow to the pastoralists, was a success. The blackfellers had learned the strength of unity, and the long wait from the start of the plan until its execution, a delay dictated by the tactful necessity of waiting for the war to end, had welded them, some six hundred souls from stations spread across thousands of square miles, into a homogeneous people of some twenty different tribes and as many languages.

Police action against the blackfeller leaders, imprisonment, contempt, and their only half-successful efforts to support themselves by hunting kangaroos for their skins, daunted the people not at all, and as the pastoralists slowly learned to do without their previously invaluable talents as bushmen, the blackfellers learned a new way of making a living. If they could not make the station owners acknowledge their worth, they would go along a different road. For years a few of them had been making a sketchy living at yandying alluvial gold and alluvial tin, and in 1950, after almost four years of privation and semistarvation, the strikers decided to go, all of them, yandying. The yandy is a narrow, long-oval dish, traditionally of wood, but nowadays almost invariably of sheet iron, which was used in early times as a dry gravity separator of edible seeds from husks, of termites from crushed termite nests, and of edible bulbs and corms from their casings. The blackfellers had learned to separate alluvial tin or alluvial gold from soil and small rocks, and now in 1950 hundreds of them, in scores of small parties, went out after gold and tin, at a score of old alluvial workings. From their main camp twelve miles from Port Hedland they moved across the face of the land, and in nameless gullies and on isolated flats, by dry creeks and jumbled hills, in barren fastnesses or rock and spinifex, and by old abandoned tin fields that had been famous in the nineties of last century, they sought gold and tin. They won these metals in quantities sufficient to prove to themselves that they could exist, as a viable cooperative venture, and even the most faint-hearted knew that they were on the road to those grand successes that their whitefeller friend, Donald McLeod, had painted for them in glowing words. "Let the whitefeller world condemn McLeod," they said, "he is the saviour of the blackfeller." By the time their mineral-getting ventures were flourishing and prosperous the mineral wolfram had become eagerly sought after by the world's metal dealers, and at last the group found a great patch of wolfram, in difficult country some seventy miles southeast of the township of Marble Bar. After enormous vicissitudes, which were the daily portion, and had been for years, of all the people, a camp of several hundreds of them was established near the junction of the Nullagine River and Cooke's Creek, at the centre of the new find. Many thousands of pounds' worth of wolfram was won by the most primitive of methods, with pick and shovel, hammer and gad, knapping hammer and the yandy. Soon the first great dream came true with the buying of an old derelict station, Yandeyarra, some one hundred miles south of Port Hedland, for a base from which to operate. At the same time, McLeod joined with a South Australian company promoter to form a company to work the wolfram field. But though a great deal of mining machinery was carted to the field, no full scale mining took place before McLeod and the South Australian interests quarrelled. Litigation, the curse of the penurious, soon followed, and the case dragged on, through minor and major courts, until the South Australian company fell to pieces

DONALD R. STUART

and the blackfellers were left holding only a fraction of their former wolfram ground. Meanwhile wolfram had become unsaleable, and McLeod, who had welcomed a handful of earnest white helpers, quarrelled with them all, and he was left in full charge of the destinies of hundreds of Souls, and with mounting debts, rapidly failing mechanical transport, no credit, and a stirring—a slight, almost inaudible, unseen stirring—of a spirit of unrest among the blackfellers. By the end of 1954, the blackfeller cooperative, of which all the assets of land, vehicles, mineral holdings, etc., were in McLeod's name, was hopelessly and irretrievably in debt, and more than half the people, disillusioned, left to go battling on their own in small parties and family groups as tin and gold prospectors.

After incredible hard times, and the formation of a new company, Pindan Pty. Ltd., to replace the Northern Development and Mining Coy. Ltd., the group, now greatly reduced in numbers but still seeing great visions, discovered a major deposit of manganese about a hundred miles east of Port Hedland. McLeod entered into negotiations with a Sydney firm of metal merchants, and an agreement was made, whereby Pindan and the Sydney firm established a third company in which each held fifty per cent of the shares, to work the deposit. Again a quarrel, again litigation. Finally, under the leadership of some of his staunchest lieutenants, the main body of opinion turned against McLeod, and he was forced to resign his position as managing director of the group's affairs. He left, taking with him a splinter group which today operates in the Roebourne area, some one hundred and thirty miles down the coast from Port Hedland. The splinter group and the main group have been at law intermittently ever since the split, and neither group seems to be doing more than keeping its head above water long enough to take another gasp of air. What the future holds no one knows. The main group now accepts advice and some guidance from the Native Welfare Department of the State Government, but the Roebourne group is still most bitterly opposed to anything that savours of "Gov'ment." There is, from the main group's Port Hedland camp, some attendance of children at the State primary school, but none from the splinter group to the Roebourne State School. Each group is in the position of having lost the original dynamic, and each is now more concerned with the pressing problems of survival as a group than with the original dream of a bloodless social and economic revolution. Ahead, undoubtedly, lie hard times, and perhaps further protracted, expensive, and time-wasting litigation. The future is cloudy and uncertain, and meanwhile the mineral resources of the Pilbarra, resources of iron in thousands of millions of proven tons, and of copper, manganese, asbestos, and a dozen other minerals, are being exploited by companies ably led in a most efficient and businesslike manner. Each year the old vision of a self-supporting, prosperous, and advancing blackfeller community grows dimmer. But as one old blackfeller, illiterate and marked by privation and deprivation, said to me, proudly, in lame English, "Well, youngfeller, win or lose, wefeller never gonna be sheepdog again."

I remember them with pride.

Tanapa, a desert man, of the Mandjildjarra people, on first seeing the Indian Ocean: "Hah! Big one!" Then, thinking of the long troughs where the cattle came to drink at the windmills on Warrawagine: "He got chement unner'neath, longa bottom?" Toodjoobalguñ, no more than about eight years old: "I been strikin' man all my life!"

Moorandi, fine old thinker, who said, " 'Sim'lation? That whitefeller Dave been tell me he mean 'swallow 'em up.' Wefellers, blackfellers, you can't be swallow us up, we just human people, same as youfellers."

Willalang, Manapoortja, and a hundred more, veterans of hungry days and empty-gutted hungry nights, of long traverses on foot in waterless country by rocky hills and shadeless plains, the temperature 120°F. in nonexistent shade. The women, staunch through all their bewilderment, the children, large-eyed, dusty, solemn. The old people, cared for, sharing what meagre ration of necessities had been won. The spirit of the camps, the acceptance of hard times and hunger, the endurance, the hope, the bitter disappointments as their dreams came tumbling down around their feet. Their pride in being a People. I remember them, in pride and humility.

DONALD R. STUART

THE TWO WOMEN WERE SITTING BY THE OPEN DOOR OF THE PUG HUMPY, looking out on to the red clearing that protruded like a headland into a sea of mallee. In the dead calm under the noon sun, that sea and the drought-bare paddocks were as tremulous with heat haze as the wings of the famished hawks hovering above them. Upside down on the far horizon stood trees of mirage.

A dog barked, and the thin woman with the baby started.

"If only he'd sleep o' nights!" she murmured wearily as she fanned the flies from his pale face. " Sh, sh! Lenny go bye-bye. Sh, sh, sh!"

"Ah, yer worritin' too much abaht 'im," the older woman said, "jest acause h'es yer first an' 'e give yer a bad time. Still, dearie," she added in a sincerer tone, "he *should* be gainin' weight."

"I can't *help* worrying; he won't take the breast now, and the cow's milk doesn't seem to do him any good. Jim says he needs goat's milk; we're trying to get a goat, you know, from Adelaide. No, I can't help worrying; it's worse when Jim's away all day—I'm just waiting *all* the time for the sun to set. This place is so lonely and empty after the town—it frightens me."

She was silent awhile, looking hard at the nearby mallees and fighting against the feeling that their motionless leaves were listening menacingly.

"And the blacks," she went on, "they scare the life out of me; they seem to pop up out of the ground, I never see them coming."

The grey-haired woman's features darkened:

"They're not 'uman, dearie, that's wot I say. And yer can't be too keerful of 'em. I always keep two guns loaded, 'andy by. Treacherous! Every one of 'em! I 'ate the sight of 'em. But my boys are the ones for the blacks: they shoot 'em like dingoes— every time they find a cow speared, or a sheep. They keep away from *our* homestead, I can tell yer."

With a horrified expression, the young mother said:

"Oh, Jim'd never do that. I . . . I like their babies, but the men . . . I'm frightened of the men; they're so fierce looking and . . . and they smell . . . ."

Though she was still fanning the baby, beads of sweat were oozing from his forehead. Just as she leaned over to wipe them off with a little towel, a crow on the ridge of the thatched shed gave a sudden cry, a ka-aak that dwindled away as if it were being slowly strangled.

The young woman shuddered:

"God above!" she cried, "those birds give me the horrors."

II

"You'll do what I tell you," the big man roared. The boy began to whimper.

"God in heaven! Jean, if he don't stop that whining, I'll belt his ears," he snarled, and added bitterly, "Five years old and can't gather eggs! God! Neil Simpson's young Jackie can ride a horse already. I can't stand a leaky watermelon of a kid. Shut up, boy!"

"But Lenny's frightened of the clucky hens, Jim. Don't be angry with him. I'll get them."

"You get those eggs at once, boy," the man demanded, dragging him by his puny arm to the door of the fowl house, "and shut up that damned snivelling!"

The child burst into loud sobs.

Flushing deeply, his father gave him a sudden slap across the mouth.

"Jim, oh Jim!" the mother cried, and took the child into her arms.

Without a word, the man strode off into the sundown.

III

His mother stood on one side of the pony's head, holding the bit ring, his father on the other.

"Are you sure it's safe, Jim? Are you sure it's safe?"

"Yes, yes," he replied impatiently, "she's an old pony and she's used to kids. God, he's got to learn to ride *some*day."

"But . . . but . . . he's only eight, and . . . ." He ignored her, saying to the white-faced youngster:

"Now, hold the reins like this. See? And don't jerk them. Just lean forward and clap your heels in to her, and she'll canter. When she trots, just hang on to this monkey-strap. See?"

Lenny licked his trembling lips.

"Yes, Dad," he breathed.

"All right, off yer go!" And the man smacked the barrel-bellied pony on the rump. In a moment it was cantering smoothly along the green track that bordered the wet stubble. The father's eyes lit up.

"Not bad! He's not sittin' bad, Jean. Jest holdin' her in nicely, too!"

When the pony drew near the fence, he shouted:

"Yer doin' a good job, Lenny. Now pull your near rein—jest a little, not hard, *not hard*!"

The pony swerved to the left, and the boy shot over its head to fall in a soft patch of paddymelon.

"Jerked it!" the man said, disappointed. "But that's nothing." And he ran to head off the runaway. Catching it easily, he led it back. The boy gave a scream.

"Gord! is he *hurt*?" he asked anxiously.

His wife, kneeling by the boy, looked up, wide-eyed.

"He's scratched his leg, it's bleeding!"

The father looked at it and frowned:

"Get up, kid, and this time don't jerk your rein. Pull it slowly. Hold both reins in your left hand, and then turn it slow, like this. See?"

The boy blubbered:

"I can't! I can't get on again. I *hate* horses. I doan wanna learn to ride."

Snivel ran down his upper lip, and the man barked:

"Wipe yer nose, and get up on to this pony."

"Mummy!" the boy cried, turning to her, "Mummy!"

"You were doing fine," declared his father, biting off each word, trying hard to be patient. "Now up into the saddle, and you'll soon be able to ride like young Jacky Simpson."

"I don't want to!" he sobbed. "I can't stop him!"

"Oh, Jim!" sighed the mother," he might break his arm next time."

"Tommyrot!" her husband exploded, "the ground's as soft as butter, after the rain. You're making a milksop of him." And peremptorily he ordered his son to climb into the saddle. At that moment the pony shook itself. Lenny gaped at it and almost screamed:

"I can't!"

His father lifted his boot, as if he were going to kick him, and then turned away silently and, with the reins in his hand, trudged back to the new stable, slowly, so slowly that the pony was able to graze on the green wild oats that grew knee-high on the fallow beside the track.

Hand in hand, the mother and son followed, lagging behind, just out of earshot.

The swelling sun dropped below the rim of scrub; a mopoke hooted from a native pine.

IV

The school—it had formerly been a storeroom—still smelt faintly of mice and wheat.

Lenny was sitting up straight at the smaller of the two long desks, waiting for the teacher to speak to him. Since she was busy writing the next day's sums on the blackboard, he turned to watch the ponies canter past, some carrying two children, one carrying three. Last of all came Jackie Simpson on his tall iron-grey.

"Lenny, come here!"

He walked up to the table, and stood there, hanging his curly head.

"Stop fiddling with that button!" she snapped. "I'm absolutely disgusted with you, Lenny Delafield. I don't know what's come over you; you've been sulking for over a month. You used to be top of the school, and now you're near the bottom. Well, your parents pay me to make you learn. *Learn*, do you understand? So, you can stay in every afternoon till you get your sums and spelling right. Now, get back to your seat."

And she took out her copy of *David Copperfield* and began to read with great relish.

After a while Lenny ceased his scribbling, and stared about him: over there was the shelf of grubby books, above it the three maps, there the picture of Queen Victoria, and next to it the six fretwork saws hanging on the wall, and by the fireplace in the corner, was the little platform where he had so often stood to sing and recite. This, the scene of the only victories he had ever won, in the days before clever Johnny Wheaton came to the school.

Suddenly he burst into tears.

"You needn't imagine you'll get out one minute sooner," scolded the teacher, in her deep voice. "Try to be a man. A boy of twelve blubbering like a girl with a broken doll! You ought to be ashamed of yourself."

Not till she made to get her cane from the cupboard was he able to stifle his sobs.

"And do another hundred words for interrupting me," she snorted, and went on with her reading.

V

After the auction, his father slipped away from the crowd and went over to the piggery where, himself unseen, he watched various neighbours drive off the sheep and cattle, and strangers lead away the horses; a bearded German, called Karl, was the last to leave, with the stripper hitched behind his bright blue wagon.

When flocks of ringnecks were settling in the mallees and the afterglow in the east was as pink as the breasts of the circling galahs, Lenny went up the rise and stood awkwardly beside the grey-haired man who was drooped against the wall, his forehead resting on the top slab.

"I'm sorry, Dad," he muttered, "I'm sorry, but I just can't understand it. You cleared the land, you built the house and the sheds, you *paid* for the place, and they've taken everything—not only the *new* block!"

"I paid far too much for the new land," his father answered hoarsely. "That bank manager talked me into it, the oily cow. And I wanted it, too—for you ter have when you marry. Then I borrowed to stock up and pay them off quick. That's why the last drought knocked me. I run me neck into a noose, son, I run me neck into a noose. A noose!" Then, in a choking voice, he added: "I don't seem to have done nothin' right since the day Mum died."

"And can't we work the land, can't we even stay here?"

"No, the bank's puttin' in a young couple to manage it."

"Where . . . what will we do?"

"We're stony-broke, Len," his father said quietly. " 'cept for a few sovereigns I got put away. We'll 'ave to go share-farmin' or contractin'. They reckon there's lots a work in the South East."

"*But the place was ours!*" the young man cried passionately. "They can't take everything—not the new house you built; you *paid* for it!"

"They've took it," his father said bitterly. "An' Mum never even seen it finished."

"She woulda liked the plaster walls 'nd the wooden floors," said Lenny softly and slowly; "She always wanted them things."

　　　　　　　　　　　　　　　　　FLEXMORE HUDSON

"Yeh, she woulda liked the walls . . . ." and, after a long pause, the old man added, in a strangled voice, "and the floors, too."

From far above there came the cries of swans.

Lenny looked up and, with difficulty, made out the dark arrowhead on the sky.

"That's a bonzer sound," he murmured sadly. "They're off to the Murray to nest."

"Yeh. They got somewhere to go."

VI

The dance had been rowdy: a sly-grogger was hawking wine in the scrub at the back of the little hall and, as a result, there was a fight after almost every dance, and a good deal of hooliganism during the lancers, too. Whenever a dance was announced, the young men rushed wildly across the floor to the row of seats against the wall where the girls were sitting; consequently, he had managed to get only two dances with Rhonda—he was too slow and too easily brushed aside.

But since she lived next door to the farm he and his father worked, she let him take her home in his buggy.

At the slip-rail he tied up the horse.

"Come for a walk by the lake first," he begged. "I want to tell you something—something important. Come on, it's not cold."

"I'm awful tired," she pouted. "Oh, all right!"

Its being midsummer, the wheat harvest nearly finished, the lake at the boundary fence was dry, and the dead trees, and the detritus that had been immersed throughout the winter, were now all encrusted with crystalline salt, suggesting fantastic images and dazzling white under the large moon.

At last he plucked up courage to stroke her lustrous red curls; then he took her hand and, blinking into her blue eyes, stammered:

"It's . . . I love you Rhonda. I . . . you're the only girl I ever loved . . . . I've loved you ever since we come here. I . . . I work hard and . . . I've saved some money. I was hoping . . . couldn't we walk out together?"

She stared at his sensitive face and short, weedy form.

"My, you're a sudden one, ain't yer?" she gurgled, and, with a toss of her red curls, she burst into peals of laughter that put to flight some straw-necked ibises roosting in a ring-barked gum on the far side of the lake.

Afterwards, while they were walking to her homestead gate, she apologised lamely:

"I didn't mean to hurt you like that . . . but, yer see, Len, you was so suddenlike, and yer not my . . . I mean, we're kind o' different . . . I mean yer don't ride in the shows . . . and yer don't dance much, and . . . ."

He swung the gate open.

"Good night, Rhonda," he choked, and, turning away, went back to stand by the lake and stare at the skeleton gum.

VII

The magenta afterglow was fading into the ultramarine of a starry summer night; uttering their weird, lancinating shrills, the early bats were swooping about the clump of native pines.

After the children were called from their play, the old man, carrying a bucket of milk in each hand, limped over to where Lenny was stripping his last cow in the shadow of one of the pines.

He put down the buckets, pared some tobacco from a black plug and rubbed it in the palm of his hand. Then he went on with the conversation begun that afternoon while they were stooking.

"It's a good offer I'm makin' yer, Lin. Fifty-fifty. And later on yer can buy the farm. I'm gittin too ould to manage thim both."

"No thanks, Mr. Malone," Len said, embarrassed. "I'm satisfied working here for you."

"But, man alive, yer don't want ter be workeen fer a boss all yer life. Haven't ye any ambition? Aren't ye afther wanteen a place of yer own?"

Len looked away from the kind blue eyes.

"I dunno," he muttered. "I don't seem ter care about nothin' much."

"Ye'd have ter do a bit o' bacheen on yr own, an' sure it might be hard goeen for a while, but the land's good, an' there's plinty o' water on it. What do ye say, eh?" And he spat at a hen that was noisily settling down to roost in the branch overhanging the cow.

"I dunno, Mr. Malone," Len replied hesitantly. "I been here five years with yer now. I'm kind of used to everything here, at home like. And the work comes easy. It does me."

The old man was disappointed.

"Well, it don't seem natural to me," he grumbled; "ye jist work and work, an' ye never go to the town, an' ye niver go to a dance at all. It's thirty-three ye are, isn't it?"

Len nodded yes.

"Thin ye ought ter be married, Lin."

Pointing with his pipe over his shoulder to the limestone homestead on the rise, he went on:

"Reckon my girl'll be wanteen another husband: it's two years, it is, since Roy died."

He paused and spat again.

"Och, that's a terrible way to die! Puffed up like a drowned sheep. An' now I'm dead scared every summer that one of the wee scuts'll tread on a snake."

He was silent a while, apparently listening to the kookaburras that nested in the polled blue gum at the foot of the yard.

"An' the kids are all struck on ye, ye've got 'em eateen out of yer hand. An' yer're fair gone on kids, ain't ye?"

FLEXMORE HUDSON

"Yeh," Len replied, and stood up. Picking up the milking stool in one hand, the bucket of milk in the other, he walked slowly across the yard, beside the bearded, old man.

From time to time, the two figures approached one another, and then drew apart, as each picked his way in and out of the slops of fresh manure.

"Yeh," Lenny murmured, "I'm gone on kids all right."

VIII

The red-haired youngster raced onto the verandah, shouting:

"Lenny's back, Mr Delafield's back!"

The old couple and their daughter and her three girls hurried out of the kitchen. Lenny put his bags down and shook hands with Mr Malone.

"So ye're back, Lin! Come in out o' this stinkeen heat."

Lenny tripped over the doormat and then flopped into the canvas deck chair.

"Too light and too short!" he said bitterly. "They even knocked Bill Travers back."

"Och, Linny!" put in the old lady, as she handed him a glass of water, "there's better things to be doin' than murtherin' people with guns."

"Thanks, Mum. That was bonzer."

"But, Mum," her daughter objected, "if we don't beat the old Kaiser, them Germans'll come out here and bayonet our babies the same as they been doing in Belgium."

Her father spat.

"Och! I don't believe a word of it. All paper talk!" And he forestalled a contradiction by adding hurriedly: "Had ter shoot two more horses, Lin—Tig and Dapple. Sand! Couldn't stand seein' 'em roll round with the pain of it any longer."

There was a long silence broken only by the cries of squabbling crows.

"And I been feedeen the seed wheat to the cows. One of 'em's got the bloat—Daisy. We'll have ter put a knife in her, Lin. There she is now."

They listened to the faint mooing.

"My old Daisy! Let's look at her!" And Len walked outside, followed by the stooped, old man, who mumbled, as they passed a dead calf:

"Flies and crows! Flies and crows, the only ones that's doeen any good now!"

The encircling red plain lay bare with drought; far ahead of them a red willy-willy, high as the hazy, blue hummocks behind it, whirled across the empty paddocks and the shimmering lagoons of mirage. The bare roofs of the sheds looked like crows' nests.

"Fed the horses every bit o' thatch, Lin. Och! 'nt's meself'll niver be caught again without a couple o' good haystacks. Five quid a ton fer straw, they're askeen in the township. Wicked! Wicked! An' there's thim agents from Yorke Peninsula and the South East buyeen up sheep fer a song, makeen fortunes!" He spat again, in disgust.

"My old Dad was always talkin' of goin' to the South East," Len said thoughtfully. "One of these days I'll take a trip down there. They say the water lies about in the lakes all through the summer."

As they climbed through the rails, Lenny swayed and slipped on to his hands and knees.

"Glory be!" the old man cried, after giving him a hard look, "ye've been drinkeen, Lin! An' ye've niver touched a drop in all these years!"

Uncomfortably, the other answered:

"Bill Travers was feelin' a bit low after we come out o' the drill hall. Said he wanted a drink. I had some, you know, just to keep him company. Gin, it was." Shaking his head, he added, with a grin, "Queer feelin', ain't it? He-he he!"

"Gin! Ah, that's the terrible stuff, gin! Me ould father died of it. Gin! If ye're goeen ter drink, man, stick to beer, stick to . . . ."

The swollen cow lying in the corner of the yard interrupted with a long moan.

IX

As he drove off, his friend called out:

"Now don't go purrin' up to the old battle-axe! Ha, ha! See yer next Saturdee, Len."

Lenny almost pranced down the track that led between rows of polled sugar gums to the severe-looking stone farmhouse. He chuckled as he thought of his afternoon in the pub. He had spent every penny of his earnings, but he had met some decent blokes and had some good laughs. He felt free, free as the wind rippling the paddocks of young barley all around him. He could see, silhouetted against the saffron sundown, the farmer and his wife milking in the yard by the orchard. Recklessly, he decided not to help them, for, after all, it was his day off.

He sat down by the stove in the kitchen and something—perhaps the glumness of the room—set him thinking sadly of the days when the old Malones were alive and he knew what it was to be welcome.

In scampered little Mary, the Grays' five-year-old daughter. She came to him prattling, and he smothered his sadness to pick her up and bounce her on his knee. Then he sang her "A Froggie Would A-wooing Go" in his light shaky voice. She was laughing happily when the wire door was flung open and Mrs Gray stamped in. She plumped down her bucket in front of the stove and snatched the child from him.

He gaped at her.

"What the . . . why . . . whatever's the matter, Mrs Gray?"

The hard-faced woman drew herself up. She made him think of a prison wardress.

"No child of mine will be nursed by a man smelling of drink."

"But that's an insult, Mrs Gray," Lenny blurted out, despite his fear of her. "I am not drunk. I'm only singing to Mary."

"Never, never will we tolerate drink in this home. Mr Gray is the Grand Master of the Rechabites of this district. We believe drink is a snare of the Antichrist."

Gray himself appeared at the door. He was a thickset, pudgy man as humourless as his wife, his surly face remarkable for nothing but a forehead so low that it allowed room for only two furrows. He prided himself that he never swore, and yet as he beat his horses across the knees when they wouldn't back, he would hiss "By Gollygosh!" so viciously that Len felt he would never forget it.

"Yeh," he said. "Thass right. A man in your position has no right ter be wastin' his wages on drink."

"Wages! Why, you only give me a pound a week, and the Government pays most of that!"

"Well," Gray said, in a sour, provocative tone, "if yer not satisfied there's hundreds o' men in the town—younger men—waitin' ter take yer place."

Lenny thought of the years of unemployment that had eaten up all his savings, and he choked back a retort. Mary began to cry. Her mother promptly smacked her legs.

"Keep quiet, your father's talking."

The child went on crying—but silently.

"And tell him now, father, about the room."

"Yeh," the farmer went on, "yeh. The wife saw a bottle o' beer in yer suitcase the other day. We told yer we wouldn't have a drop o' strong drink in this home. So we're shiftin' yer out to the shearer's shed. Yer've 'ad yer chance, and...."

"It's quite good enough for him, too," Mrs Gray said harshly. "He hasn't enough clothes ter need a wardrobe, and a stretcher's a good enough bed for anyone who's been a common swagman."

Pale and trembling, Lenny stood up and said with dignity:

"Mrs Gray, there are millions of men unemployed in the world today. Through no fault of their own. I can't understand why there's a Depression, but I do know it's not their fault."

"It's Sin, that's why." Mrs Gray pronounced. "Man's Sin! God looks after His own! Sin, isn't it, Father?"

"Sin." said Mr Gray sombrely. "The Flesh!"

"Sin!" Lenny echoed, flabbergasted. "Flesh? Gawd!"

"Yeh. Now look at yerself. You're over fifty—and yer've got nothing. Now, if yer'd been real hard-workin' and god-fearin', do you think yer'd be just a stony-broke farm hand today?"

"I've never done anyone any harm, never, in me life. Yer so wrong ... it's ... it's hopeless. I can't argue with you. All I know is you've no right to complain." His voice grew warm with indignation. "I work from half past five in the morning to about nine at night—and sometimes six days a week. And all for a measly quid ...."

"And your board," Mrs Gray insisted, "and your board. The best board in the district."

"And then you make me stay after tea for Bible readings and nag at me to go to church with you Sundays and . . ."

Gray talked him down:

"We always expect our working man to set an example to the children. And a God-fearin' man'd be *glad* to come to church."

"But I don't belong to your religion."

Mrs. Gray looked alarmed:

"Don't tell me he's a Catholic! I *thought* he was a Catholic. Are you a Catholic?"

"No, I'm not."

"Well, what are you then?"

"That's no business of yours, Mrs Gray."

"Don't you talk to my wife like that," Gray blustered. "You'd better get out to yer own room—in the shed, or . . ."

"Yes, I've put his things out there," Mrs. Gray crowed. Then she thrust her face close to Lenny's—so close that he could see three fine hairs on a little mole by her nose—and grated:

"And in future, Mr. Delafield, you can wait there till I ring the bell for tea."

Stone-sober, sick in the stomach, Len Delafield walked out. He passed the two older daughters on the porch—they looked too scared even to signal him any sympathy with their eyes.

Trembling all over, he stumbled down to his new room. It was the sight of the dirt floor that made him cry like a child.

X

As the cell door opened, he threw aside the grubby blanket and sat up on the wooden shelf that served as a bed. His head swam for a few moments.

A dark, burly young fellow entered and slapped down a tin pannikin of water and a chipped enamel plate on which lay two rounds of bread and apricot jam.

Fingering the bruise on his sunken cheek, Lenny spluttered with sudden fury:

"Yer won't get away with this, Mr Johnny Tarrant. Everyone in the town'll hear about this, and the J.P.s too."

The policeman flushed and, with his open hand, gave him a contemptuous push in the face. The back of Lenny's head struck the rough stone wall, and he cried out, in pain.

"You shut your trap," Tarrant hissed, "or you'll get another dose. Who'd take the word of an old soak like you, eh?" He laughed. "Just you bring it up in court, and you'll be up on another charge as well—resisting arrest. See?"

"But what did yer want to hit me for, Johnny?" Lenny asked, in a quavery voice. "I wasn't doin' yer any harm. What did yer want to hit me for?"

"Ah, I'm sick to bloody death of you old wine-dots," said Tarrant, and thought of how he had missed a party. "I got better things to do than stay home just because *you're* in here."

Lenny drank the water, and then leaned back against the wall because his head began to swim once more. After a while he murmured, half to himself:

"Well, them half-castes yer locked up last shearin', they kept sayin' yer bashed 'em around, but I reckoned it was a lot o' lies. But now I know." And he repeated, with a shake of his head, "Yeh, now I know."

Tarrant gritted his teeth.

"Will you shut your bloody trap?" he snarled, "or . . ."

And he made to give the little grey-haired man a backhander across the face.

"Don't hit me, Johnny!" Lenny cried, suddenly cowed. "Don't hit me again!"

Scowling with distaste, the policeman continued:

"I'm puttin' you under the Blackfellers' Act, you old soak. And I'm goin' ter see if I can get you put in some Home or other. They'll grab yer pension, and all you'll cop is a coupla bob a week for tobacco. *They'll* fix you: old nurses with dials you could crack Brazil nuts on—slog all day in the garden, or polishin' the floors—up at five—lights out at eight—no meat, no cake—jist Jesus Christ and cabbage three times a day!"

The old man was incoherent with distress:

"But I . . . I gotta have a drink now and then, Johnny . . . I gotta . . . and . . ."

"I've only gotta say the word," Tarrant lied, "and the magistrate'll commit you. And the Home'll grab yer pension."

"But I . . . how can . . . I can't work much . . . ever since I had the pneumonia bad . . . . I'd die in a Home, Johnny, I'd die with me legs in the air."

"That's your headache," Tarrant gloated, "not mine."

"Aw, have a heart, Johnny, I'm an old man. Old enough ter be yer father. Don't put me in a Home. Look, I'll sign the Pledge again. Give us a chance, Johnny!" And because the policeman scowled, he added obsequiously, "Mr. Tarrant."

The policeman grinned.

"But you're goin' to charge me with usin' third degree!"

"Dinkum, Johnny . . . er . . . Mr. Tarrant—I'll never breathe a word . . . Only don't put me in a Home. Gawd, a man'd dry up like a . . . like a . . ."

"Huh! say what you like. No one'll take *your* word against mine. But I'll give you one more chance. I won't get yer put into a Home, but all the same, I'm puttin' you under the Blackfellers' Act fer a year."

"A year! Gawd!" the old man sighed, "That's a helluva long time."

"Do you know when I picked yer up last night you were tryin' to undo yer fly outside the pub, in the main street? Women and kids coulda been passin'. Anyone."

The old man's face puckered with self-disgust.

"Gord, that's terrible, that's a terrible thing fer a man to be doin'. Was there any . . . any woman around?"

"No," Tarrant admitted reluctantly, "but Mrs Drayton was comin' out o' the store. If I hadn't grabbed yer, yer'd have been pissin' against the tely post, and she'd have spotted yer, sure as eggs."

"Gord, thanks, Johnny!" Lenny said fervently. "I'd hate to offend her. Ah, she's a fine young woman, that. Knitted me this sweater . . . ."

"I'm goin' to let you out on bail. Yer old cobber Mitchell can't come in till to-morrow. Who'll go bail fer you this time?"

"Oh, Tim McCabe, he'll be in today; or B.M., or Charlie Taylor."

"I'll ring Charlie."

Tarrant looked at the plate on the bunk.

"Better eat yer breakfast."

Lenny looked at it and shuddered.

"Gord, I couldn't touch it."

Tarrant glared.

"I mean," he said quickly, "I don't feel hungry, Johnny." Then he asked, in a wheedling tone: "Couldn't yer give a man some aspirins for 'is head?"

"Ah, all right," Tarrant answered, flushing again. "I'm leavin' the door un-locked. You can go to the dike and wash up at the tap, and then come back in here. See?"

"Yes. Thanks for the aspirin—you won't forget, will you?"

"Gord, bugger me days, didn't I say I'd give yer some?" Tarrant snapped, and he stepped outside.

The old man listened till he heard him scrape his boots on the wire grill at the back door.

With a shiver, he drew the blanket round his shoulders, as if it were a cloak.

"I know it," he murmured to himself. "He *does* bash them up. I *know* it."

It gave him a curious satisfaction to be absolutely certain of something about which the rest of the community were in doubt. He felt a sore spot on his ribs, and winced:

"The dirty little Hitler!" he cursed, and then inspected the bread and jam.

"Gord!" he exclaimed, slamming the plate down on to the floor. "Not even a skerrick o' butter! The dirty, mean sod!"

He stretched himself out and very gingerly laid down his aching head.

XI

Lenny and the teacher were leaning against the rails of the stockyard gates and talk-ing while they watched the children playing circle chase on the grassy slope in front of the school. The teacher was a studious-looking man in his early thirties, with a high, lined forehead and a deep voice that rather overawed Lenny.

From time to time, a tall boy standing in the centre blew a whistle, and, at the sound, the runners in the ring immediately turned about and began chasing the ones in front of them.

"Who's that girl in the green, Mr Drayton, the one with the red hair?"

"Jill Butson; you know, her father's the new ganger."

"Oh, Darky," said Lenny, his finger in his mouth. "Pretty hair. Real pretty. Re-minds me of someone. I can't think who. Red hair looks good on a girl, I reckon.

FLEXMORE HUDSON

Best of all. Someone it reminds me of . . . ."

His speech was wavery like the flight of a butterfly.

"Yes," the teacher said, "it looks just like my red setter's coat in the sun, doesn't it? I mean the *colour*!"

"Damn these bloody teeth! They're new," the old man explained, "and they fit like a mouthful of screws. I gotta take 'em out to eat. I don't reckon I'll ever be able to eat with 'em."

The teacher chuckled:

"Oh, everyone finds 'em queer for a while. They *look* tip-top."

"Huh! Fat lot I care how they look! Gord, they feel so big in me mouth I wonder if he give me the right set." He put his forefinger into his mouth and fiddled with his top plate.

"I like watchin' kids," he went on. "Them kids are happy. I been here thirteen years and I never seen such happy kids before. Yer can see they don't get knocked around. I reckon you're right not usin' the cane."

"I did use it a bit in other schools," the teacher said ruefully.

"Ah, if I had a kid I'd never lay a hand on her," Lenny murmured, his eyes on the red-haired girl as she jumped over a little hurdle. "She can jump all right, too. Yes," he went on earnestly, "I'd help her every night with her homework and I'd never lay a hand on her. Never lay a hand on her."

The teacher scrutinized the pinched, lined face with its weak, bloodshot eyes, and nobby red nose, the grey hair, the scrawny neck with its bobbing Adam's apple, and the sloping shoulders. He resisted an impulse to run his eyes down the wasted form to the narrow feet.

Touched, he said:

"It's a pity you haven't children, Mr Delafield. You never married, I heard."

"No. Could have been lots o' times when I was young. A man wasn't a bad looker *then*," he smiled. "I was a good horseman then, too; used ter break 'em in. But I put it orf till it was too late, I suppose." Then he added in a slightly apologetic voice: "Too old to be ridin' nags too, now."

The spring sun was making the teacher drowsy: he yawned, and said quickly:

"Sorry, I was up late last night—reading."

"Yeh?" Lenny said, his mind on the children. "Now my old dad, he was the one to bring up kids. He never hit me once. Never laid a hand on me. Never laid a hand on me." His reedy voice trembled. "I often wish I was a kid again, don't you?"

The teacher looked thoughtful and did not answer at once.

"No, not often; well, not very often. My dad was pretty hard on us all, and we were usually broke. But still, I had some wonderful times. We lived for a good while in the Hornsby hills near Sydney—that's about thirty miles out. The bush was pretty thick there in those days. You ought to have seen the boronia there—the red sort. Ever seen it? No? Well, it smells better than any other scent I know. I learnt to swim there—in an orchard owned by an old bloke that used to fire saltpetre at us from a big shotgun."

He threw back his head and laughed; and Lenny joined in the laughter.

"And I remember," the teacher continued with animation, "I was always pinching fruit. I knew just when everybody's peaches were getting soft and just when everybody's oranges turned sweet!"

An ugly little boy ran up to them, grizzling and waving his hand in the air.

"Please, sir, Billy McDonald's gone and pinched my apple, sir. I had two, sir, and I put them on top of the strainer post, sir, and there's only one left, sir. And Billy was standing there, sir, and they all saw him eating an apple, sir, and . . ."

The teacher cut him short:

"Now, now! That won't break your heart. I know lots of people who lost shirtfuls of apples and it didn't even break their legs. I'll see Billy later. Off you go now and play."

The two men grinned at each other.

"That's the one they call Pongo. Young Billy's always as hungry as an emu."

"Ah, if I had a kid," Lenny panted, pumping up his tire, "I'd give 'im things so he wouldn't want ter be pinchin' from his cobbers. Now, Billy's ole man's a good bloke, but he's tight—he don't give Billy enough money ter spend. Too tight. I know—I put up his fowl sheds."

He continued in a very earnest tone, as though he had considered the matter for a long time:

"I'd give 'im a deener a week, every Saturday. And when he was ten I'd give 'im, say, another zac. And when 'e was twelve I'd give him three or four deeners."

Just then Jill ran past them again, carrying a little red flag, and a few yards behind her a boy carrying a blue one.

"Look at that kid's red curls shinin'! Gord, I bet her ole man's proud of 'er, eh?"

They cheered the youngsters on. In a few moments, two handsome black-haired boys (obviously brothers) returned with the flags. Though the older one was ten yards in front, the younger one fought out a hard finish, to cries of:

"Come on, Jimmy, you're catching him!"

"Gord, them Taylor kids again! Good at everythin', aren't they!" the old man exclaimed. "Must be wonderful ter be like that . . . do everythin' so easy . . . ."

Something in his voice made the teacher look at him curiously.

"Young Jimmy was tellin' me," Lenny went on, "that he's goin' ter be a Spitfire pilot when he grows up. Thank Gord, it looks as if the war'll be over before long." And he returned, with great seriousness, to the subject they had been discussing: "Do yer *reelly* reckon the Japs'll surrender?"

"I think so . . . . I hope so."

"It'll be the best day of me life when it stops. I can't sleep fer thinkin' of that atom bomb 'nd all the kids that musta gone up like . . . like a gas explodin' . . . . Hell, human bein's aren't evil when they're kids."

"No," agreed the teacher. "I don't want another one dropped—not even on the

FLEXMORE HUDSON

Japs. But they'll surrender. I've got a feeling the news'll come over the air any time now. We're keeping our wireless going, night and day."

"Gord, my ole humpy don't run to a wireless," Lenny replied dolefully, "and I gotta get back ter sharpen some axes. I mightn't hear the news till I ride in again; and I'd like ter know the minute it comes over . . . ."

"You'll know all right, Mr Delafield. The kids are going to ring the bell for hours. And then we're all going for a chop picnic in the scrub. I'm closing the school— whether it's declared an official holiday or not. Look, what about coming with us? Would you like to?"

"Gord, like to! I'd walk barefooted through a paddock of star thistles ter go ter a kids' picnic. These clothes'd do, I suppose?"

"Of course. Just come along when you hear the bell. And I think you'll be hearing it soon."

Old Lenny was excited.

"I better get 'ome and wash me shirt then."

He picked up his derelict-looking bike.

"Gord, I dunno, but I hate war. I nearly went ter the first one . . . but they couldn't rope *me* in. Me and me cobber, a bloke called Bill Travers, we was goin' down to enlist one day. It was in the drought—you know, the big '14 drought. Well, we talked it over, and we reckoned it was a racket. No, they wouldn't *get me* ter go ter no wars."

Then, placing his fingers in his mouth, he mumbled:

"Damn them! I'm goin' home ter take 'em out . . . . I'll be listenin' for that there bell. Hope I can get me shirt dry in time . . . . I wouldn't miss a kids' picnic fer quids."

When he mounted his bike, it wobbled so badly that the teacher feared for a moment the old man was going to have a spill; and when he reached the level road and had to push against the slight wind, his wheels turned so slowly he seemed to be stationary, performing a balancing feat.

XII

Old Lenny's home was a galvanized iron shed that had once been a smithy and work-shop. It was the size of an ordinary farm garage. Of the old homestead nearby, which had been demolished for its stone, only the kitchen chimney remained standing, surrounded by heaps of rubble.

Because in winter the water lay about in pools knee-deep, Lenny had dug a trench round the shed, and a drain leading from it to a big hole. But the trench stayed full after the first heavy rain; frogs and toads and crickets in it kicked up a rumpus all night; mosquitoes in summer hung about it like a cloud.

Two limestone boulders and a ten-foot length of railway line held down the loose sheets of the roof. The door opened outwards: when Lenny was off to the township he always propped a wagon wheel against it to shut out the township dogs. Innumerable holes had been stopped with clay, chewing gum and paint-soaked cotton waste, so that the hut, though always draughty, was usually rainproof.

Asked why he didn't accept the room at the back of the store shed, Lenny explained that he stayed in the swamp because it was a good place to have the horrors in . . . . "It's dirt cheap, and I can swear and yowl me head off without disturbin' no one." And he always added: "But one o' these days them mosquitoes're goin' ter get me down."

He fell into his trench so often that people marvelled he didn't get pneumonia every winter.

Having drunk nearly a flagon of cheap muscat on the night before V.P. Day, he slept in late. The tolling of the school bell set an empty milk tin vibrating loudly against a tin plate on the bench . . . .

> *Slowly the girl's pale face and red curls dissolved into the white radiance surrounding them . . . moonlight on snow or salt . . . . Then a child with red curls appeared, smiling as she looked up at the school bell and pulled the rope . . . . A huge chrysanthemum of golden light turned into the light on the post opposite the bank . . . . Now half awake, he dreamed a scene he had often watched from the baker's verandah: The summer afterglow was fading into night. A ring of children stood round the lamp post, and their faces were glowing as they looked up at the bats that were flitting about the big globe. The face he could focus most clearly was Jill Butson's under her curls of red light, but he could also make out Jimmy Taylor grinning from ear to ear. When Jill threw up a little stone and the bats swooped after it, all the children laughed and called out gaily to one another.*
>
> *Then a haggish voice screeched:*
>
> *"Jill, yer mother's waitin' tea. Youse kids oughta be on yer way!"*
>
> *The laughing group broke up . . . .*

Old Lenny struggled to bring them back, but he could not; the harsh voice insisted on returning, and not a child would stay. It was the kind of thing that happened in all his dreams.

He gave a little pah! of disgust, and, without opening his eyes, he reached under the bed for the flagon of wine.

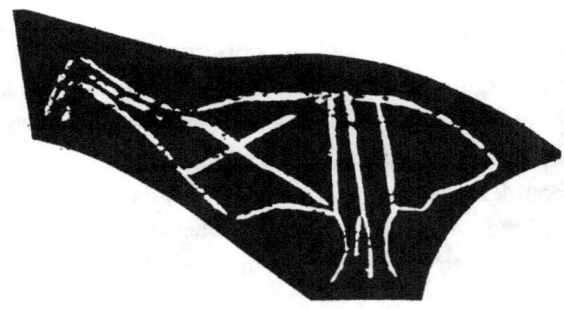

FLEXMORE HUDSON

A Little Marriage Ode

For Sylvia Dowling and Jim Morrissey

I

"Most of the life we have we give
Into this common life we live,
That all our years remaining be
So bound into its unity
That all divergent actions seem
A counterpoint upon that theme."

II

"Within this clear circumference
There is no manner or pretence,
The words and voices are our own;
All things are natural and known,
And in this union each is free
To learn his true identity."

III

"Together now we celebrate
Surrender of our liberty
—Voluntary, deliberate—
So that at last we might be free:
Thus understanding as we can
The central paradox of man."

Address to the Pure Scholars

Phi Beta Kappa poem, Stanford, 1959.

Gentleman scholars in an age of violence,
Clear readers of the insensate and the past,
You are betrayed by your unbalanced calm
To the indifferent forces of destruction:
Scrupulous indeed has been your learning,
Inadequate indeed has been your vision.

For only in the context of a vision
Passionately opposed to mere destruction
Can you bring to its fruition your cold learning;
In the historic present, not the past,
Must you, facing its obscurity and violence,
Labour to build in time a juster calm.

Sheltered you are and should be by the calm
Conditions that are traditional to learning;
You are seduced by this until your vision
Loses its apprehension of old violence,
Gathering stillness from an unreal past:
Thus you betray the present to destruction.

Look westward to the remnants of destruction
Under the cone of Fuji; try to envision
People still crippled, dying from the violence
That blossomed from the physicists' new learning.
Remember the rain of fallout in that calm;
Envision it as present, not as past.

What man or men should answer for that past,
This present and whatever future violence?
All those, perhaps, indifferent to destruction,
Who wait impassive in impassive calm,
Failing to know or speak that juster vision
Which well might be concomitant with learning.

Teachers, you should have more to teach than learning:
Scientists, there is no mere natural calm;
Historians, you are not plighted to the past:
You are servants of society, your vision
Must fight at every point against destruction
Until perhaps our wisdom outweighs our violence.

An age of such great violence, such great learning
Dragging destruction with it from the past:
Who should be calm to see such lack of vision?

A Voice from Inside

After all the talk was done,
And the questions were dismissed
As merely language with a twist,
I and I were only one.
This wearing body in a sense
Is my true intelligence:
It is past actions that recall
How all flesh gathers to a fall,
And all I do is what is done.
But what I know is not the known.

JOAN SUTHERLAND

Photographs and commentary by HANS BEACHAM

WHEN OPERA IS BEING DISCUSSED NOWADAYS, THE NAME OF JOAN SUTHERLAND IS apt to dominate the conversation. Her stature as a prima donna was established internationally in February 1959, when the Royal Opera, Covent Garden, presented her in the title role of *Lucia di Lammermoor*. Critics began seeking new adjectives to describe her coloratura technique. Her rubato, they have declared, is in the grand tradition. Even *The New Yorker* was enchanted: "Her *bel canto* flows away like crystal bubbles of sound; her pianissimi are technically marvellous, as perfectly shaped as if they were miniature versions of full-throated song."

A native of Australia, Miss Sutherland says she was born on November 7, 1926, in Sydney. Her schooling was at St. Catherine's, but she received her first singing lessons from her mother. While working as a secretary, Miss Sutherland continued her music studies and appeared in many concerts and oratorio performances throughout Australia. In 1947, in Sydney, she made her first public appearance in opera as Purcell's Dido. At the Sydney Conservatory of Music she sang the title role in Eugene Goossens' *Judith*.

In 1950 she won an aria competition staged by the Sydney *Sun*. From Mobil Quest, an oil company, she received a substantial award for the best young Australian singer of 1951. With these practical assets she set out for London to enter the Royal College of Music. There she studied voice for a year with Clive Carey and was able to join the Covent Garden company in the autumn of 1952. She made her debut as the First Lady in *The Magic Flute*.

Almost immediately she began making notable appearances—on six hours' notice she sang Amelia in Verdi's *A Masked Ball* at the Hamburg State Opera. She sang Jenifer in the world premier of Tippett's *The Midsummer Marriage*. Other roles included the Countess in *Le Nozze di Figaro*, Agathe in *Der Freischütz*, Pamina in *The Magic Flute,* Eva in *Die Meistersinger,* and the title role in *Aida.* She also sang *all* of the three soprano roles in *The Tales of Hoffman.*

Left and opposite:
Scenes from the third
and fourth acts of *La
Traviata*. Close-up
of Sutherland's eyes was
made just before the
death scene.

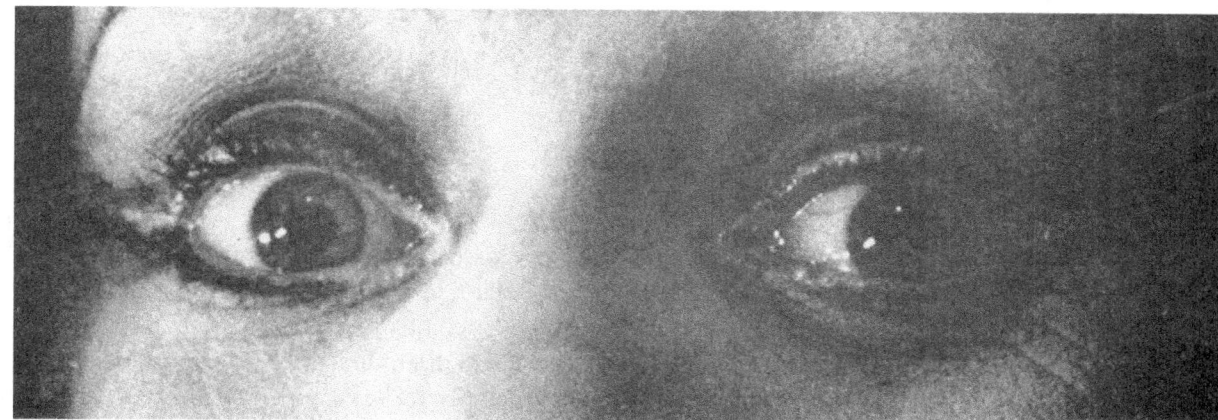

Miss Sutherland had known Richard Bonynge, the pianist, when they were both students in Australia. They met again in London where he, too, was studying at the Royal College of Music. After their marriage in 1954, he gave up his career to become her manager, coach, and accompanist. A keen student of baroque opera, Bonynge persuaded his wife to abandon heavier roles and concentrate on *bel canto*. Together, they have contributed importantly to the revival and performance—with authenticity and style—of works by Donizetti, Bellini, Mozart, and Handel.

Today, Miss Sutherland can recount successes wherever grand opera is produced: Vienna, Paris, Genoa, Palermo, Milan, Venice (where the enthralled Italians first began calling her "La Stupenda"), Barcelona, Cologne, London, and Glyndebourne. Her first American appearance in November 1960 was with the Dallas Civic Opera in the title role of Handel's *Alcina*. Her debut at the Metropolitan Opera was as Lucia on November 26, 1961.

Although she now enjoys a secure place in the loftier realms of her profession, Sutherland's status as a prima donna is more artistic than temperamental, despite a recent refusal to sing with a tenor whose taste displeased her. She is disarmingly unpretentious. She is devoted to her young son, Adam Carl. She is cooperative, with much aplomb and professional poise. In her dressing room she may calmly nibble an apple just before doing the Mad Scene, or, giggling at her own reflection, dance a little jig in her Zeffirelli peignoir while arranging her hair for the last act of *La Traviata*. In the Birthday Honours of 1961 she was made a C. B. E. in recognition of her important services to music. Her busy schedule, which often includes radio and television performances in America and Europe, leaves little time for leisure, but during spare moments she and her husband collect such nineteenth-century memorabilia as autographed scores, operatic lithographs, and books on singers of the period. She also enjoys reading history and biography.

Left, opposite, and following page:
A series showing Sutherland in
the Mad Scene from *Lucia di
Lammermoor*, the role which
helped establish her international
fame in 1959.

At present Miss Sutherland is recording *Alcina.* She has completed full-length recordings of *Lucia di Lammermoor, Rigoletto,* and the *Messiah,* along with two albums of arias. Her musicianship, usually discussed in superlatives, is further displayed by her versatility as an artist. In concert she has sung works from Piccinni, Scarlatti, and Weber. She has sung the Prioress in Poulenc's esoteric work, *The Dialogues of the Carmelites;* Desdemona in *Otello;* Elvira in *I Puritani;* Donna Anna in *Don Giovanni;* and Amina in *La Sonnambula.* She has given memorable performances in Handel's *Samson* and Bellini's *Beatrice di Tenda. Les Huguenots* will be staged for her at La Scala.

The accompanying photographs of Miss Sutherland were made during actual performances in London and in Dallas, Texas.

R. F. BRISSENDEN : *Some Recent Australian Plays*

W HEN RAY LAWLER'S *Summer of the Seventeenth Doll* WAS TO BE PRO-
duced in London in 1957 it was clear that, whether the production were a
success or not, theatrical history would be made. For the first time a play
set in Australia, written by an Australian, was to be presented on the London stage:
presented, moreover, by an Australian company, including the author, fresh from a
brilliant opening season in their own country. The company, and those backing the
production, had justified confidence in the play itself, but there were doubts as to
how the Australian idiom of the dialogue and the accent of the actors might go down
with an English audience. The doubts did not survive the first night: critics and
ordinary members of the audience were equally enthusiastic, and *Summer of the
Seventeenth Doll* had an excellent run.

Its idiosyncratic Australianism may have had something to do with its relative
failure on Broadway (just as—paradoxically—it may have had something to do with
its success in London). The New York critics were, for the most part, respectful, but
the play enjoyed only a short season. It created sufficient of an impression to interest
Hollywood, however, and a film, in which Ernest Borgnine, Angela Lansbury, Anne
Baxter, and John Mills appeared, was made shortly after. In the motion picture a
fatuously sentimental happy ending was substituted for Lawler's soberly realistic
conclusion, but in other respects it gave a faithful and sympathetic rendering of the
script. As a whole it certainly conveys a more authentic impression of some aspects
of Australian life than do most of the recent crop of films set in that country.

Lawler's *Summer* soon proved to be no single swallow. Not long after its success,
The Shifting Heart, by Richard Beynon, was also produced in London. *The Shifting
Heart* had already gained an award in a competition sponsored by the London *Ob-
server*, and it was warmly received when it reached the stage.

Since then several Australian playwrights have seen their work performed outside
Australia. Ray Mathew had a play produced recently in London—a production
worth mentioning not because it was a success (in fact it failed to take) but because
the play had not previously been produced anywhere. Works by Ric Throssell have
been performed in the United Kingdom and on the Continent. *Black Diamonds*, by
Frank Hardy, best known for his crude but forceful novel, *Power without Glory*,
has been filmed for television in Czechoslovakia, and in February of this year was
reported as being in rehearsal with the Brecht Berliner Ensemble. Morris West's own
dramatizations of his novels, *The Devil's Advocate* and *Daughter of Silence*, have
been presented on Broadway, the former with marked success. Most recently, *The
One Day of the Year*, by Alan Seymour, a play which, unlike those of Morris West,
is unashamedly Australian, was staged by Joan Littlewood's Stratford Theatre in
London after a very well-received opening run at home. The number of plays and

playwrights grows rapidly: a recent issue of *Australian Theatregoer* carried a list of fifty-one scripts, the work of twenty-four dramatists, available for production at the present time. Some of these were written well before *Summer of the Seventeenth Doll* appeared—but the total volume (despite considerable variation in quality) is impressive. *Australian Theatregoer* itself bears lively witness to the growing interest in drama: modelled partly on *Theatre Arts* it carries theatrical news, reviews, and articles, and prints in each issue the text of a new Australian play. The Australian drama has clearly, in some sense or other, arrived.

II

Why the drama should have emerged at this point in Australian history is an interesting question. Distinguished work in fiction and poetry has been produced for many years—why not in drama? Three reasons suggest themselves: first, a general cultural and intellectual burgeoning is taking place in Australia at present, and the new playwrights are part of this wider movement; second, there has been a renascence in Australian theatre; third, drama and theatre, along with the other arts, have received in the last few years a certain measure of governmental and public assistance.

The second of these reasons is in some ways the most interesting, for the birth of drama in Australia has been preceded and to some extent made possible by the rebirth of theatre. At one period theatre in Australia was a lusty and vigorous institution, capable in its golden days of attracting such notable and varied performers as Sarah Bernhardt, Dion Boucicault, Lola Montez, Marie Lloyd, W. C. Fields, and others—including Janet Achurch, the original English Norah, in a performance of *A Doll's House*, shortly after the London production. The stage did not appeal, however, to the best writers of that period; and in the nineteen twenties the motion pictures, followed by the depression and a stupid and brutal entertainment tax, crippled the Australian theatre severely.

The current revival has many links with these earlier days. But it is characterised by the presence of certain new elements. The little theatre, both amateur and professional, plays an unusually large role today in the theatrical life of the nation; and Australian audiences are much more sophisticated than they once were. In recent years, plays by Samuel Beckett, Eugene Ionesco, Arthur Miller, Bertolt Brecht, Tennessee Williams, Jean Genet, N. F. Simpson, John Osborne, Jean-Paul Sartre, Harold Pinter, and others, have been produced, mostly in the theatre, sometimes only on the air. It is natural that theatregoers should look hopefully for the appearance of native playwrights of comparable power and ability.

It has been the policy of public agencies, notably the Australian Broadcasting Commission, the Commonwealth Literary Fund, and the Elizabethan Theatre Trust, actively to encourage and assist playwrights. Lately their example has been followed by community bodies—the Adelaide Festival Committee, for instance—and some private business organisations, such as General Motors Holden, who have offered prizes for plays. The activities of the Elizabethan Theatre Trust, though open to

R. F. BRISSENDEN

certain criticism, have been most important. *Summer of the Seventeenth Doll, The Shifting Heart*, and *The One Day of the Year* were all given their first professional productions by the Trust; and it has guaranteed against loss the presentation, often by little theatre groups, of other Australian plays which in ordinary circumstances might not have reached the stage. The Trust has in general had a remarkably catalytic effect on the development of both theatre and drama.

III

Among the plays which have been produced in recent years, there are a few which seem to me of particular importance: *Summer of the Seventeenth Doll* and *The Piccadilly Bushman*, by Ray Lawler; *The Shifting Heart*, by Richard Beynon; *The One Day of the Year*, by Alan Seymour; and *The Ham Funeral*, by Patrick White. By confining my discussion to these plays I shall perhaps be dealing unjustly with the work of certain other playwrights. This essay does not pretend to be a comprehensive survey of Australian drama, however—indeed, since productions are sporadic and scattered, and since many plays are not published, such a survey would be difficult to make. The plays I shall be dealing with do for the most part have the merit of having proved themselves in professional production and of being available in printed form (the exception is *The Ham Funeral*).

My omission of Douglas Stewart may seem strange. Apart from his being dealt with elsewhere in this journal there are two reasons for the seeming neglect: first, I am not convinced that he has yet produced a verse play for the stage which is completely effective in theatrical terms; second, his one clear achievement in verse drama, *The Fire on the Snow* (for which my admiration is unqualified), is a radio play, and so falls somewhat outside the area of this essay. This play, which has for its subject Scott's heroic and disastrous polar expedition, is an extraordinarily impressive piece, both dramatically and poetically: Tyrone Guthrie's comment, when directing it for the BBC in 1951, that it is "one of the few important works of art which radio has so far produced," is more than justified. Stewart's stage plays, however, though animated with fitful bursts of energy, seem static, episodic, wordy, and extremely uneven in tone. This is particularly true of *Ned Kelly*, where Ned the introspective bush Hamlet and Ned the son of the people never quite coalesce. Stewart's work is always interesting and impressive, and he may eventually produce something which is not only poetically effective but also theatrically viable. Up to now his plays seem to lie out of the main stream of dramatic development in Australia.

This stream has flowed fairly evenly so far along the conventional channel of naturalism and social realism. Many playwrights have contributed to it: Louis Esson, an awkward but forceful pioneer in the twenties, Vance Palmer, Henrietta Drake-Brockman, and others. But the first Australian stage play to have been a complete success—at the box office as well as with the critics—is Ray Lawler's *Summer of the Seventeenth Doll*. In some respects it is still the best play yet written in Australia. Those which have followed it (including Lawler's own *Piccadilly Bushman*) have sometimes attempted more difficult and more challenging subjects. None has been so effective within its own terms as *Summer of the Seventeenth Doll*.

These terms may seem to some persons not very ambitious. The play presents a simple—or apparently simple—situation, and presents it in a straightforward manner. For sixteen years, Barney and Roo, Queensland cane-cutters, have been spending the annual summer lay-off down south in Melbourne on a paradoxically respectable spree with their permanent girl friends, Olive and Nancy. In the seventeenth year the passage of time finally overtakes them and the association disintegrates. The themes—the conflict between romantic illusion and reality, the painful recognition of the fact of age—are universal. But the situation in which they are displayed is fresh and original. Lawler's story bears the stamp of authenticity: it seems to have sprung directly from his own observation of life, rather than from his knowledge of literature or the theatre. It is a play with no obvious pretensions: it explores no timely social problem, it carries no overt political or religious message—it merely presents an interesting and unusual (but by no means unrecognizable) instance of a general human predicament. Though in the naturalistic mode, *Summer of the Seventeenth Doll* is no raw slice of life. It is an honest, well-constructed piece of craftsmanship by a man who thoroughly understands his medium. The situation lends itself naturally to the dramatic treatment it is given, and the strong, unsentimental conclusion emerges with a satisfying inevitability.

One of the main strengths of the play is Lawler's confident and enthusiastic rendering of the Australian scene and the Australian language. With *Summer of the Seventeenth Doll* the Australian character stands forth firmly and unmistakably on the stage. And the Australianness of the play is all the more effective because it is not there for its own sake: it is subordinate to the main theme. At the same time much of the force of the play derives from the manner in which it presents and also examines and questions certain long-established Australian values and modes of action. The situation—the annual spree with one's mates in the "big smoke," knocking down the fat cheque earned up the country, and the happily pagan ideals of beer, girls, and loafing in the sun which it embodies—these things are part of the Australian tradition. In Lawler's play they are presented with a good humour and a wholehearted enjoyment which perhaps blind some persons to the way in which they are being exposed, criticised, and assessed through the dramatic action. Simple and unpretentious the play may be, but it has an intellectual toughness and honesty which make it more than merely entertaining.

Lawler's concern with the values of his native society emerges more clearly but less effectively in his next and latest play, *The Piccadilly Bushman*. In this he examines that struggle between English and Australian loyalties which fights itself out in the heart of every Australian who visits the mother country. Lawler's hero is an actor who, by destroying every marked trace in voice and manner of his Australian origins, has acquired a considerable reputation in the English theatre. The play deals with the personal conflicts set up by his temporary return to his native country to

R. F. BRISSENDEN

make a film. *The Piccadilly Bushman* has many virtues: it is mature, intelligent, and sophisticated, and presents a revealing and shrewd study of certain theatrical types, and of certain Australian pretensions and vulgarities. But it has an air of contrivance; and the inability of the characters to carry with ease the symbolic burden Lawler places on them leads him to overwrite and strain for effect. Although only partially successful the play is a stimulating and courageous attempt to grapple with a very complex issue—an attempt which it was clearly important for Lawler to make.

The Shifting Heart, by Richard Beynon, is also concerned overtly with Australian attitudes and values. Beynon's subject is topical: the problems of adjustment faced by an Italian immigrant family, the Bianchis, and the Australians they come in contact with. Since the war, under a government-sponsored programme, there has been a steady flood of European migrants entering the country. The resulting clash of cultures has been stimulating and enriching, though not always comfortable: Australians, isolated from the rest of the world for so many years, have had an insular distrust and contempt for the alien which has died hard.

This is especially so in the social environment in which the Bianchis find themselves: Collingwood, a semi-slum area in Melbourne. There the problems they have to overcome range from the comic to the tragic—from devising new strategies of defense and retaliation in the running fight of garbage and blocked drains waged by their next-door neighbour, to forgiving and reconciling themselves to the community which has produced the gang of hooligans who kick Gino, the son of the family, to death. The action of the play centres on the relationship between the daughter, Maria, and her Australian husband, Clarry. The climax comes with the birth of a child to Maria, and the accompanying recognition by Clarry of the full implications of his marriage into the immigrant family.

Beynon's rendering of his characters and their situations is warm and sympathetic, and the play offers a palatable blend of humour and tragedy. With its plea for tolerance it is not surprising that *The Shifting Heart* should have been successful. One English reviewer described it as having "something very near greatness." Such praise is excessive: the play may be theatrically compelling, but it has a contrived and melodramatic structure; and its realism is weakened by a certain sentimentality. The action, for example, occurs over Christmas Eve and Christmas Day, during which brief and conveniently symbolic period Gino is murdered and Maria gives birth to a son. This is a little too pat. Beynon's basic situation is real enough, however, and one must admire the honesty and compassion with which he has tackled it.

An even more direct and searching light is thrown onto the Australian's image of himself in *The One Day of the Year*. The "one day" of Alan Seymour's title is Anzac Day, the most significant holiday in the Australian calendar. The name, "Anzac," comes from the initials of the Australian and New Zealand Army Corps, a force, consisting entirely of volunteers, which landed against strong Turkish opposition at Gallipoli in the Dardanelles during the first world war. Anzac Day begins at dawn on April 25th—the hour and date of the attack—with solemn memorial services for the fallen. In all large cities this is followed by a march of ex-servicemen. The afternoon is given over to informal reunions of old comrades—reunions which by tradition are earnestly alcoholic.

Alf Barnes, the central character in Seymour's play is, in his own often repeated phrase, a "bloody Australian." He is one of the richest characters who have yet appeared in Australian drama. He is a little man, materially defeated by a world which refuses to recognize the abilities he believes he has, and which condemns him to work as a lift driver. He retaliates by continuously asserting in language rich with slang and sardonic vulgarity his democratic Australian independence, by enjoying proudly the vicarious satisfaction of contemplating his son, Hughie's, progress as a university student, and by looking forward to, celebrating fully, and recalling fondly for the rest of the year each annual Anzac Day—a commemorative occasion that means more to him than it does to most people.

On the particular day with which the play deals a crisis occurs: Hughie refuses for the first time to attend the dawn service with his father. In fact, he spends the day collecting photographic evidence of the debauch which follows, evidence used to illustrate an article exposing the hypocrisies of Anzac Day written for the university newspaper by his girl friend, Jan.

Hughie's relationship with Jan, a wealthy young student from the North Shore, brings a new dimension into the play and makes it more than an investigation of Anzac Day. One of the most cherished Australian myths is that Australia is a classless society. In *The One Day of the Year*, Seymour exposes the clash of different classes and social attitudes in a way which is new, at least in Australian drama. The struggle between Hughie and his parents is crystallized by the Anzac Day issue, but basically it is the old conflict between youth and age, a conflict saddened and sharpened by the fact that the parents, in the desire to realise in their son the fulfilment of their own dreams, have ironically educated him out of their social group. This is a problem to which there is no easy solution, and it is to Seymour's credit that he concludes his play not with a reconciliation but with an uneasy truce.

Seymour's intuitions are greater than his ability to express them: *The One Day of the Year* is an uneven piece of work, and its weakest element is the characterization of the young intellectual rebels, Hughie and Jan. Beside the robust working-class vigour of the parents they seem pallid and unconvincing; Jan, especially, is an almost embarrassingly artificial sketch of the little rich girl gone slumming, and in places she throws the play seriously out of balance. But in general it is a stimulating and vital rendering of a significant area of Australian life.

The successes of Lawler, Beynon, and Seymour are evidence not only of the extent to which the tradition of naturalism is established in Australian drama, but also of the opportunities which this genre offers to the dramatist for presenting an illuminating and authentic recreation of his society. It is likely that many of the plays produced in the future in Australia will be cast in this most conventional of moulds. But it is possible also that some dramatists may begin to move in directions which, at

R. F. BRISSENDEN

least from the technical point of view, are more exciting. If there are any followers attracted by *The Ham Funeral*, a new play by Patrick White, it is possible that they will produce something which is both less conventional in technique and less narrowly Australian in subject.

Patrick White has gained in the last few years an international reputation as a novelist—in particular for *The Tree of Man, Voss*, and *Riders in the Chariot. The Ham Funeral* is not his first play, but it is the first to be produced in his own country, and the first to have met with a generally favorable reception.

Approval has not been unanimous, however, and in this its career parallels in an interesting way that of *The One Day of the Year*. Both works were nominated (in successive years) as prize-winning plays by the Drama Committee of the Adelaide Arts Festival, only to be rejected by the timid and hidebound directors of the Festival because of their dangerous unconventionality. Seymour's play was considered an insult to the Anzac tradition, *The Ham Funeral* to be too daring in other ways. Both pieces received their initial production in Adelaide, however, in each case by an amateur group at the University.

There the similarities cease. *The Ham Funeral* does not put before its audience a "bloody Australian," but a young man who has no name and who announces: "the time doesn't matter. The same applies to my origins. It could be that I was born in Birmingham . . . or Brooklyn . . . or Murwillumbah." The action is set in a London boarding house. In the basement live the landlord, Will Lusty, a fat man, once a wrestler, and his still vital wife Alma. Upstairs live the young man, in one room, and in another, a girl. They never meet, and we see the girl as the young man imagines her to be in his poetic reveries—grave, dressed in white, "remote but radiant"—and as she really is—"Phyllis Pither . . . a young lady as works for a firm of gas-fittters in Kennington. . . . Gives 'er wages to an auntie 'oo suffers from Bright's Disease. . . . Most nights she goes to bed with an aspirin and a cold." In the course of the play, Will Lusty dies and is mourned at a wake for which his wife provides an expensive ham. The wake is followed by the consummation of the sexual attraction which has been developing between Alma and the young man, and which has partly caused the husband's death. The play concludes with the departure of the young man for the world outside the boarding house.

White describes *The Ham Funeral* as a "tragi-farce," and its tone is a wryly dissonant blend of unillusioned realism and wild comedy. It is at once heavily symbolic and starkly naturalistic. At one level it presents the ritual pattern of growth towards sexual, social, and artistic liberation and self-knowledge on the part of the young man; at another the cyclic, organic stability of ordinary life represented by the landlord and his wife. In manner the play is expressionist; and it also exhibits many of the elements of what has come to be called the Theatre of the Absurd. In his creative response to the poetic possibilities of ordinary speech, with all its irrelevancies and repetitions, White achieves effects similar to those of Harold Pinter; and in his preoccupations with the isolation of the individual, with the problem involved in the search for self-identification and the attempt to communicate with others and to formulate a meaningful picture of a possibly meaningless universe—preoccupations which have already been revealed clearly in his novels—White demonstrates obvious affinities with Beckett and Ionesco. And in the bold theatricality of his technique he shows a creatively imaginative and highly individual grasp of the potentialities of his medium. He demonstrates in particular that a poetic revitalising of dramatic language is possible without the dramatist's having to revert to the more conventional forms of the verse play. One of the most remarkable things about *The Ham Funeral* is the way in which the author subtly heightens the common language in order to make articulate characters who would normally not be able to express themselves. It is an unusual but exciting and beautiful play.

According to the final stage direction in *The Ham Funeral*, the play closes with the young man "walking into the distance through a luminous night." The image comes too aptly to my purpose for me to resist the urge to borrow it. Like the young man Australian drama has at last made a mature gesture of independence and has broken out of the limits of its adolescence. The future towards which it now can move is luminous with possibilities.

R. F. BRISSENDEN

HAROLD J. OLIVER : *Douglas Stewart and the Art of the Radio Play*

IN AUSTRALIA, AS IN ENGLAND AND AMERICA, THE RADIO PLAY—PERHAPS BE-cause it was that rare phenomenon, a new literary form—tempted not only those who made broadcasting their profession but also authors of established reputation. Not surprisingly, it appealed particularly to poets: as Archibald MacLeish has put it, in radio drama "there is only the spoken word—an implement which poets have always claimed to use with a special authority. There is only the word-excited imagination—a theatre in which poets have always claimed peculiar rights to play." MacLeish's own *The Fall of the City,* perhaps the best known of all radio plays, may well have been the work that inspired Douglas Stewart to write his verse plays for broadcasting: it might even be said that Stewart's place in the history of broadcast drama in Australia is equivalent to that of MacLeish in the United States, or that of Louis MacNeice in Britain.

It is in a sense ironical that Australia should be represented in this way by one who is by birth and education a New Zealander. Stewart has been living in Australia, however, for most of his literary career, and nearly all his work has been published in Sydney, where he has won for himself a unique place as a man of letters and is known as poet, playwright, short-story writer and critic—and not least as the editor for many years of the "Red Page" of the Sydney *Bulletin,* the most famous of Australian weekly journals.

His plays were not all written for radio: at least three, *Ned Kelly* (1943), *Shipwreck* (1947), and *Fisher's Ghost* (1960), were composed for the stage, although radio versions exist. The two to be considered here, however—*The Fire on the Snow* and *The Golden Lover* (1944)—are radio plays in the strictest sense, even if stage performances were later authorized, and it is their special use of the broadcasting medium that I wish to examine now.*

The better known of the two is *The Fire on the Snow,* a dramatization of Captain Robert Falcon Scott's march to the South Pole with Wilson, Bowers, Evans, and Oates, and the death of all five on the return journey. In the words of the Prologue, "the time of the play is from 4th January 1912, when the last supporting party returned, to 29 March 1912, when Scott's diary ceases." Here, then, Stewart is dramatizing recorded history; his sources he has acknowledged to be "Scott's diary and Apsley Cherry-Garrard's *The Worst Journey in the World.*" The second play, *The*

---

* The dates are those of publication. *The Fire on the Snow* was first produced, by the Australian Broadcasting Commission, in 1941. Stewart has written at least one other radio play, *The Earthquake Shakes the Land,* but it has not been published. The text quoted throughout this article is that of *Four Plays* (Angus and Robertson, Sydney, 1958). Quotation is by permission of Angus and Robertson and of the author.

Golden Lover, which I myself consider to be the better, is quite different. It is based on the Maori legend of the beautiful young wife Tawhai who was kidnapped by, or ran away with, her golden lover Whana, the chief of the fairylike people of the mist (who could even *be* the mist) and tried to make husband, father, mother, and lover accept the bargain that she should spend each night with the lover in the forest and each day with the husband in the village—until race, or tradition, or magic, or common sense triumphed and she reluctantly came back to her people. The radio play, always the perfect medium for fantasy—as Louis MacNeice's March Hare programmes proved—undoubtedly lends itself splendidly to this fairy tale. The Golden Lover need only be described; there is no physical appearance to break the illusion of his romantic perfection; and because Whana cannot be seen in the flesh, it is easier for a listener to find in the story, if he pleases, a development through symbols of the theme that the perfect lover is merely the creation of the romantic mind:

> You have dreamed about me. All your life you have dreamed.
> I know you, Tawhai. You have had lovers, a husband,
> And lovers and a husband they were not to be despised;
> But always beyond them, Tawhai, there was a dream.
> You lay, I know you have lain, with your lover in the bracken,
> You have lain with your husband in the bed of fern in the whare,
> But who did you lie with in dreams? With your golden lover!

Yet the story may also be taken as an allegory of woman's desire to have at one and the same time the solidity of married life and the perfect romance with no ties whatever—or simply as a fairy tale.

Far from being inconvenienced by his medium, then, Stewart, like other good radio dramatists, can turn to his own advantage the fact that this new form of drama lacks the solid flesh. What cannot be seen can always be, and often must be, described —and as the Elizabethan drama so brilliantly demonstrated, description can be a dramatic virtue. Stewart's plays similarly show that lack of scenery, for example, is no handicap if the author is skilful enough to paint his scene in words:

> I do not know what it means. I am frightened of it.
> The seven great fires, flaring against the stars,
> And the steam rising from the pots; and behind the steam
> Wera and Koura kneeling, and the other old women;
> And behind the women, Nukuroa and Ruarangi
> And Tiki too, standing there straight and silent;
> And behind those three, the warriors, row on row,
> With their spears and clubs and axes—eh, the fine men!—
> Row after row from the firelight back to the shadows
> Where we who are not important may stand and watch.

Nor need the description be in a set passage, such as this; indeed, any lines that hold

HAROLD J. OLIVER

up the action are doubly dangerous in a broadcast story, and description is therefore better given in truly dramatic comment or, better still, in dialogue. A good example of the use of dramatic comment is found at the opening of Scene V of *The Golden Lover,* when Tawhai returns to her husband Ruarangi after her first night with Whana:

> *Sound of* RUARANGI *snoring.*
> *Tawhai.* Aha, the song of the husband! Sleep on then, fat one.
>   The day is bright but I do not think you will like it.
>   [RUARANGI *snores.*]
> When you wake, Ruarangi, you will have some reason to roar.
> Eh, the same old husband and the same little whare,
> The posts of tree-fern, the thatch of raupo from the swamp,
> The flax mats on the floor and the bed of fern.
> How long since I left you? Only a night? And yet
> How dear you are since that one wild night in the bush,
> That night with Whana. Eh, my dear little whare,
> I might have lost you for ever!

A good example of description through dialogue occurs in *The Fire on the Snow* as the polar party get nearer to their goal:

> BOWERS. . . . My eyes are playing tricks—
>   I thought for a moment I saw a cairn ahead.
> SCOTT. What's that? A cairn?
> BOWERS.   Only sastrugi.
> WILSON.   Sure?
> OATES. I had a feeling Amundsen would beat us to it.
> EVANS. I can't see anything.
> BOWERS.   Look there. I can see it still!
>   But it's only sastrugi. I'm sorry, I feel like a criminal,
>   Startling you all like that.
> SCOTT.   I can't see anything
>   Either; look carefully, Bowers. If this is Amundsen . . .
> BOWERS. It's so confusing, all these waves of snow.
>   I wish the light were clearer; but it's not a cairn.
> OATES. Cairn or no cairn the Norskies will beat us.
> EVANS. I believe I can see it. A cairn. I can see it.
>   What will we do if it is?
> WILSON.   You can't see anything.
>   It's not a cairn, and if it is, it doesn't matter.
> BOWERS. It's nothing. I shouldn't have spoken. I apologize.

The wind's heaped up the snow a bit more than usual,
    That's all it can be.
SCOTT.   Let's march. And haul, men, haul;
    Whatever it is we'll find out soon enough,
    And if it's the worst I want to get it over.   ...
BOWERS. There's something there I can see. I have to tell you.
    There's something black on the snow.   ...
SCOTT. Yes, I can see it. I don't like the look of it.
EVANS. Couldn't it be a rock?
OATES.   There aren't any rocks.
EVANS. Then a bird or something.
OATES.   There aren't any birds, curse you.
BOWERS. I'm afraid it looks like a flag.
SCOTT.   Yes, it's a flag.
OATES. Oh, blast the luck. And blast the Norwegians. Damn them.

This passage illustrates the further point that, because it has no scenery, the radio play, again like Elizabethan drama, has no limitation on space. It can move as far as the author pleases and as quickly; and like the film it can move continuously. A play in the theatre—even probably on a revolving stage—has to rely on action at certain places and at certain selected points of time; radio drama can keep moving. This simple fact makes possible a play like *The Fire on the Snow;* the audience really can be given the illusion that they are travelling with the five men for most of the eight hundred miles to the pole and the six hundred back again. Indeed, one may maintain, hypercritically, that the very ease with which the radio play can cover ground operates paradoxically once in *The Fire on the Snow* to lessen the heroism of Scott and his men. In historical fact, they pushed on some distance beyond Amundsen's tent, to what they considered to be the true location of the Pole; it has even been said that their action in doing so put them the few miles behind schedule that cost them their lives. Stewart knew of the fact, and allowed for it in his dialogue:

SCOTT. Let's get on.
BOWERS. It's not far now. This is the Pole.
    This is the Pole, as near as I can fix it.
SCOTT. All right then, Birdie, get the camera ready.

In a broadcast play, however, this is not enough; precisely because the characters can move so easily, one must place more stress on a particular movement if it is to be noticed and to be significant.

Radio drama differs from both Elizabethan drama and the film in that its characters, in addition to its scenery, cannot be seen. Their costume, their features, their limbs, their gestures must all therefore be described if these are relevant; and again the economy and vividness of poetry will be invaluable. So Stewart will put into the mouth of Tawhai a description of the Maori witch doctor:

> He is old and yellow and evil and feeds on horror
> Like fungus on a rotten log

and if that is all we know, it is all we need to know. In a different way, because the fatness of the husband Ruarangi is a relevant fact in the story, it is made the subject of joking comment—and because the picture has to be kept before us, and not forgotten, the jokes are repeated throughout the play. Stewart is also well aware that if a change in physical appearance is important for our understanding of the action, that change must be put into words; accordingly he gives us his unforgettable picture of Seaman Evans, in the words of Scott:

> I've seen this coming and been afraid of it;
> Each day since he took that fall I've watched him failing,
> His poor hands rotting with frostbite, his face all eaten,
> As if there were rats in the ice. The worst thing
> Was to see his reason going, see him losing heart,
> His movements slowing and his speech becoming wooden.
> Each day we've seen him nearer this collapse,
> And it's made my heart bleed, watching him.

The danger is that when characters cannot be seen the listener may find it difficult to know who is speaking. The dramatis personae must be immediately identifiable and, if possible, not only by voice but also by what they say and how they say it. There is no weakness here in *The Golden Lover*; I am not so sure about *The Fire on the Snow*, where the fact that the five characters are all men perhaps set an insoluble problem.

Just as physical appearance must be translated into sound in a radio play, so must physical action (a fact that explains the unfortunate fondness of so many radio dramatists for the slap, the slamming door, and the moving car). As Val Gielgud has pointed out, radio is therefore particularly limited on the side of comedy and farce and mystery; it suffers from its "inability to make use of the mysterious hand groping between the curtains; of the curate being deprived of his trousers or sitting on the bishop's hat." Many actions, in fact, cease to be funny when described. One must admire Stewart's skill in *The Golden Lover,* where the humour is in situation and contrasts of character and is in the dialogue even when that dialogue refers to physical action. In *The Fire on the Snow*, where there is little humour, the problem with physical action is with the marching and the hard work with the sledges, and again the solution is to rely on what can be put into the words of characters or announcer, not always naturally perhaps, but nearly always vividly:

> Stumbling. Oates. Crashing. Scrambling to his feet
> And shambling on, and crashing, and rushing on . . .
> Falling. Oates. Hauling. Falling in to-morrow,

Recalling yesterday and suddenly finding to-day
When comrades look at him with eyes of sorrow
And the mind holds like a pebble the thought of dying,
Curious, cold.

In all these ways, the word predominates in the radio play; it has all the functions that it has in ordinary drama and others as well. One disadvantage is that since silence is, so to speak, unnatural on the air, the great dramatic effect of silence may there be lost; one other disadvantage is that the characters of the radio play may become too loquacious, may talk too much about themselves (as, I fear, the characters in Stewart's stage play sometimes do) and may *say* what is better implied. Here, quite unfairly perhaps, I should like to compare the scene of the death of Oates in *The Fire on the Snow* with its great original in Scott's Journal. The play reads:

OATES. I had hoped not to wake this morning. It's cold.
   A blizzard outside?
SCOTT.   A blizzard. We must march if we can.
OATES. I'm glad there's a blizzard. The sunlight here's too cruel,
   Lighting the ice and everything looking naked.
   When it's grey and snowy it makes me think of home,
   I suppose because of December and the fires.
   I see my mother quite clearly, lighting the sticks,
   Stooping, as over the garden in the summer.
   Colours and flowers and flames came out of her hands.
   There were good days in the regiment, too, in winter,
   Hard, brisk days and wine at night
   And the horses steaming and bucking on frosty mornings.
   It's good to have lived.
BOWERS.   Good to be living, too.
   We'll make it yet.
OATES.   Living is over for me.
WILSON. Wait till the doctor tells you, Soldier. Hardly
   Thirty more miles and we'll be at One Ton Camp.
   Cherry and the dogs'll be there and we'll haul you home
   Like a prince, lying back on the sledge and watching the scenery.
OATES. Don't. Don't, Wilson. You only make it
   Harder, for me and for all of us. No more pretending.
SCOTT. At lunch-time yesterday you thought you couldn't go on
   Yet you managed to march, and the same can be done to-day.
OATES. And to-morrow? And the day after that? No.
   Not even to-day.
BOWERS.   I'll help you along.
OATES. Thank you. You're all very kind. Too kind

To a man who's been a burden these past three weeks.
Too kind, too kind.
SCOTT.   Soldier!
What are you doing? For Christ's sake, where are you
Going?
WILSON. You mustn't! Bowers, hold him! Hold him.
BOWERS. Soldier, you fool, it's blowing hell outside,
A howling blizzard.
OATES.   Nobody move, don't move.
I am just going outside. I may be some time.

THE ANNOUNCER

They let him go.
In grief and shame
They let him go
Out to the flame
Of wind and snow
Where he burns for them.

They are silent for a while. They like to play with the notion
That it hasn't happened, for it seems too monstrous to happen.

The original is as follows:

"Should this be found I want these facts recorded. Oates' last thoughts were of his Mother, but immediately before he took pride in thinking that his regiment would be pleased with the bold way in which he met his death. We can testify to his bravery. He has borne intense suffering for weeks without complaint, and to the very last was able and willing to discuss outside subjects. He did not—would not—give up hope to the very end. He was a brave soul. This was the end. He slept through the night before last, hoping not to wake; but he woke in the morning—yesterday. It was blowing a blizzard. He said 'I am just going outside and may be some time.' He went out into the blizzard and we have not seen him since.

"I take this opportunity of saying that we have stuck to our sick companions to the last. . . . We knew that poor Oates was walking to his death, but though we tried to dissuade him, we knew it was the act of a brave man and an English gentleman. We all hope to meet the end with a similar spirit, and assuredly the end is not far away."

Can there be any doubt that the passage from Scott's Journal is the more moving? I make the point not in criticism of Stewart, who brings out the tragedy more than adequately (even if he ought not to have allowed the Announcer to comment on it) but because I wish to suggest that there are themes and incidents of which *no* radio version could be perfect. The radio play has one great defect, that the characters in it must talk; and perhaps one feels this difficulty again in the dying speeches of Scott and Wilson in *The Fire on the Snow.**

I do not mean to imply that characterization in these two plays is a weakness; certainly I do not mean to imply that the characters are inadequately distinguished from one another (although I have pointed out that in a broadcast performance of *The Fire on the Snow* a voice is not always immediately identifiable as that of a particular character). In *The Golden Lover,* which, unlike most stories of unsophisticated people, never sentimentalizes, there are most skilful portraits of the beautiful, romantic, attractive but flighty young wife Tawhai and of her fat, lazy, pompous old husband Ruarangi—the latter a figure of farce, perhaps, but one who never loses his dignity, or quite loses our sympathy (although one speech at the end of Scene III seems to be completely out of character, when the poet in Stewart takes over from the dramatist). In *The Fire on the Snow* the leader Scott, the staunch Wilson, the good-natured but impatient Bowers, the strong but less intelligent Seaman Evans, and the gallant but unintellectual Captain Oates are all clearly shown—and it is perhaps graceless to complain, as I must, that Stewart does not seem always to have interpreted the characters correctly according to the historical evidence and that in particular one speech by the Announcer

> This journey is one man's dream
> As it is one man's burden
> And the man is Scott, the leader.
> The others do what they're bidden,
> Bearing their share of the load,
> But cannot tell what it means

is almost a libel on Dr. Wilson, the most intelligent member of the party, its scientist, its artist, and to my mind incomparably the finest personality of them all. Perhaps, however, this is not strictly a *literary* criticism of the play.

There is one other character in most radio plays—the Announcer—whom Archibald MacLeish has called "the most useful dramatic personage since the Greek Chorus," the choric commentator whose presence "as natural as it is familiar . . . restores to the poet that obliquity, that perspective, that three-dimensional depth without which great poetic drama cannot exist." The ready availability of the announcer provides temptations, and a listener is sometimes uncertain whether the announcer is, so to speak, a character within the play or one outside looking in (I confess to feeling this difficulty even in *The Fall of the City*). In *The Golden Lover* Stewart makes only the simplest use of the announcer, to introduce the play:

> The story of Tawhai and her golden lover, Whana, of which this play is a free interpretation, is told in James Cowan's *Faery Folk Tales of the Maori* . . . . Quite possibly it is a true story, for, if the rationalistic explanation is accepted, the patu paiarehe, as a fair-skinned red-haired people of dif-

---

* Stewart—wisely, in my opinion—does not rely heavily on the fact that soliloquy and aside are less incongruous on the air than on the modern stage.

HAROLD J. OLIVER

ferent origin from the Maoris, once really existed as a wild tribe of the forest . . . . On that basis of fact is built this fantasy . . . . The first scene is set in the early morning in the whare of thatched reeds where Tawhai lives with her husband Ruarangi.

In *The Fire on the Snow,* however, there are two announcers, one outside the play, one within it. The first, called "Prologue", makes the introductory announcement, in the plainest of prose:

Captain Scott's Antarctic expedition landed in McMurdo Sound on the Antarctic Continent on 4th January 1911 . . . . This play opens at the point when Scott, Wilson, Bowers, Evans and Oates are about to leave the last supporting party before setting out on the final dash to the Pole. The Announcer speaks first.

Then the voice of the second announcer is heard (and this part is sometimes spoken by a woman):

I am to break into the conversation
With a word that tastes like snow to say;
I am to interrupt the contemplation
Of the familiar headlines of the day—
Horses, divorces, politics, murders—
With a word cold to hear or look at,
Colder to speak. These are my orders,
. . . I say what I have to say: "Death."

This second announcer has many functions in the play. He (or she) creates the tragic atmosphere, and helps to preserve it; he introduces the symbolism of the fire of human courage burning brightly against the harsh whiteness of the snow; paradoxically and ingeniously, he establishes the fact of the overwhelming silence of the Polar plateau:

In the beginning was the Word,
Before the Word was silence.
Man was born of a word
And he dies back to silence.
It is quiet in the white South.

Life is a word, a shout:
The aeroplane roars in the sky,
Factories crash and clang,
The traffic thunders by.
It is quieter in the South;

he describes the scenery, and if necessary fills in parts of the story:

The surface breaking like glass,
The snow slowing the sledge
Like waves of white iron.

The wind like a wall of ice
That has to be forced, broken
For every inch of the way.

The sledge heavy to haul,
The limbs aching, the sweat
Freezing on bearded faces . . . .

And yet their lives are simple. They forget
Most of the time that life was ever different
And each day's march is a matter of mere routine
Like going to work at the office. I see them hauling
Grimly, not talking much, then making camp.
Evans, the giant worker, has cut his hand
But still attends to the sledges, pitches the tent,
The strongest man of the party;

and, less justifiably, he offers editorial comment. The difficulty is that any narration and comment given by an impersonal voice, one that is not really part of the action of the play, is apt to seem stilted; the intrusion of a commentator can be annoying, as is, I fear, the intrusion of this announcer after the death of Evans. The alternative adopted by many radio dramatists is to have a character in the play do the announcing, as it were. The result is a discomforting fondness for flashback, retrospection, reminiscence. This danger Stewart does avoid, except possibly in the final speeches of Scott and Wilson and in one undramatic narrative passage in *The Golden Lover*, Nukuroa's otherwise fine account of a famous journey of the Maoris to the coast.

By considering Stewart's radio drama in this way—by concentrating on the opportunities offered by the different medium and so creditably taken—I may well have done less than justice to the plays as literature. I hasten therefore to add that they have many merits quite apart from their radio technique. *The Fire on the Snow,* for example, does show what the hardships of the Polar journey were and convinces us of the courage necessary to endure them; in particular, when men like Scott, Wilson, Bowers and Oates face up to the fact that they are in one sense relieved that Evans has died, we are made to understand what the journey involved.

Nevertheless there is some evidence that the pendulum of critical opinion may be swinging; Australian readers have been told (by David Bradley, in *Westerly* Number 3, 1960) that because of Australia's lack of good drama, *The Fire on the Snow* has been greatly overrated. I think more highly both of the principles of Australian literary criticism and of the play. I could almost be reconciled to a lower opinion of *The Fire on the Snow,* however, if this meant that *The Golden Lover* was to receive more attention. It, no doubt, goes on too long, and there are times when what is intended to sound romantic comes close to sounding prosaic or platitudinous (a fault not unknown in Stewart's nondramatic verse). Yet the language does rise to the necessary level for Whana's lovemaking; without ceasing to be poetical, it is more than adequate for the comedy:

    TAWHAI. . . . We must find a way—
    WHANA. I could find a way to turn you over and smack you.
    TAWHAI. Although, Whana, you are certainly my golden lover
      And of faery blood, and handsome as the sun to look at,
      You behave at times surprisingly like a husband.
    WHANA. Although, Tawhai, I could not doubt for one moment
      That you are my crimson blossom and the song of a tui,
      You argue at times disconcertaingly like a woman

and it even at times has an epigrammatic force:

    There have always been two moments
    When a man is deaf to argument; one is the time
    When he asks you to smile on him; and the other time
    Is when he forbids you to smile on someone else.

Indeed, *The Golden Lover* has a varied but a consistent charm. In theme, as Leslie Rees has pointed out,* it is rather similar to W. B. Yeats's *The Land of Heart's Desire*, of which there may also be one verbal echo; Stewart's fantasy, however, is far more lighthearted and, in the best sense, less intense. It is the work that one would most wish to recommend to those theatregoers and readers outside Australia who might otherwise base their judgment of Australian plays on the different kinds of dramatic skill shown in Ray Lawler's *Summer of the Seventeenth Doll*.

  * *Towards an Australian Drama* (Sydney, 1953).

WHEN MONICA, TIRED OF WAITING LUNCH, SAT TO EAT SHE MERELY picked at the meat loaf for she was tense with apprehension. She had imagined Ludwig's arrival a hundred times since he had rung last night to say, in his still slightly accented voice, that as he would leave the ski lodge early in the morning he should be home about lunchtime. So this is what it is like to be a betrayed wife, she thought flatly as she prepared some coffee and reminded herself that she had only the faintest grounds for suspicion of Ludwig. The pattern of life was unchanged, the externals remained in place but it was all husk. Your husband rang, he still called you darling, you continued to run the house and the second car, even if he was out on loan. Civilized was the word for it, frightfully European, which made it part of the stereotype Monica had scoffed at when she married Ludwig thirteen years ago and there was dire talk of the unfaithfulness of European husbands.

She took her coffee to the patio, which was flanked by the driveway and overlooked the harbour, and lay back on the cushioned cane lounge. The harbour held the grey of the overcast sky and, even though it was June, the atmosphere had a March warmth. Monica took the binoculars from the coffee table by the lounge to scan the section of harbour she commanded but the Manly ferry and a two-masted yacht were the only craft in sight. Perhaps she could have accepted Ludwig's betrayal if it had taken place with anyone but the Lonergans. She thought of it like that—not only Wilma Lonergan, but the Lonergans. For Ludwig to betray her with the Lonergans came close to incest: Monica could not think of them without her own parents coming to mind.

Determined to relax, Monica had barely closed her eyes when she head Ludwig's Jaguar; it slowed, swung, then crunched the driveway's gravel. She checked her impulse to run to meet him and, foxing sleep, watched until the Jaguar rolled into the garage. She really closed her eyes as the car door slammed and kept them closed until Ludwig sprang onto the verandah and kissed her on the lids.

"A sleeping living doll!" said Ludwig, all mock surprise. "Does she walk and talk?" Usually his dark skin and hair, together with his strong features, made his face hard but now it seemed boyish.

Monica swung her legs off the chaise lounge as if they were held in a plaster cast. "If anyone will listen she's liable to bouts of total recall. Walking's not so easy."

This was not quite true but it was meant to awake sympathy. Monica had homed after wrenching her knees skiing, saying that she would be more comfortable convalescing in her own place. She had not added that it was torture to be confined to bed in the ski lodge while Ludwig and Wilma enjoyed each other's company.

Ludwig kissed her cheek diplomatically. "That's tough Monica." He frowned as he gripped his beard-shadowed jaw. "The Lonergans drove up with me—I asked them to drop in . . . ."

Monica felt her scalp flinch.

"It was one of those last minute things—I couldn't say goodbye now without even asking them in for a drink."

A car drew up at the front gate. Ludwig went to greet the Lonergans, then Mick Lonergan rounded the corner with Wilma and Ludwig, laughing together, following. Although stooped, Mick Lonergan, a strong-framed six foot two in his prime, was still an imposing figure. He greeted Monica as if she were a daughter.

Wilma turned from her joke with Ludwig to ask Monica whether her knees had improved. Monica lied that she could not walk without a stick, hoping that would induce the Lonergans to drive straight on but instead Wilma ordered her to stay on the lounge while she prepared drinks. Monica felt then that she really was a victim. Mick Lonergan eased himself into a chair to tell her how they had passed the time since she had left the ski lodge while Ludwig, of course, showed Wilma about the house. Monica listened with only half an ear when she realised that Mick Lonergan would tell her nothing of the relations between Wilma and Ludwig.

As far back as Monica could remember there was always Lonergan. Her father and Lonergan had been officers together in the first world war and until her father's death they had kept the memory alive even though their fortunes had been so diverse: Lonergan had returned to run his family's wealthy property in New England while Monica's father had become an accountant. He prospered in the immediate postwar years, but Monica's memories began as the depression of 1929 blighted business. They were the years in which Monica choked with panic as the shouting matches between her father and mother became fierce; her father had the upper hand for he had the advantage of an overbearing personality and a Catholic faith in which he found dogmatic answers to every problem even, eventually, to that of living with a non-Catholic wife: they separated.

In Monica's young eyes the Lonergans were fabled creatures, for her father constantly praised Lonergan's drive, intelligence, commanding personality, he listed his holdings and stock, and promised Monica that she would ride in the Lonergans' Lancia. And while the Lonergans were in town he recaptured some of the dash of the just-discharged officer; he regarded himself as host and Sydney as his property. At what cost though, at what cost! They all paid when the Lonergans returned to the country.

Monica at that time sensed a connection between the Lonergans' visits and her parents' quarrels but not until she was older did she realise it was due to both religion and snobbery. Her father enjoyed his contact with the intellectual, as well as the social, assurance of the Lonergans. They moved exclusively among Catholics and had never a moment's doubt about their faith; Monica's father's efforts to impose the same iron doctrines on her unbelieving mother had met with such resistance that he welcomed a yearly respite with the massively certain Lonergans.

The cosy colloquy between Ludwig and Wilma as they prepared drinks in the kitchen abruptly gave away to an argument which Monica listened to without being able to pick up its sense. There was a rapid exchange which could have been a lovers' quarrel before Wilma emerged with the tray of drinks, smiling as if she were hostess.

"Has Daddy given you all the news Monica? You should have been there dear, the last week's been superb."

"I wouldn't have enjoyed it," said Monica, "not cooped up."

"The Burnetts arrived the day after you left—Gordon, Melanie, and the Monster. You just should have met them."

The name Burnett meant nothing to Monica but she could imagine them: they would barely be back from an overseas trip, they would be regular theatre first-nighters, they would drive the latest model cars and keep to the more exotic makes, their home would be a functional, architect-designed box.

"Didn't Ludwig tell you about them?"

"I'm sure Ludwig has lots to tell me Wilma."

"Let's go down to the Burnett's P.B. house instead of driving home Daddy," said Wilma, saved from boredom by this improvisation.

Wilma was one of those whose forebears had pioneered so successfully that there now seemed little left to do other than trip off to Europe, America, and, lately, even Asia, to adopt the latest overseas styles, and to compete to appear in the social columns of the Herald and the Telegraph. She had given signs of such development when attending the Rose Bay convent with Monica. Wilma, a few years younger than Monica, started later at the convent but within a short time she was attracting more attention. Monica was outstanding for her fervour: she assiduously amassed spiritual bouquets, she was a regular communicant, she ran up a rosary of novenas for years in the vain hope that her mother would overcome her invincible ignorance and, receiving the gift of faith, return to serve her husband. Moreover she was one of the better students, quiet and conscientious, whereas Wilma was mechanical in the practice of her religion and careless in her studies. None of this counted, however, against the fact that Wilma was one of the rich country set while Monica was a Sydney girl, a boarder kept there because her mother was not a Catholic and, as the girls were constantly warned, mixed marriages did not work out. As confirmation of this, Wilma had supplied fulsome background information about Monica's home life to the other boarders.

Monica appraised Wilma's downswept dark hair, her dramatically emphasised eyes and mouth, her golden, silk, skin-tight slacks, and Italian silk straw top piece as she begged her daddy to run down to Palm Beach, and wondered why she had been so happy to introduce Ludwig to her at the ski lodge the year before. The reason was patent: after losing her parents while she was at the convent, and her faith

　　　　　　　　　　　　　　　　　　　　DESMOND O'GRADY

while at university, Monica led an almost solitary life until she met Ludwig. She had lost touch with all her convent friends while Ludwig, a plastics-factory owner, could introduce her only to dreary businessmen. So she had been pleased to present Ludwig to the Lonergans when, the previous year, they had chanced to arrive at the same ski lodge. Ludwig had appreciated their company from the start but Monica had never imagined a liaison with Wilma would result. The nuns at Rose Bay would be surprised at their pupil's progress, thought Monica, but then it struck home: what could be more Catholic than such a situation, for wasn't divorce unthinkable?

"Has Gregory settled in at that school yet?" asked Ludwig with a heaviness which broke Wilma's light chatter. Monica, surprised at the question, said their son had settled in splendidly but Ludwig persisted, asking whether Gregory studied sufficiently for a boy in his first year of secondary school.

"It's not what they study," said Wilma, "it's who they meet."

Mick Lonergan raised two fingers hieratically. "Wilma sees things superficially, which would be all right if she would only stick to wearing skirts." Turning to Ludwig, he spoke with even greater deliberation than usual. "What weighs, Ludwig, is the atmosphere in which they learn."

Monica had the impression that she was hearing the conclusion of a long conversation. She presumed that Lonergan was so old he adopted this paternal attitude with everybody but she was surprised that Ludwig, who was dominating in his own way, should listen as if he were a son.

"Rose Bay had atmosphere enough, didn't it Monica?" Wilma accepted a light from Ludwig and fixed her cigarette in a long holder.

"It was right out of this world." Monica, who could smile now at the memory of the convent, sat up and wished she could rise to walk without seeming a hypocrite.

"We've learnt a lot that they never taught us." Wilma smiled at Monica as if they shared an understanding.

"I spent a long time unlearning what they taught us."

"Monica is a philosopher." Ludwig spoke loudly, half jolly, half annoyed. He was impatient with Monica's way of discussing things without ever reaching a conclusion, detecting in it a fear of the definite.

That's exactly how Wilma would have summed me up when we met on her return from her first trip abroad, thought Monica. She recalled that she had received a printed card, with a scribbled note from Wilma attached, inviting her to lunch at Princes'. Not until she arrived did Monica realise it was a gathering of Wilma's former school friends. It was barely eighteen months since they had left the convent but the changes in the girls were striking. Some of them, like Wilma, had already been overseas and had discovered an interest in theatre and art which they would continue to ignore in their own country. Others had returned to the country so that they could frequently descend on the city, as they had that day, in pomp; some of them had found husbands with an acreage equal to that of their own families, and the rest were looking forward to the Bachelors' Balls. A few were at the university which, from their talk, seemed a social club; but not one of them, no one they even *knew*, had fallen as low as Monica. They had all felt she was painfully out of place: not only was she dressed in some puritan uniform of skirt and jumper which was just too drab altogether for Princes', but she had a dull academic glaze to her eyes. The point was, of course, that the luncheon group was made up of the convent country set and it was only because of Lonergan generosity that Monica had been invited at all.

Monica did not appreciate all this until later. Possibly she was too absorbed in her own problems to take much notice, for the university had made her question all the certainties which had comforted her in the convent and one by one they dissolved. She stayed with Wilma after the others had gone to see whether her beliefs had likewise been shaken but Wilma, as she should have guessed, had no patience with such problems. Monica understood just how much she had been out of it when a friend pointed out, in the Telegraph's women's pages the next morning, a 'Lonergan back from London' paragraph: every girl was mentioned by name except Monica.

"She was always the studious type," Wilma told Ludwig, and Monica attempted to cover the paperback which lay beside her on the lounge.

Mick Lonergan, pointing with his athritic left hand, asked what it was. He would recognise it only if it was a Catholic book.

"A book of stories" said Monica, tossing it on to the coffee table.

"No name?" Mick Lonergan sometimes had the manner of a police sergeant.

" 'The Wrong Set,' " said Monica.

"Who's that by?" Wilma apparently guessed it was her sort of territory, even if a bit off the map.

"Angus Wilson."

"He's that young fellow," said Ludwig going in to set up more drinks, "who's just written a book on murder."

"It would be wonderful to be a writer," said Wilma. "Daddy is always talking of writing a book about the family, you know, pioneering saga and all that jazz, but he never gets underway."

Perhaps Mick Lonergan did not hear; his face, always red because the capillary veins under the skin had burst, was aflame; his head drooped.

"I reckon he should get someone to do it for him. But it would be wonderful to be really creative I mean. I love Morris West, don't you? I've just read 'Daughter of Silence'."

Ludwig had no opinion.

Monica waited until Wilma addressed the question silently to her.

"He's a fake," she said with a flat intensity, "a phony." It was quite final. Monica could be a conversation stopper, thought Wilma, discovering that Monica, who had

DESMOND O'GRADY

never made it socially, was a snob in her own way.

Monica wished only that the Lonergans would leave so that she could rise and confront Ludwig before Gregory returned from school. It was pretty clear that he was having an affair and trying to carry it off with a sophisticated flourish: Monica felt like a character in a Schnitzler comedy, only it would have to be a paralysed character. She longed to walk. She looked at robust Ludwig wrestling his Alsatian Bismarck and wondered just how much she understood him. He certainly had a taste for Sacré Coeur girls and, it seemed, a talent for moving up the social scale in his choices; but even here she felt there was something which eluded her. Still she would not let an affair ruin her marriage. She felt grateful for the bitter knowledge that an affair was not the worst that could happen; what she really feared was the bigotry that had torn her parents' lives to pieces. She and Ludwig had already compromised wisely: after living for some years without beliefs Monica had returned to the Church but with a different, newly liberal concept of its role. She believed in Christ as the Church did but thought the Church itself more fallible than it claimed to be. She had been discreet on the subject of religion with Ludwig. He was a Jewish agnostic and agreed to a church marriage solely to satisfy Monica while she, in turn, agreed that any children would not attend Catholic schools: they would have a chance to make their own choice of religion. Monica passed her hand across her brow. It was oppressively humid, and tiresome Wilma was discussing, of all things, the view. She told Monica how fortunate she was to have it.

"The harbour is a bit hackneyed," said Monica, then cautioned herself to be less boorish.

"Hackneyed or not," said Ludwig, "Monica is always studying it through those binoculars."

Wilma yawned expansively.

"Ludwig calls that side Buda" said Monica, "and this side Pest."

This information sent Wilma into disconcerting giggles.

"It's a nice touch," Monica spoke drily, "it makes you think you're in old Europe."

"I'd love to go to Hungary now that things have quietened down."

Ludwig rose to pace the patio rapidly.

"Spain will always be my favourite, though," Wilma continued. "It's a pity Australia and Spain aren't closer. You'd love a bullfight if you saw one Monica."

"What about El Porco? Just the thought of him running the place is enough for me. I'm sure you'd like Portugal even better if you went there Wilma—it's *really* picturesque. I don't suppose you went to the prisons in Spain—you'd have found them full of colourful political prisoners."

Wilma, discomfited, started on a description of the pleasures of Spanish life but Ludwig cut in heatedly, "If Franco hadn't won, Europe would be completely Communist today. Franco has his faults but he's one of the best dictators—Spaniards are grateful to him for securing law and order for thirty years."

"They're waiting for elections to show just how grateful they are. How nice can a dictator be?" They had been through the argument many times and Ludwig always roared Monica down. Wilma was lost in the crossfire and her presence would stop it from developing into a long, comprehensive battle. Ludwig hated Monica's reluctance to face the hard realities of life; at times he felt himself Spanish—he would know how to kill for Christ.

"You thought that after the civil war an English parliament would rule in Spain?" Ludwig was shouting loud enough to stir Mick Lonergan. "That's the trouble with living in Australia, you're so far away you don't understand a menace like Communism."

Monica kept her peace: Ludwig was so rabid in these political discussions he always had the final say and it was best not to provoke him.

"Can you see more of the harbour from down there?" asked Wilma uncertainly, and Monica suggested to Ludwig that he take Wilma to the back of the garden.

"I'll watch through binoculars," said Monica, and they went off, Wilma asking Ludwig what he thought of Santamaria. Mick Lonergan awoke slowly, looking old, stuffy, even stupid. Monica's hope that the Lonergans would go rose now that Wilma was out of the comfortable deck chair. As they strolled across the lawn, Monica noted that Wilma was the same height as Ludwig; his fawn slacks and loose blue cotton sports shirt made it seem they were dressed in His and Hers outfits. Ludwig somehow looked a natural companion for Wilma while Monica had the strange impression that she was a bitter, fragile woman of Mick Lonergan's generation.

Wilma cavorted springily across the lawn as they returned. "You don't know how lucky you are Monica to have that spread out in front of you," she called. "It would make living in a wheelchair a pleasure. Seeing it like that anyone would think you *owned* it. I can't live without the sea." She waved a silk scarf breezily. "It gets so dry around Walgett. We *are* going to the Burnett's Daddy." She dived at him to kiss his cheek with the swiftness of a girl of eighteen. "I'll drive, now don't make a fuss. You can sleep at the Burnett's Daddy." Wilma was helping her father out of the chair and Ludwig took his other arm. "Why don't you two come with us?"

Ludwig referred the question to Monica but she pleaded her painful knees so at last, after farewelling Monica, the Lonergans left her. As soon as they had gone Monica came to her feet and, taking the ash tray filled with Wilma's cigarette butts, entered the house. She tipped the butts into the water closet and continued to the front lounge where, from behind the curtains, she could observe Ludwig farewelling the Lonergans. They were grouped by the car, with Wilma eyeing the house critically and Ludwig in earnest conversation with Mick Lonergan. Monica saw no threat in the old man so she took the opportunity to examine herself in a wall mirror: she was reassured to see an austerely handsome face, neatly boned and narrow, which had kept its form even though the fair skin, blue eyes and straw coloured hair were quick to show the first signs of age. She was happy to find her face: stretched on the lounge during the Lonergans' visit she had felt featureless, as if she had only a past and no present. Now that they were about to enter the Citroen, Ludwig placed his arm about Wilma's shoulders to give her a fraternal hug.

Ludwig stayed to wave the Lonergans out of sight for he felt a real gratitude towards them. He had not met anybody quite like the Lonergans before and he was annoyed that Monica had not been more cordial. Granted their visit had been unexpected and her knees were still troubling her, but weren't the Lonergans old family friends? Perhaps Monica was jealous of their assurance. Ludwig recognised that Monica, in some respects, was insecure and fragile; what exasperated him was that she seemed to prefer precarious indecision to anything clear and decisive. It was, decided Ludwig as he walked along the driveway, a neurotic state of mind.

Ludwig had been disposed to believe in miracles for only a few days and here, it seemed, one had happened: Monica was walking towards him along the patio.

Arms akimbo, Ludwig said, "That was a quick recovery!" He sounded more angry than pleased but Monica ignored the remark.

"We'll be seeing a lot of the Lonergans, will we?"

She wanted the whole question settled before Gregory's return but she did not know how to go about it; perhaps Europeans had conventions to cope with such situations.

"You introduced me to them," said Ludwig coming onto the patio. "Why are you suddenly so down on them?"

"I didn't know it would finish like this . . ."

"Like what?" asked Ludwig, at a loss.

Monica saw she was on the verge of making herself ridiculous. Ludwig obviously did not know what she referred to and she wondered why she had such a persistent sense of threat.

"Nothing Ludwig, I was just surprised that you became such a friend of the Lonergans." Monica sat in a bamboo chair because her legs were trembling now that it had all ended in an anticlimax.

Ludwig, concerned, perched on the edge of the chaise lounge. "There's few men I admire as much as Mick Lonergan," he said.

Monica accepted the switch from Wilma to Mick Lonergan; all she knew now was that she had not understood at all.

"He's a success" she admitted, "but he had it made—their property has been in the family for three generations."

Ludwig waved that consideration away. "Not that—everything about him. That's what I call to be on top of life."

A curious expression, Monica thought, probably a translation of an idiomatic one. Anyway it was Ludwig's greatest encomium.

"Despite the Australian legend to the contrary," said Monica, "established families have an assurance that others can't attain all of a sudden."

"I don't agree with you at all Monica."

She asked herself how she could have imagined him conducting an affair when he had become so ponderous.

"The Lonergans have a certainty, and you could have it too."

It was a delphic answer as far as Monica was concerned but she let it pass; Bismarck had brought his ball for Ludwig to throw, and now that the menace had proved illusory she wanted to relax. The atmosphere was less close now and the lowering sun penetrated the clouds sufficiently to strike a glittering sheen from the harbour. The sight of Ludwig tossing the ball for Bismarck, and the Alsatian leaping for it, then backing and growling as Ludwig tore the saliva-smothered ball from his mouth, seemed cosily domestic to Monica. She regretted her dryness with the Lonergans but her instinct had warned her and, as a victim of a broken home, she was particularly sensitive to anything which could injure Gregory. Seeing Ludwig engaged now in a mock fight with Bismarck, she reproved herself for her suspicion; he was so direct, she told herself, that if anything like that had happened he would have told her himself.

"Greg's due any minute, isn't he darling?"

Monica confirmed it.

"There was something I wanted to settle with you before he arrived."

She felt the slightest quaver of disquiet.

"Stop strangling Bismarck then."

Ludwig came on to the patio again and stood above Monica. "You're quite happy with that school of his."

"We went through this earlier." Bismarck deposited the slimy ball in Monica's lap.

"You might be happy but I'm not. I'm surprised at you Monica. In any case I want him to change straightaway."

Ludwig's face had taken on a peculiarly rigid expression.

"It would be foolish to make him change at this time of the year."

"It would be foolish to let him stay."

"Why? Where did you get this idea Ludwig? And where would you send him?" Monica, amazed by the proposal, felt panic at his tone.

"He'll go to Riverview."

The full force of it hit her then. There had been a Lonergan threat after all.

"Riverview!" Her voice was faint. "They won't take him at this time of the year."

"Well we'll send him to some other Catholic school."

Monica could hear her father using the same words. She looked up to see Ludwig's face set in the same stern mask as her father's.

"It will upset Gregory to switch over like that."

"He'll be grateful for it when he realises what it means." Bismarck was at Ludwig to toss the ball again and as he had, in his fashion, settled the question of Gregory's future he returned to the lawn.

Monica watched Ludwig put Bismarck through his paces and tussle with the beast in perfect content until she felt weak in face of their combative spirit. The sheen had died from the harbour, once more the air pressed in on her, and she was choked by the past. She took up the binoculars.

After a short time she called excitedly to Ludwig: "Sharks! Look Ludwig—sharks!"

This, at least, made him cease his violent struggle with Bismarck. But as soon as Ludwig took the binoculars he saw Monica's mistake.

"Have you ever seen sharks carrying on like that—they're porpoises. You just couldn't pick when you're in danger, could you?" And, hot from his battle with Bismarck, he bent to kiss Monica hard on the cheek, for she did not offer her mouth.

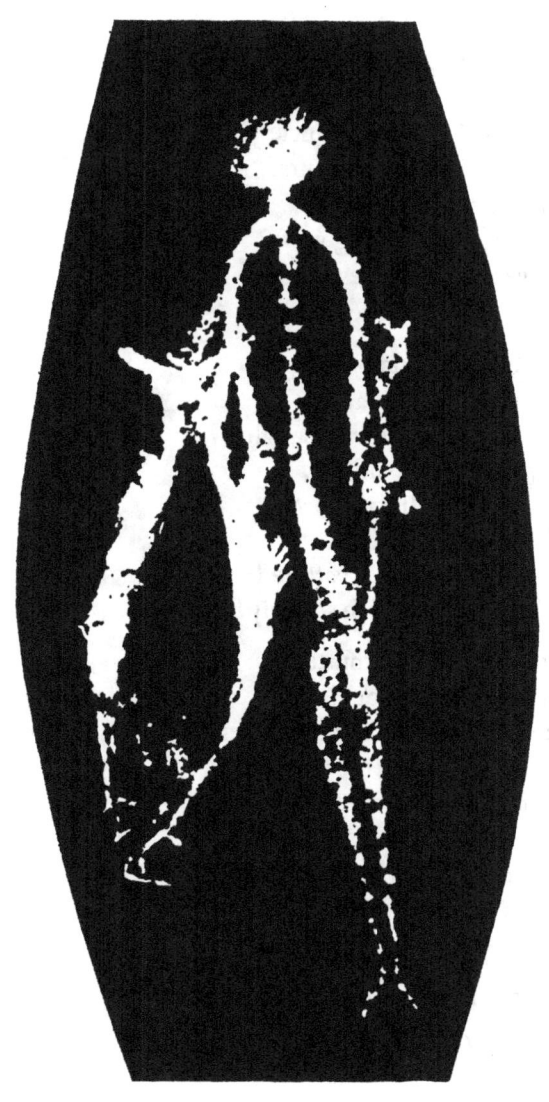

A. D. HOPE : *Conversation with Calliope*

'Finierat dictos e nobis maxima cantus'

The proper way to start a poem
Built on the old high generous plan
Is to invoke the Muse; and, though I'm
Bound to placate the harridan,
She can't expect an epic proem:
The trick's been lost; the best she can
Look for in these degenerate times
Is an *O Thou* to start the rhymes.

'*O Thou!*'—You see it does sound silly—
'*Descend, my Muse!*'—and that sounds worse.
'Descend and—' 'Don't be Uncle Willy!'
She says, appearing just like nurse,
The antiseptic smile, the chilly:
'Well, Master Alec, writing verse?
I'm sure I've told you times enough
I can't be bothered with your stuff.

Now that you're fat and over forty,
It's rather odd, you must agree,
My sisters having all proved haughty
Though wooed with assiduity,
You find that after all your *forte*
Was writing epic poetry;
And offer me this slightly battered
Bald rhymester—well, I'm scarcely flattered!'

'I'm very sorry, Miss;' I mutter,
'Indeed I beg your pardon, Ma'am!
But though we poets spread the butter,
The Muses must supply the jam.
The flood of things I have to utter
Threatens, you see, to burst the dam,
Without your aid, to whom belong
The lost arts of heroic song.

You may be right about my figure;
It has perhaps filled out of late.
There's no denying that a wig or
Toupee might enhance my pate.

But while you name with wonted vigour
Defects I grant without debate,
Yet there is one aspersion I
Must categorically deny:

Your imputation of neglect,
That only in the last resort
With failing powers or prospects wrecked
I turn to pay you tardy court,
This, with concern, I must reject.
At fifteen years, or less, I sought
Your aid, and with that aid began
An epic on the Doom of Man

Though I suppose its verse was far
From mastery and blank at best,
Though Browning was the avatar
The style too well made manifest,
While Renan's *Abbesse de Jouarre*
Supplied my scheme, yet all the rest
Was mine: contrivance, persons, tales
Made up in Bathurst, New South Wales.

I gave it up, as you recall,
Before the end of Canto Two,
But not till I had planned it all,
Nor, though a child, until I knew
My bent and heard the poet's call
That brings his promised land in view.
Though forty years have passed I still
Have not forgotten Pisgah's hill.

Who that has known it can forget
That first fierce moment of elation
When a young poet feels the jet
And vigour of his inspiration?
Not fame achieved compares, nor yet
Can Love's supreme intoxication.
And at that moment you were there
And smiling bent above my chair'.

'I own', she answers less irately,
'That once you seemed a likely lad.
But think of all I've suffered lately,
The family troubles that I've had.

A sister can't sit by sedately
And see things going to the bad:
There's poor Miss Clio's lost her wits;
Euterpe cursed with sinking fits;

Terpsichore reels home each night
As drunk as any fiddler's bitch;
And, since the time has passed you might
Behold the Muse without a stitch,
Turned prude at last and laced too tight
Thalia's caught a nasty itch;
Unhinged by neurasthenic dreams
Melpomene just sits and screams;

Erato—though, I won't deny it,
She keeps her health and earns her crust—
Has lost her figure, needs a diet
And uplift for a sagging bust,
Spends half her nights in maudlin riot
And works for an Amusement Trust;
Urania's lost the common touch
And only talks in Double Dutch;

And Polyhymnia's on a pension:
The sacred arts are out of date;
Gods are not asked for intervention
To save a technocratic state;
And if by chance or by intention
She's present when they celebrate,
It is with an embarrassed air
She mumbles some archaic prayer;

As for myself, I must admit I
Am on the shelf, and that's a fact,
The ramparts of my Trojan city
In ruins and its temples sacked,
And not by poets, more's the pity,
Critics and scholars range the tract
Where Milton sang the world's *Te Deum*,
To pick up bits for their museum.

For since society has ended
Its ancient pact with the divine,
The public actions which depended

A. D. HOPE

On common faith to make them shine
Once gone, what use is left the splendid
Impetus of the epic line?
The chronicle of prose survives
For the small beer of private lives.

My sister Clio shares, of course,
At least a measure of the blame;
An epic loses half its force
Not built round some historic name,
Some legend which at least for source
Has deeds that Truth will not disclaim;
Its greatness rests on a conviction
That heroes happen outside fiction.

And since historical research
Has lost the name of noble action,
Proved most ideas in state and church
Mere subterfuge of greed and faction,
That great men do not lead: they lurch
Between rebellion and reaction,
By documented texts it can
Abolish the Uncommon Man.

And as for the Uncommon Woman
Who blessed the Hero's hearth and bed,
Divine Calypso or the human
Penelope he chose instead,
Your psychological acumen
Thrusts in where angels fear to tread
And proves her something in between
A mirage and a love-machine'.

'Madam', I say, 'although no stranger
To the misfortunes you relate,
I can't believe your fame in danger
Or think the mode so out of date;
For though the dog is in the manger,
No hand has locked the stable gate:
The wingèd horse is free and still
May light upon your sacred hill.

The Muses and the modes you mention
Have fallen, I grant, on evil days;

Slovenly craft and cheap invention
May parch the spring and blast the bays,
Your art alone, without declension
Preserves its splendour and its praise'.
'Poor comfort', she retorts, 'and small
When no one writes it now at all.

The epics of the past perhaps
Survive like Tadmor in the waste,
Impressive still, but in the lapse
Of ages men first lose the taste
And then the skill; while, on the maps
Their sites forgotten or misplaced,
They wait, as ancient ruins should,
For Horace Walpole's Mr. Wood.

There was a time the poet's mission
Was to give men their daily bread,
The crown of life, the timeless vision
Which linked the living with the dead.
When Homer spoke, the great tradition
Of verse commanded, taught and led;
With Milton it began to nod,
And Cowley was its *Ichabod*.

"Who now reads Cowley?" Who indeed
Reads Homer now or his translator
But schoolboys and the dons who breed
Their kind in every empty crater?
Can some fresh Milton rise to feed
Blind mouths in Learning's incubator,
Or Pegasus his flight renew
Boiled down for academic glue?

For after Cowley came Defoe's
Invention of domestic fiction;
The comic epic dressed in prose
Drove out heroic deeds and diction;
Pamela's budget of chaste woes
Pleased more than Homer's whole depiction
Of Troy and Milton's War with Hell
Less than the Death of Little Nell.

So by a sort of Gresham's Law
The novel rose, the epic died,

A. D. HOPE

Nor could be resurrected nor
Remade, for all that Arnold tried.
"What did they kill each other for?"
Old Kaspar's small granddaughter cried,
Which marked, since Kaspar could not say,
How a whole world had passed away.

Well, if you still would venture on it,
Go in and try it: you will find
To poems longer than a sonnet
Your readers deaf, your critics blind.
Even the few prepared to con it
Will lack enlargement of the mind.
No lion-soul acquires its habit
From close acquaintance with the rabbit.

Long narratives are out of fashion;
Sustained invention does not please;
And sacred truth and moral passion
Belong to former centuries.
Yet epic stakes its reputation
On public taste for things like these.
Readers who give your poem a glance
Will settle for a police romance'.

'All that you urge is cogent, Madam',
I say, 'and sure the Muse knows best;
Yet if a simple son of Adam
May speak and venture to contest,
The epic gifts, suppose I had 'em,
Will quickly put me to the test
And if I fail, I may at least
Make way against the Blatant Beast'.

'Well, if you must, you must, my hearty'
She answers with a little frown.
'If *con amore* match *con arte*,
My scholar yet may grace the gown.
But if we must prolong this party,
You might invite me to sit down,
For legs, though not of mortal clay
Will tire and I have more to say'.

'A thousand pardons, pray be seated;
Allow me to pull up a chair!

Forgive me, being somewhat heated,
If I forget the proper care
With which the Muses should be treated:
Their visits are extremely rare.
To honour this poor house of mine,
May I suggest a glass of wine?'

'Thank you, although the drink I treasure
I don't suppose you have—I mean
Of course to ask you for a measure
Of pure, unblushing Hippocrene?
No? Well, I should accept the pleasure
A drop of anything between
From nectar down to mortal pottle;
No glasses though: bring out the bottle!'

The wine poured out, I take my chair.
She tastes and nods and says: 'Not bad!
Now let's get back to where we were:
Your epic poem. Suppose you had
The wit, have you the time to spare?
That *jeu d'esprit*, your *Dunciad*,
Cost you six months, as I recall,
And only four books, after all.

Four books and comic stuff at that,
And yet it caused you quite a coil
Before you had it neat and pat,
Long days of unremitting toil
And nights of labour when you sat
Keeping your modest pot aboil
Or tossed in fever on your bed
With verses seething in your head.

Can you conceive the dedication
Those mighty works demand? Or can
You summon up the concentration,
That service of the entire man
Required to plan, to mould, to fashion
To grind the grain and bolt the bran?
A task so long, so great, so dread,
So Pope, my foster child, once said,

As leaves a man, this side the grave,
Scarce time to breathe, no time to be

Friend, neighbour, husband, nay, to have
The care to plant and tend a tree,
Much less in the long run, to save
His soul or meet eternity.
If not, just fold the napkin round
And hide your talent in the ground'.

'Ah, there's the rub indeed', I say;
'The doubt you raise, I feel and share it.
Most poets are employed today,
Own cars, eat well, drink vintage claret
—Your glass is empty by the way—
Hogarth's poor poet in his garret
Or truckling at a patron's board
Has gone forever, praise the Lord!

But though the Lord be praised, I wonder
Are poets so much better off?
Though now they have their share of plunder
And get both forefeet in the trough,
To earn their bread they have to squander
The hours they once were masters of;
In fact the poet's calling pays
Much worse than in the bad old days.

Those bad old days (would they were with us!)
Saw Ariosto trim his light
Debase his art, deploy his mythus
To lick the boots of Este's knight.
Well, let it wring the critic's withers,
At least he had the time to write.
Odd jobs as envoy or commando
Still left him years for his *Orlando*.

Admit he flattered, grant the note
Of adulation gross and crass,
The King of France who turned his coat
Considered Paris worth a mass.
And shall I sneer while I devote
My days to lecture-room and class?
There's nothing sours the Muses' soil
Like eight good hours of honest toil.

And while that garden blights and sours
On which a full sun rarely shines,

The poets labour after hours
To raise a crop of stunted lines,
Like serfs who round the baron's towers
By day manure the baron's vines
And, while exhausted muscles groan,
By moonlight cultivate their own.

The serf well knew the serf's condition;
He knew his wine was harsh and thin.
The well-fed poet's dwindling vision
Soon cuts his coat to suit his skin,
Thinks the great tuns of the tradition
Not equal to his kilderkin,
And that no House of Fame surpasses
His week-end cottage on Parnassus.

See Esau tamed, in Jacob's lobby
Run errands now for Jacob's house;
His birthright bartered for a job, he
Plans mountains that bring forth a mouse;
For art diminished to a hobby
Yields just what hobby-time allows.
Why does he do it? Save your breath:
As poet he would starve to death.

Take my own case: the world of letters
Is what, God help me, I profess;
For lecturing about my betters
Each year they pay me more or less
Four thousand pounds. Ask what I get as
Poet!—at a random guess
For poems forged with sweat and tears,
Four hundred pounds in forty years!

Now take the Greeks'—Says she, 'Young fellow
I'd rather hear you on the purse.
Your theme grows warm as you grow mellow
(Though frequently your rhymes get worse.)
Let's take the Greeks; but please don't bellow.
You argue prettily in verse.
Go on! I like to hear you speak,
Especially as you know no Greek.

And on the Greeks, you might recall,
The towns which strove for Homer dead

To build him a memorial
Were those where Homer begged his bread.
There never was an age at all
Gave poets three meals and a bed
Though every age is apt to cast
Regretful glances at the past.

In every Paradise, professor,
The charmer lures, the serpent lurks;
When academic chores depress or
Committees gall and teaching irks,
Just think of Chaucer, the Assessor
Of Customs and the Clerk of Works;
And yet by candlelight he made
The time for *Troilus and Criseyde*.

Think of Camoëns as trustee
Serving the absent and the dead;
Hated, reviled, imprisoned, he
Could still contrive his *Lusiad*;
View Milton in his misery
Unfaltering, and Tasso mad,
And judge if your condition bears
The least comparison with theirs.

What genius has a mind to speak
Mere circumstance will rarely throttle,
But, if the wine is thin and weak,
It makes no sense to blame the bottle.
Our hidden cause is still to seek;
It is not found in Aristotle
For he was born before the long
Decline and fall of epic song.

He knew it at its peak and prime
And gave no thought to its decay.
Longinus too, on the sublime,
On this had nothing much to say
And Vida looked to see it climb
To greater triumphs in his day.
But what the worthies never knew
The steadfast Muses keep in view.

The gift of prophecy they hold,
Although it is the lesser gift,

The past and future they behold
And poets sometimes catch its drift,
Catch glimpses of the Age of Gold
And sometimes see the curtain lift
Upon the face of things to come
When other oracles are dumb.

But though the Muse bestows the vision
She very seldom gives it scope,
Lest prophecy subvert his mission
By fostering the poet's hope
Through dim surmise and intuition
To cast creation's horoscope:
The task for which we grant the bays
Is still to celebrate and praise.

That task in which he may not shirk or
Falter, on his hope of bliss,
Die unbegreiflich hohen Werke
(The Devil himself once vouched for this)
Is, nobly, without crank or quirk or
Default, to show it as it is,
And through his art to bring to birth
New modes of being on the earth.

This is the task that we assign,
Not to haruspicate or scry;
The poet's part in the divine
Stops this side of divinity—
Let's have another flask of wine
Before I start to prophesy,
For now the time has come to show
Things that the Muse alone can know'.

I fetch the second bottle out
And while I draw the cork, I ask:
'First would you please resolve a doubt?
If celebration is our task,
I think I know what *that's* about;
The second part still wears the mask.
What does it mean—or must I wait?—
New modes of being to create?'

'Some truths can not be uttered save
By myth', she says, 'or like recourses:

(Socrates' Fable of the Cave;
Swift's Fable of the Talking Horses).
Though Wittgenstein turn in his grave,
The mind has other means and forces
"Whereof one cannot speak" to show
The inenarrable we know.

So, *pacè* Wittgenstein, I shall
Tell you my meaning in a fable;
And, though you may not grasp it all,
It has a grace which may enable
The heart to answer to its call;
While Logic built its Tower of Babel
The truth it seeks and seeks in vain
May fall like dew upon the plain.

In the beginning was the Word
—My myth, you see, is scarcely new—
But though it *was*, it was not heard;
The earth was void and nothing grew
Upon the barren rock; no bird
Flashed singing through the barren blue,
And in the blue and barren deep
There was no life to swim or creep.

It was as wild a world to see
As e'er returned its Maker thanks:
Mountains in savage majesty
Thrust upward in colossal ranks
And searing ice and scorching scree
Ground slowly down their ragged flanks,
While plains upheaving from their beds
Dried out in desert browns and reds.

And then the Word began to move,
Itself unmoved, the quickening Will,
By infinitesimals it wove
As in the womb it quickens still.
The endless edifice of love
Felt life's first step upon its sill
And in that primal globule furled
Lay all the orders of the world.

Orders of being come to birth
Evolving in the cosmic dance.

Each fills and each creates a dearth
Filled by the next in its advance:
Enfolding to transform the earth
First came the mantle of the plants
And with the beasts in their degrees
Made up the living entities.

The joy to see that green brocade
Bald scarps and shadow lake and rill,
Carpet bare clays with lawn and glade
Is something hard to grasp, until
One sees the dead moon-landscape made
By an abandoned copper mill
(As in Tasmania you have seen)
Breathe, burgeon and resume its green.

Then gradual in the womb of kind
The second mystery began:
The order of the conscious mind
Perfected in the race of man,
Gave eyes to groping needs and blind
And freed the will to search and plan,
A revolution as profound
As that which clothed the barren ground.

Civilisation when it came,
After long ages in the mould,
Formed the new hearth for a new flame,
Though kindled first in tribes too old
To leave a history or a name,
Or see from magic arts unfold
Within the world of mind the third
Order of being from the Word.

Freed from those ends which men foresee
And meet with predisposing skill,
The arts themselves propose the free
And unknown ends which they fulfil.
To shape the new entelechy
Of life, the autotelic will
Transfigures and transforms the span
Of all we mean by social man.

But here I ought to make a pause.
You catch my drift?—So far, so good.

New modes of being, till their laws
Prevail cannot be understood
Beyond the process and the cause;
The end will still be misconstrued
By minds unable to apply
The logic of analogy.

For instance, scientists agree
In thinking, and they may be right,
There was a time when none could see
Except in shades of black and white.
What must it have been like to be
The first few born with colour-sight,
And how could they explain or find
Words to convince the colour-blind?

That passion of scarlet, turquoise, gold
In feather, scale or leaf or shell,
Orchid or rose as they unfold
Their delicate, breathless miracle,
How could those drab, grey minds be told
With only grey, drab words to tell,
And lash or straitjacket, no doubt,
For those who dared to brave it out.

Anger or pity, or derision
Would be the least they could expect
Yet, see, they have imposed their vision
And made their foes a dwindling sect,
Achieved by means of binary fission
What argument could not effect;
So, *verbum sap.*, don't preach or shout—
Just work to bring the thing about.

But now, my friend, we have to turn
To that deferred, prophetic answer;
You cannot guess, divine or learn
The cause, so hear it while you can, sir,
Why epic cannot yet return.
I promised in an earlier stanza
Footnotes to Malthus and remarks
On certain doctrines of Karl Marx.

But what I have to tell embraces
Much more than Marx or Malthus guessed.

Conversation with Calliope

The future of the human race is
Somewhat precarious at best.
The day when mere survival places
All other values to the test
May not be far away; indeed
Man's deadliest instinct is to breed.

And breeding as he does unchecked
By Nature, Law or Common Caution,
No cornucopia can expect
To pour forth plenty in proportion,
Nor human skills for long perfect
New means to eke his dwindling portion:
Since self-control is too much bother
They'll end by eating one another.

My main concern of course is not
This anthropophagous dilemma;
Not last decay but that first spot,
The earthquake's first foreboding tremor.
The final inference is what
Should be implicit in the lemma
And what must bring man to the worst
May well pervert his nature first.

A plague like locusts, lemmings, lice
Breaks out like fire, typhoon, or flood,
And swiftly as it grows, it dies;
The human plague, less understood
Through slow millenia takes its rise,
At every step, so far so good!
And yet as each divide is crossed,
Some measure of the whole is lost.

Man wants but little, even so
By little wants he is misled:
"Man wants but little here", you know,
"Nor wants that little long", was said
By Edwin just about to throw
Fair Angelina on his bed;
Which lost the girl her pilgrim's permit,
And left him an unlicensed hermit.

Their vows abandoned with their habits
The "Law of Measure" set aside

Alas, the phrase is Irving Babbit's,
This precious hermit and his bride
Bred, as you might expect, like rabbits
And had produced before they died,
Counting greatgrandchildren as well,
Two hundred from that single cell.

But death by then was just the stitch in
Time devoutly wished by both.
They'd seen the life their love was rich in
Imperilled by its very growth.
It is not only in a kitchen
Too many cooks can spoil a broth,
And families perish by inflation
Into a tribe, a horde, a nation.

What Edwin found to be the case
Proves true in history's arena:
Huntress or victim of the chase,
Angelica or Angelina,
Each future mother of the race
So ravishing in her demeanor,
By instinct still, and natural bent, is
Another Sorcerer's Apprentice.

No hunter of the Age of Fable
Had need to buckle in his belt;
More game than he was ever able
To take ran wild upon the veldt;
Each night with roast he stocked his table,
Then procreated on the pelt.
And that is how, of course, there came
At last to be more men than game.

No matter: man's invention can
Snatch triumph from his worst mistakes.
Soon cuts of beef and pork began
To take the place of feral steaks,
Next bread, and sifting out the bran
He turned his plain loaf into cakes.
—And as for cake, mankind will do
Their best to eat and have it too.

It does not work: a time must come
—A fact that man is slow to learn—

Patch, plan, put off, explore and plumb,
You face the point of no return;
The Providential Voice is dumb,
And Wisdom, weeping by her urn,
Proffers in place of Nature's fruits
Synthetic pulps as substitutes.

Effects of over-population
Converge, no matter where you start;
The economics of inflation
Follows the same curve on the chart
To where *ersatz* provides the ration
Alike for belly, mind or heart.
Then Muses geared for mass production
We make, to save *us* from seduction.

For though it once made Plato groan,
Deceptions in the cause of grace,
We use at times and freely own.
The singer of the Works and Days
Watching his lambs on Helicon
Learned this and told it in a phrase:
"The Muses speak true things at will,
Though falsehoods lie within their skill."

Already these factitious muses
Spread their synthetic wares abroad;
Their sooterkins promote their views as
Members of Trust and Fund and Board;
The Great Society produces
Only the arts it can afford,
Stamped, sterilized and tinned and tested
And standardized and predigested.

Quite soon, let Observation view,
As systems and their nostrums cramp us,
The world from China to Peru,
The wild from taïgá to pampas,
The last tame bison in the zoo,
The last tame poet on the campus
Is all she'll find, poor Observation,
Of all the former free creation.

Well, there's your answer! In a word
To look for natural forms from this

Synthetic template is absurd.
The Word itself, their genesis
And goal withdraws and is not heard:
With Man disposing, God in his
Good time can scarce propose, or move
By patient, prescient, procreant love.

So first the great forms, as I said
A while ago, must disappear.
Epic, like tragedy, is dead;
The doom of all the rest is near,
Just as this wine whose living red
Delights the sense must go, I fear,
For where the vineyard stood, will be
A coca-cola factory'.

So saying she takes her glass in token
And drains it off and sets it by,
The silence as we sit unbroken
By motion, syllable or sigh,
While in my face she reads unspoken
Sad scrutinies of how and why,
And then at last to my relief
She smiles and intercepts my grief.

'There is no need for you to ask it:
If this is how the arts collapse,
Are all the eggs then in one basket?
Do all the poets then, poor chaps,
Labour in vain? And is the task it
Pleases us to set, perhaps
Mere throwing dust against the wind,
As pointless as it is unkind?'

'Why yes', I answer, 'while agreeing
That Sodom's arts prevail of late,
Shall no just man succeed in fleeing,
Leaving salt witness at the gate?
And what of those new modes of being
The Muse assigns us to create?
Can, while her mysteries unfold,
She palter, and blow hot and cold?'

'Look in my eyes', she says, 'and read
The answer to that doubt, my friend!'

And in that depthless gaze indeed,
Where all uncertainties have end,
Where lights in endless Light recede
And all the partial visions blend,
Rapt by its Universal theme
I hear her speak, yet seem to dream:

'Although the great Un-culture wins,
Though Sodom's values tip the scales,
Another providence begins,
The Word withdraws but never fails:
As in past ages, dressed in skins
And following the forest trails,
In those vast woods, each little clan
Preserved the entity of Man.

So in this next barbarian age,
Small clans we choose and hold apart,
Some few in whom the heavenly rage
Still blazes and keeps pure the heart;
The human jungle sets the stage
Where these new Levites learn their part:
To guard the coals and keep them fanned
And bear them towards the Promised Land.

Goodbye my friend, the gift of sleep
I leave you, not my gift of song—
That epic power alone I keep
For one unborn. You waited long
But did not sow and shall not reap.
To you the lower slopes belong,
To him the peaks when time is due.
Now sleep—for I have much to do'.

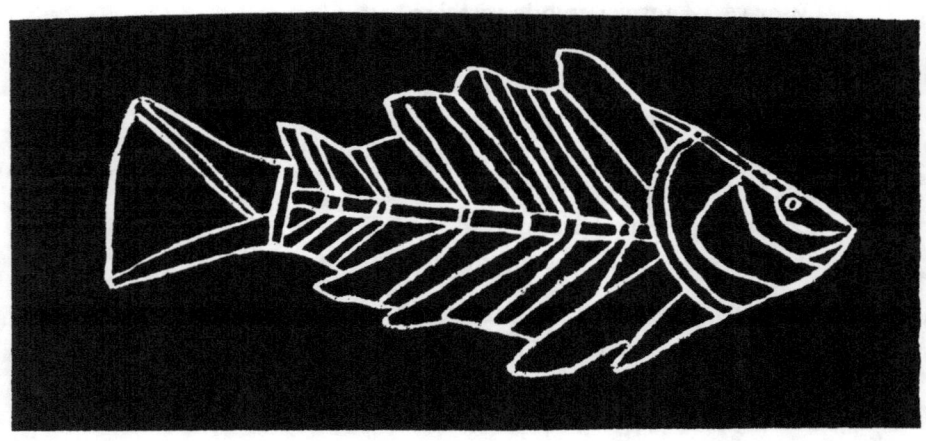

MOLNAR

HANS BEACHAM, whose photographs of Joan Sutherland appear in this issue, needs no introduction to *Quarterly* readers. His principal work, as stated in the Winter 1960 number, continues to be "making unorthodox portraits of famous persons"—a phrase in which the adjective "famous" may soon have to be used twice.

JOHN BLIGHT, born in South Australia in 1913, now works as an accountant in Queensland. Two books of his verse, *The Old Pianist* (1945) and *The Two Suns Met* (1954), have been published and two others are nearing completion. The marine life of the Great Barrier Reef, which Blight has often visited, is the subject of a series of ninety poems to which the sonnet "Mud" belongs.

ROBIN BOYD is a member of the architectural firm of Grounds, Romberg, and Boyd, Melbourne. Just past forty, Mr. Boyd has already a distinguished career behind him both as practicing architect and as interpreter of Australian architecture in numerous contributions to periodicals and in three books: *Victorian Modern* (1947), *Australia's Home* (1952), and *The Australian Ugliness* (1960). His next work is to be a monograph on Kenzo Tange of Japan.

ROBERT F. BRISSENDEN, with his wife Rosemary and small son Michael, recently drove a "Minibus" from California to New York, visiting American universities on a Carnegie Corporation travel grant. He is Senior Lecturer in English at the Australian National University, Canberra; is thirty-four; holds the M.A. from the University of Sydney and the PH.D. from Leeds; is a contributor to *Meanjin* and other Australian periodicals.

DAVID CAMPBELL, who describes himself as "farmer," would be called a rancher in Southwestern U.S. parlance. Campbell was born in New South Wales in 1915 and after a career as student and athlete at Sydney and Cambridge and as pilot in the Royal Australian Air Force (D.F.C. and bar) he returned to the land. His published poems are contained in magazines, anthologies, and two volumes: *Speak with the Sun* (1949) and *The Miracle of Mullion Hill* (1956). *Evening Under Lamplight* (1959) presents him as a short-story writer.

GAVIN CASEY of Manning, Western Australia, contends that "you have to work like a horse at writing in Australia in order to survive." Casey's numerous novels and books of stories published during the 1940s and 50s are proof not only of his survival but of his equine energy, which earlier was expended at such occupations as salesmanship and laboring on the Kalgoorlie gold mines. (He was born at Kalgoorlie in 1907.) During World War II he was a war correspondent with General MacArthur's forces in the Pacific, and from 1945 to 1947 served as Director of the Australian News and Information Bureau in New York. His latest novel, *Amid the Plenty*, appeared in March, 1962.

C. B. ("CLEM") CHRISTESEN, O.B.E., celebrated late in 1961 a twenty-first birthday—not his own (he was born at Townsville, Queensland, in 1911), but that of *Meanjin Quarterly*, which he founded and continues to edit. Mr. Christesen and his wife Nina (who teaches Russian at the University of Melbourne) live close to the "bush" on the outskirts of Melbourne but are a vital part of the city's cultural life—as *Meanjin* over nearly a quarter century has become a vital part of the cultural life of all Australia. Besides pursuing his career at midwifery for *Meanjin*, "Clem" has done lecturing, served as a publisher's branch manager, been a journalist, published a considerable amount of verse, and paints.

ROSEMARY DOBSON (Mrs. Alec Bolton), the poet-granddaughter of a poet, Austin Dobson, lives in Sydney where she was born in 1920. She has studied and taught art, besides working for publishing firms in England and Australia, and is the author of three books of poems: *In a Convex Mirror* (1944), *The Ship of Ice* (1948), and *Child with a Cockatoo* (1955). Her poetry often blends, with unusual success, the worlds of visual and verbal art.

GEOFFREY and HENRIETTA DRAKE-BROCKMAN, both native Western Australians and long-time residents of Perth, are distinguished examples of parallel achievement by husband and wife not at all unusual in Australia. So much of such achievement is apparent in their twin contribution to this issue that biographical detail seems superfluous. It should be added, however, that Gen. Drake-Brockman is the author of a recent autobiography, *The Turning Wheel* (1960), and that Mrs. Drake-Brockman is one of the best-known personalities in Australian literature, through various novels and books of plays and short stories which she began publishing in the 1920s, in addition to several collections for which she has served as editor. Her most recent publications include a novel, *The Wicked and the Fair* (1957) and a collection of plays, *Men Without Wives* (1955).

MARY DURACK (Mrs. H. D. Miller), born in Adelaide in 1913, grew up in Western Australia and has made Nedlands (a suburb of Perth) her home. Mother of several children, social worker, and an active officer in the Fellowship of Australian Writers and other organizations, she has somehow salvaged time for the writing of poems, articles, stories, a Book Society Choice novel, *Keep Him My Country* (1955), and a major work on the Western Australian cattle country, *Kings in Grass Castles* (1959). A sister, Elizabeth Durack, is a well-known painter and has illustrated several of Mary's books.

ANDREW FABINYI, PH.D., O.B.E., as publisher and continuing sentryman of the profession, surveys periodically for *Meanjin* and other journals the state of Australian publishing. Born in Budapest in 1908, he migrated to Australia and is now publishing director for the Melbourne firm of F. W. Cheshire, Ltd. "I seem to be," writes Dr. Fabinyi, "the Australian book trade's sole publicist," adding that during the past fifteen years he has published more than fifty articles, in and outside Australia, on Australian literature, library development, publishing, and journalism.

GEORGE FARWELL, born at Bath, England, in 1911, has become a leading interpreter of the Australian scene as suggested by such titles as *Traveller's Tracks* (1950), *Australian Setting* (1952), *Land of Mirage* (1953) and *Vanishing Australians* (1961). An Adelaide journalist with interests in many directions, he has recently completed a stage play on Northern Australia, has a novel in progress, and commissions in hand for books on the development of North Australia, the explorations of Capt. Charles Sturt, and a critical study of modern Australian life.

ROBERT D. FITZGERALD, O.B.E., lives at Hunters Hill, near Sydney, where he was born in 1902 and where his forebears lived for several generations. By profession a surveyor, FitzGerald has published seven books of verse, won several important literary prizes, and been Gold Medalist of the Australian Literature Society. His most recent books, *This Night's Orbit* (1953) and *The Wind at Your Door* (1959), will be followed by a volume titled *Southmost Twelve*, forthcoming. He has served also as critic-lecturer for the Commonwealth Literary Fund, and has just accepted an appointment as Visiting Lecturer in

English at The University of Texas for the spring semester of the 1962–63 session.

DAME MARY GILMORE, now 96, lives in an apartment in the heart of King's Cross, one of the busiest sections of Sydney. Her remarkable career as teacher, poet, journalist, social reformer, and much else, has spanned virtually the whole history of Australian literature: she knew, for example, the pioneers of the efflorescence in the 1890s, all long since departed, and was herself one of them. In 1937 she became Dame Commander, O.B.E., for her literary achievements, has worn her laurels modestly for twenty-five years, and has never stopped working: writing, publishing, thinking ahead of most of her young contemporaries, stoutly refusing to cease creation and become a symbol. No other career in modern literature, unless it be that of G.B.S., is quite a match for hers. "I find," said FitzGerald, writing in 1960, "in her idealism and in her abiding sense of tradition the foundations of the edifice of her life-work."

LYNDALL HADOW, of Scarborough, Western Australia, was born at Kalgoorlie in 1903. She has received prizes and commendations both as writer and broadcaster and has published stories in numerous Australian periodicals as well as in several anthologies. Her plans, she says, are "to continue to experiment within the field of the authentic Australian short story."

ALEC D. HOPE, Australian National University professor-poet who converses with Calliope, converses critically also with his fellow Australians. He was born at Cooma, N.S.W., in 1907, educated at Sydney and Oxford, and lectured at both Sydney and Melbourne before settling in Canberra. Long known as a poet-critic in magazines and anthologies and as a broadcaster, Hope published his first volume of poems, *The Wandering Islands,* in 1955. His *Poems* appeared in 1961 in London and in New York early this year. "Conversation with Calliope," which "began as an experiment in writing tetrameter *ottava rima,*" is one of several finished or projected poems on similar themes.

FLEXMORE HUDSON was born in Queensland in 1913 but came early to live in South Australia, where he is Senior English Master and Rowing Coach at Scotch College, Adelaide. From 1939 to 1947 he edited the quarterly *Poetry,* and has published several volumes of poems. He was awarded the Commonwealth Literary Fund Fellowship in 1946. "Twenty years ago," he writes, "while a head teacher in lonely outback schools, I got to know several men whose lives gave me the conception of 'Lenny.'"

EVAN JONES, of the English faculty at Australian National University, Canberra, is one of a younger generation of poets, having just turned thirty. In 1958 he was awarded the Australian-endowed biennial "Stanford Writing Scholarship" and spent two years at Stanford University, where "Address to the Pure Scholars" was read before Phi Beta Kappa. Like Hope and McAuley, Jones is also interested in the long poem and has completed sections of a rime-royal narrative, "A Dream of Barricades." His first book, *Inside the Whale* (1960), is composed of poems written before he left Australia.

ELWYN LYNN, of Sydney, is editor of the monthly *Contemporary Art Society Broadsheet,* a teacher of English and History, a contributor to *Quadrant, Meanjin,* and other periodicals, and—by no means least of all—a painter. His canvases have been exhibited at the São Paulo Bienale (1961), the Whitechapel Exhibition of Recent Australian Painting, London, and various one-man shows. He was born at Candowindra, N.S.W., in 1917.

JAMES MCAULEY, before going to the University of Tasmania as Reader in Poetry in 1961 and being subsequently appointed Professor of English there, was Senior Lecturer in Government in the Australian School of Pacific Administration, Sydney, concerned with New Guinea affairs. He was born at Sydney in 1917; has edited the quarterly *Quadrant* and published two books of poems—*Under Aldebaran* (1946) and *A Vision of Ceremony* (1956) —as well as one of essays, *The End of Modernity* (1959). The long poem *Captain Quiros* is now complete, he reports, and he hopes to return to personal and mainly lyrical poems.

ALAN MARSHALL, of Melbourne, was born at Noorat, Victoria, in 1902. Despite the handicap he describes in "Work in Progress" and its predecessor devoted to his childhood, *I Can Jump Puddles* (1955), Marshall has seen much of Australia and described it in such volumes as *These Are My People* (1944), and *Ourselves Writ Strange* (1948). A novel, *How Beautiful Are Thy Feet* (1949), a book of stories, *Tell Us About the Turkey, Jo* (1946), and one of humorous sketches, *Bumping Into Friends* (1950) are among his other published works. "I have in mind two further books," he says, "to continue the story of my life up to the present day. When the complete plan is finished I hope it will give a picture of Australian life for the first fifty years of this century."

The word "shout" as used in Marshall's narrative, incidentally, is Australian for "treat" (to drinks).

T. INGLIS MOORE, O.B.E., professor at Australian National University, Canberra, was born at Camden, N.S.W., in 1901. He holds the M.A. from Oxford. "A story told me by the late Percy Lindsay, artist, in 'the *Bulletin* pub,' Sydney, over beers," he writes, "suggested distinctive national characteristics, leading to a study of these in our literature. The place was especially fitting, as the *Bulletin* weekly paper was once a leading force in Australian nationalism and the development of a distinctively national literature." Professor Moore teaches Australian literature and has edited several collections of it (*A Book of Australia*, 1961, is the latest) but has been a producer, as well, in three volumes of poems, a novel, and published plays. A sociological analysis, *Image of Australia: Social Patterns in Australian Literature,* is forthcoming.

DESMOND O'GRADY, literary editor of *The Bulletin*, Sydney, was born at Melbourne in 1929. He has had stories and articles published in England, Italy, America, and Australia. His play, "Heart of the Wise," was performed in Melbourne in 1958 and he won the 1961 *Quadrant* Award with a story. During 1955–57 he lived in Italy, mainly in Rome.

HAROLD J. OLIVER, born at Sydney in 1916, is Professor and Head of the School of English at the University of New South Wales. He is the author of numerous articles on English, American, and Australian literature; has published *The Problem of John Ford* (1955) and *The Art of E. M. Forster* (1959), and edited *Timon of Athens* in the Arden Shakespeare series (1959). Professor Oliver has served as Commonwealth Fund Lecturer in Australian Literature at several universities, and during 1955–56 he visited the U.S. and Canada on a Carnegie fellowship.

HAL PORTER, born at Melbourne in 1917, left Hedley, Victoria, for London in May of this year with plans to be away several years while working on an autobiography, a novel, and a further collection of stories. He wishes, ultimately, to write a novel on Francis Xavier in Japan. "Great-Aunt Fanny's Picnic," he says, is based closely on a pioneer family of Tasmania and an actual happening, "pruned, moulded, etc. to short story form." Porter published his first collection of stories in 1943; his latest, *A Bachelor's Children,* this year. He is the author also of two novels, *A Handful of Pennies* (1957) and *The Tilted Cross* (1961), for which translations into French and German are under way. He held Commonwealth Literary Fund Fellowships in 1956 and 1960, and has won prizes in short story competitions on several occasions. A book of poems, *The Hexagon,* appeared in 1956.

DOUGLAS STEWART, O.B.E., for many years literary editor of *The Bulletin* before recently joining the publishing firm of Angus & Robertson, was born at Eltham, New Zealand, in 1913. He studied law at Victoria University College, Wellington, and came to Australia in 1938 for a career in journalism and literature. Most of his fourteen books have been poetry or dramatic verse, but he has published criticism and short stories as well. Students of folklore are well acquainted with an extensive collection of Australian bush songs edited by Stewart with Nancy Keesing.

DONALD R. STUART describes himself as "bushman, drover, prospector, machine gunner Australian Imperial Forces World War II, Native Welfare assistant, writer, broadcaster, P.O.W! Thailand Railway." This varied career began in 1913 at Cottesloe, Western Australia, and Stuart remains a Western Australian, living at Scarborough, near Perth. He has interested himself specially in aboriginal life and culture. One of the most recent Australian novelists to appear, he published *Yandy* in 1959 and *The Driver* in 1961 (Melbourne, London, and New York). *Yaralie* is scheduled for 1962, and a fourth, *The Conjuror's Years,* is in progress. Stuart holds a Commonwealth Literary Fund Fellowship for 1962.

JUDITH WRIGHT (Mrs. J. W. McKinney), grew up in farming country near Armidale, N.S.W., where she was born in 1915. Although she has travelled, and has worked in cities, she still prefers rural surroundings, living now near Tamborine, not far out of Brisbane. *The Moving Image,* her first book of poems, appeared in 1946, followed by *Woman to Man* (1949), and by others in the 1950s, including *A Book of Australian Verse* published by Oxford in 1956. In the introduction to this volume, Miss Wright explores the growing involvement of Australia in world events and world issues and concludes, "It seems time for the emergence in Australian poetry of some new impulse which may give it strength to deal poetically with this movement of a country from its position of shelter into the storm."

www.ingramcontent.com/pod-product-compliance
Lightning Source LLC
Chambersburg PA
CBHW081147020726
47504CB00009B/2028